The Wandering Signifier

The Wandering Signifier

℘

RHETORIC OF JEWISHNESS IN THE LATIN AMERICAN IMAGINARY

Erin Graff Zivin

℘

DUKE
UNIVERSITY
PRESS
Durham & London 2008

Library of Congress Cataloging-in-Publication Data
appear on the last printed page of this book.

Permissions:
Sections of chapter 1 first appeared as "Reading Max Nordau:
Unspeakable Difference in Spanish American Modernism," *Chasqui*
34.1 (2005): 102–13; "Traducir lo raro: Darío, Ingenieros, y Silva leen
a Max Nordau," in *Literatura y otras artes en America Latina: Actas del
34th Congreso del Instituto Internacional de Literatura Iberoamericana*, ed.
Balderston et al., 203–11 (Iowa City: University of Iowa, 2004); "The
Face of the Other: Diagnosing Jewishness in Latin American Literature," *Modern Jewish Studies* 14 (2004): 91–101; "Cuerpos errantes,
sujetos patológicos en la obra de Luisa Futoransky y Margo Glantz,"
in *Memoria y representación: Configuraciones culturales y literarias en el
imaginario judío latinoamericano*, ed. Alejandro Meter and Ariana
Huberman, 249–62 (Rosario, Argentina: Beatriz Viterbo Editora,
2006); and "Sick Jews: Disease and Deformity in Luisa Futoransky's
De Pe a Pa: De Pekín a París and Margo Glantz's 'Zapatos: Andante
con variaciones,'" in *Luisa Futoransky y su palabra itinerante*, ed. Ester
Gimbernat González, 123–32 (Montevideo, Uruguay: Hermes Criollo, 2005). An earlier, Spanish-language version of part of chapter 2
was published as "Transacciones judías y discursos promiscuos en
'Emma Zunz,'" *Variaciones Borges* 22 (2006): 191–99.

For my parents

✿ CONTENTS

ℬ ACKNOWLEDGMENTS

There are many people without whose support I would not have been able to write this book. At New York University, I had five exceptionally talented and warm dissertation-committee members. Sylvia Molloy's role in the fashioning of the conceptual framework of this project was vital, and her unceasing moral support has provided me with confidence at critical moments during the process of writing my dissertation and book. Gabriela Basterra's brilliant work on ethical subjectivity has been an inspiration: the seminars I took with her at NYU, as well as our many conversations outside of the classroom, have impacted my work in a profound way, and I am deeply indebted to her generosity. I would like to thank Marta Peixoto for numerous unscheduled conversations in her office during my years at NYU (and delightful Princeton coffee dates since then), as well as Mary Louise Pratt and Georgina Dopico Black for their provocative insights, questions, and interventions during the dissertation phase of my academic career.

I was able to conduct research in Rio de Janeiro and São Paulo thanks to the Susan Eliakim Siman Scholarship in Sephardic Studies, the King Juan Carlos I of Spain Center Dissertation Summer Travel Grant, and the Tinker Field Research Grant. In Brazil, Beth Brait, Heloisa Buarque de Hollanda, Lilian Cardia Guimarães, Alberto Dines, Eduardo Diniz, Monica Grin, Keila Grinberg, Beatriz Kushnir, Beatriz Resende, Nancy Rozenchan, Silviano Santiago, Bila Sorj, Ilana Strozenberg, and Berta Waldman welcomed me into their homes, introduced me to colleagues, and provided me with references that I would not have found on my own. I am indebted to each of them.

At the University of Pittsburgh, I have had the good fortune of encountering true interlocutors among the faculty and graduate students in the Department of Hispanic Languages and Literatures. In particular, I would like to thank Citlali Martínez for her meticulous translations and rigorous proofreading, as well as John Beverley and Joshua Lund, who were immensely supportive throughout the long process of finding a publisher for this book. The dialogue and debate I shared with the participants of the 2005 graduate seminar "Ethics, Alterity and Representation in the Hispanic Atlantic" helped me to refine many of the arguments I make in this book. Finally, a Center for Latin American Studies Faculty Research Grant enabled me to complete the final version of this manuscript.

Earlier versions of chapters 1–4 have appeared in various publications, and I would like to thank the publishers for granting permission to reproduce revised versions of these essays here. The anonymous referees at Duke University Press provided invaluable criticism and insight that, simply put, made this a better book. I would also like to thank Reynolds Smith, Sharon Torian, and Molly Balikov at Duke for their professionalism and good cheer.

I feel blessed to have been surrounded by friends and colleagues who have read countless versions of this book. Nathalie Bouzaglo, Emily Maguire, and Erin Williams Hyman know this work almost as well as their own, and I feel incredibly grateful to have three such loyal friends who are also intellectual companions. Edna Aizenberg, Vivaldo Andrade dos Santos, Daniel Balderston, Soledad Falabella, Nora Glickman, María Cisterna Gold, Gabriel Giorgi, Jeffrey Lesser, Graciela Montaldo, Anna More, Ronnie Perelis, Mariano Siskind, Diana Sorensen, and Karina Wigozki have contributed to this project by reading earlier versions of the chapters included here, and I would like to thank each of them. The conversations I have had with Luisa Futoransky,

Margo Glantz, Francine Masiello, and Doris Sommer have been invaluable as well.

While they have not been directly involved in the writing and editing process of this book, Ali, Dana, Deb, Harriett, Len, Lisa, Michael, Rocco, and Tracy have provided unconditional support (and free babysitting!). Simon and Josh bring an immense amount of joy into my life on a daily basis and have been incredibly understanding about the amount of time this book has taken to complete. Finally, this book is dedicated to Barry and Bonnie, who taught me to read.

"Jewishness," Alterity, and the Ethics of Representation

W hile issues of racial, sexual, and economic difference have become central to debates on Latin American culture, both within the social sciences and the humanities, little has been written about representations of "Jewishness" in the Latin American literary imaginary.[1] Despite the fact that Jews inhabit every Latin American country—from a small community in Nicaragua to a significant population in Argentina—they are not generally considered a substantial presence in the literature of that region.[2] Indeed, when I was beginning my research, interviews with numerous Latin American literary scholars yielded such answers as "Are there any Jewish figures in Latin American texts?" or "Do you mean Jewish writers?" or "That's not my area of specialization—why don't you talk to someone in Jewish Studies?" And yet, Jewish characters and other representations of "Jewishness" can be found in writers as canonical as Machado de Assis, José de Alencar, José Asunción Silva, Mário de Andrade, Jorge Luis Borges, Roberto Arlt, Gabriel García Márquez, Mario Vargas Llosa, Ricardo Piglia, and Silviano Santiago.[3] It is curious that despite the substantial incidence of Jewish figures in widely read texts, the phenomenon has gone largely unnoticed. This paradox of simultaneous invisibility and prevalence merits further investigation: what is it about the notion of "Jewishness" that lends itself to such diverse texts, written in dramatically different historical, intellectual, and political moments, and why has such a dynamic been overlooked?

In order to address this lacuna in the existing scholarship this book traces the symbolic presence of "Jews" and "Jewishness" in late-nineteenth- through late-twentieth-century aesthetic works from Argentina, Brazil, Peru, Mexico, Colombia, and Nicaragua,[4] and analyzes the uncanny but repetitive use of the "Jew" in order to articulate original aesthetic and political subjectivities. By reading "Jewishness" as a *wandering signifier*, a mobile sign that travels between literary texts and sociohistorical contexts, I simultaneously pursue two avenues of inquiry: literary representations of "Jewishness" and anxiety surrounding difference in modern Latin American culture.[5]

The issues I raise in this introductory chapter can be understood as falling into three concentric circles that mirror the levels on which each textual reading can occur. I devote a section to each level. In the first section, which corresponds to the innermost circle, I treat inventions of "Jewishness," how this concept is constructed as a rhetorical device and to what ends. I argue that "Jewishness" functions as a wandering signifier that, while not wholly empty, can be infused with meaning based on the needs of the textual project in question. By engaging with work by European and North American intellectuals who highlight the prevalence of the signifier "Jew" in the Western imaginary, I aim to expose the constructed nature of "Jewishness."

In the second section I broaden, and relocate, this question in two ways. First, I bring the problem of representing "Jewishness" to Latin America, to a new and radically unique set of cultural, ideological, racial, and political circumstances. Within the context of Latin America, not only do Jews possess distinct histories relative to their European and North American counterparts, but they also come to occupy new spaces within the cultural landscape on a symbolic level. Second, I suggest that anxiety, desire, paranoia, attraction, and repulsion toward "Jewishness" are always in tension with (or representative of) larger attitudes toward otherness, whether racial, sexual, religious, national, economic, or even metaphysical. This is particularly significant in Latin American countries, in which ethnic others are more often of indigenous or African descent, and in which Jews tend to make up a smaller minority relative to other ethnic communities. This raises the question of representing "other others" through the figure of the "Jew."

In the third section I take into account the idea of representation in general. Engaging with the concepts of ethical and rhetorical language in the work of the Jewish-Lithuanian philosopher Emmanuel Levinas, I ask if it is possible to ethically represent the other within the literary text, or whether the act of representation necessarily involves the objectification and, therefore, a kind of figurative obliteration of the other. Questioning Levinas's critical stance with respect to art, I search for possible holes in thematizing discourse through which what Levinas calls "the face of the Other" can enter the literary text.

THE SIGNIFIER "JEW"

Though the idea of the symbolic life of the "Jew" has not been discussed within the context of Latin American letters, a number of scholars have analyzed representations of "Jewishness" in European (and, to a lesser extent, North American) culture and art in recent years. To what can this surge in research be attributed? Have the Inquisition and the Holocaust, both of which targeted Jews as their primary victims, stimulated such interest? When grappling with issues of violence, evil, and the collective and individual subjectivities that these events uphold, have intellectuals turned to the question of the "Jew" to explain such phenomena? Or is it simply that the "Jew" has marked—historically or symbolically—the limit of subjectivity in the European imaginary? Regardless of the motivation, these debates have raised the critical issue of how "Jewishness" works on a figurative level, exploring diverse representations of the "Jew," that other which has stood at the center of pre-modern and modern European cultural and political discourse.

Max Silverman, Zygmunt Bauman, Slavoj Žižek, Bryan Cheyette, and Laura Marcus are among those who have considered the fascinating existence of the "figurative Jew," that is, the idea of "Jewishness" that pervades Western culture and that, while related to "real" Jews, is not always grounded in the experience of Jews and Jewish communities historically.[6] These thinkers— who range from philosophers and literary critics to social scientists— explore codifications of "Jewishness" that function on a metaphorical plane, underscoring the radical flexibility of "Jewishness" as a rhetorical concept;

as the French literary scholar Max Silverman contends, "Jew" is one of the most malleable signifiers" (1998, 197). Bryan Cheyette, in his work on Jewish figures in British literature and culture, also alludes to the malleability of the "Jew," highlighting the "protean instability of 'the Jew' as a signifier" (1993, 8). Zygmunt Bauman, who in his sociological research has analyzed questions of modernity, postmodernity, ethics, and the Holocaust, describes "Jews" as "flexible and adaptable; an empty vehicle, ready to be filled with whatever despicable load 'them' were charged of carrying" (1991, 52). What is remarkable is that beyond serving as a scapegoat for the ills of society, "Jewishness" is imagined with remarkable liberty: Jews have been viewed as dominant by the lower classes and as parasites of society by social and political elites. As the Slovenian radical philosopher and cultural critic Slavoj Žižek argues, "The figure of the Jew condenses opposing features, features associated with lower and upper classes: Jews are supposed to be dirty *and* intellectual, voluptuous *and* impotent, and so on" (1989, 125). Moreover, they have been appropriated "by the most disparate of ideologies" (Cheyette and Marcus 1998, 5), as well as within distinct historical periods.[7]

It is this rhetorical malleability alluded to by Silverman, Bauman, Žižek, Cheyette, and Marcus that I would like to highlight in my study of Latin American texts. I propose the idea of the wandering signifier both as a play on the hackneyed image of the "wandering Jew" and as a way to think about the mobility of the signifier "Jew" itself. To begin with, the stereotypical configuration of the "wandering Jew" possesses its own contradiction. This mythical figure—which emerges in the medieval Christian imaginary and is explained as both a punishment for the allegedly "Jewish" responsibility for the crucifixion as well as a personification of diaspora—reappears in the modern period through the German concept *der ewige Jude*, which literally translates as "eternal Jew."[8] Cheyette and Marcus have commented on the paradoxical use of the eternal to refer to an itinerant figure: "The fact that 'the Jew' can be perceived to be both 'wandering'—unfixed and contingent on historical circumstance—at the same time as being 'eternal'—or unchangeable and immutable—points to an equivocation at the heart of the timeworn German phrase" (1998, 5). Second, the idea of the wandering signifier highlights the consistent use of the "Jew" as a rhetorical figure, one that always appears within the order of representation. The signifier "Jew" is unique in that while it behaves as any signifier does (empty form ready to be infused with content), it exhibits the particular ability to signify contradiction; thus, for example, the "Jew" can simultaneously be represented as both oppressor and pariah, rich and poor, doctor and patient, asexual and hypersexual. The wandering signifier, like der ewige Jude, takes part in simultaneously fixed and mobile discursive practices. Unease surrounding "Jewishness" is intrinsically connected to the ambivalence with which it is read and to the paradoxes inherent in its form.[9] There is a double movement at work: society creates an ambivalent figure out of its anxiety, and its anxiety is in turn fueled by the contradictory figure it has imagined.

These formulations of "Jewishness," furthermore, are not restricted to modernity; indeed, similar representations of "Jewishness" date back to antiquity. In pre-modern times (dating from antiquity to the Middle Ages), the "Jew" represented Christianity's other. The French art historian Tamar Garb elaborates on the contradictory position of the "Jew" within the Christian imaginary: "Placed at the source and origin of Christianity whilst representing an eternal witness to the possibility of its denial, the Jew has provided a crucial point of differentiation for Christian theologies, a referent in relation to which the specificity of Christian belief and practice has been demarcated and defined" (1995, 20). Bauman signals a similar paradox in pre-modern Christian views of Jews and Judaism: "[Jews] were venerable fathers of Christendom and its hateful, execrable detractors. Their rejection of Christian teachings could not be dismissed as a manifestation of pagan ignorance without serious harm to the truth of Christianity" (1991, 37). The precarious positioning of the "Jew" as both source and limit of Christian theology creates a double bind for the Christian subject, as "Jewishness" simultaneously represents the conditions of possibility and the impossibility of its existence.

Yet in his discussion of modern anti-Semitism, Bauman contends that the Jewish other did not present as great a threat to pre-modern Christian society as it did to modern secular European society. He argues that rather than embodying the wholly other, Jews represented yet another caste in a multiple-caste system: "In pre-modern Europe the peculiar flavour of Jewish *otherness* did not on the whole prevent their accommodation into the prevailing social order. The accommodation was possible because of the relatively low intensity of tension and conflict generated by the boundary-drawing and boundary-maintaining processes. . . . In a society divided into estates or castes, the Jews were just one estate or one caste among many" (1991, 35). While Bauman focuses on medieval Christian society, the case of Jews in Muslim Spain supports his view that coexistence is possible within a pre-modern social structure. In their work on medieval Spanish culture, the cultural historian Américo Castro and the literary critic María Rosa Menocal both describe an environment of relative tolerance among Jews, Muslims, and Christians in the Iberian Peninsula under Muslim rule.[10]

After the commencement of the Reconquest, of course, the social mixing of the three religious groups began to pose a formidable threat, leading to the Inquisition, the obsession with *pureza de sangre* (purity of blood), and the eventual expulsion of the Jews in 1492. The particular situation of the *conversos* (Jewish converts), who provoked a great deal of suspicion even after their conversion to Christianity, highlights the fear and apprehension toward that which cannot easily be defined as other. The converso perhaps best exemplifies the dynamic that within modernity took the form of assimilation and secularization. In both cases the unrecognizable, hidden Jew was difficult to identify and hence define; thus, the seeds of modern ambivalence toward the Jew can be traced back to the fear of the converso.

But if pre-modern definitions of Judaism are expressed within a religious vocabulary, with the Inquisition and Expulsion serving as the most violent consequences of such discourse, the Enlightenment's secularizing tendencies redefined the idea of "Jewishness" throughout the West. As Christian theology ceased to be a dominant narrative, scientific discourse took over as modernity's central paradigm. Because the religious alterity of Jews no longer held the same weight as it had before this period, a new pseudoscientific category was imagined in order to maintain the attempt to articulate Jewish difference. With the invention of race, Jews were no longer cast as spiritually other, but rather as biologically distinct from the non-Jewish subject. This rationalization became especially crucial as Jews themselves began to secularize. As they assimilated to the dominant culture and shed visible signs of difference (beards, *peyot*, *kipot*, *tzitzit*), it became impossible to distinguish Jews from their non-Jewish counterparts.[11] In some ways, Jewish difference became even more threatening as it grew increasingly difficult to identify, as the French essayist Alain Finkielkraut suggests: "'Anti-Semitism turned racist only on the fateful day, when, as a consequence of Emancipation, you could no longer pick Jews out of a crowd at first glance'" (quoted in Nochlin and Garb 1995, 11).

Žižek, for his part, explains modern anti-Semitism by turning to the example of the film *Invasion of the Body Snatchers* (Siegal 1956), in which the aliens' resemblance to humans makes them "all the more uncannily strange." He likens this phenomenon to the treatment of Jews: "This problem is the same as anti-Semitism. . . . Jews are 'like us'; it is difficult to recognize them, to determine at the level of positive reality that surplus, that evasive feature, which differentiates them from all other people" (1989, 89). Indeed, the French anti-Semite Edouard Drumont claimed to feel sympathy toward the traditional Jew, who exhibits his otherness, but remarked, "I do have it in for the Jew who is not obvious" (Bauman 1991, 58). In the Nazi propaganda film *Der ewige Jude* (Hippler 1940) images of religious Jews from a Polish ghetto are juxtaposed with images of assimilated, clean-shaven German Jews while the narrator explains, "Hair, beard, skull cap, and caftan make the Eastern Jew recognizable to all. If he appears without his trademarks, only the sharp-eyed can recognize his racial origins." The same voice details how the German Jew changes his outward appearance in order to deceive non-Jews: "It is an intrinsic trait of the Jew that he always tries to hide his origins when he is among non-Jews." Those Jews who are second and third generation, and who have intermarried, look even more like Germans; even the elite German Jews are foreign bodies, and therefore dangerous to the German people. While the "Jew" as a paradoxical figure may have already been in existence before the onset of modernity, Jewish secularization and assimilation hinder the ability to distinguish between self and other, adding to the anxiety and inflating the malleability of the "Jew."

Contemporary continental philosophical discourse on difference and displacement has also appropriated the "Jew" as its figure, further highlighting the flexibility of the signifier "Jew." Jacques Derrida, for example, posits Hellenism against Judaism as a way to articulate the competing logics of Western philosophy and its others. In "Violence and Metaphysics" Derrida illustrates the impact of Levinas's work on the "Greek" philosophy of Heidegger and Husserl, calling his influence "a dislocation of the Greek logos" (1978, 82). Even his attempt at the end of this essay to complicate the dichotomy between Judaism and Hellenism by asking, "Are we Greeks? Are we Jews? But who, we?" fails to fully dismantle the oppositional categories that structure and strengthen his critique of Levinas's ethical philosophy (ibid., 153). Similarly, the French philosopher Jean-François Lyotard (1990) utilizes the concept of "the jews" to signify a broader notion of alterity, a category into which he would place himself (note the quotation marks and lower case "j," which he uses to emphasize the fact that he is not talking about "real" Jews).[12]

Yet where can the line be drawn—and I pose this question to my own work as well—between critically exploring appropriations of the figure of the "Jew" and reifying notions of "Jewishness," even "Jewishness" as signifier? Does the analysis of the use of the "Jew" as signifier allow the Jewish other to be present, or is it, too, a tool to discuss a secondary agenda (in my

case, Latin American representations of difference and the ethics of representation)? Or is the question posed by the Jewish cultural theorists Jonathan
and Daniel Boyarin—where are "real" Jews here with a specific history?—an
inevitable road to the essentialization of the notion of "Jewishness"?[13] Going
by the Boyarins' research, which complicates, rather than reduces, notions
of "Jewishness," I would say that the answer cannot be a simple "no."[14] Their
argument brings up the issue of the connection between symbolic "Jews"
and real Jews, that is, Jews with specific local and translocal histories.

In order to address the Boyarins' question it is important to consider several issues. First, it is crucial to focus on the chasm between imaginary "Jews"
(whether characters in a novel, images in a painting, or Lyotard's "jews") and
real Jews, that is, living and breathing people (or people who once lived and
breathed) who either define themselves or are defined as Jews. But this classification itself is infinitely problematic, and one hits a dead end when attempting to clarify this category. Are Jews those who observe the laws of the
Torah? Keep kosher? Live in Israel? Are born to a Jewish mother? A Jewish
father?[15] These questions are interminable and ultimately reductive. Like the
art historian Linda Nochlin, I am not interested in "some 'real,' essential Jewishness lurking beneath a surface of lies and clichés, a reduced essence beyond the excessiveness of the stereotypical Jewish persona of art, literature,
and propaganda, but rather that excessiveness itself; the almost hysterical re-
petitiveness of myths and exaggerations . . . which constitutes the repertory
of represented Jewishness in modern times" (Nochlin and Garb 1995, 10).
The insistence on excavating "authentic Jewishness" is risky and potentially
more reductive than the stereotypes that would hide such "Jewishness." In
this sense, I am in agreement with Žižek, who warns against the temptation
to replace prejudiced attitudes with "accurate" perceptions: "It is not enough
to say that we must liberate ourselves of so-called 'anti-Semitic prejudices'
and learn to see Jews as they really are—in this way we will certainly remain
victims of these so-called prejudices. We must confront ourselves with how
the ideological figure of the 'Jew' is invested with our unconscious desire,
with how we have constructed this figure to escape a certain deadlock of our
desire" (1989, 48).[16] For this reason, throughout this volume I will remain focused on the excessive constructions of what ultimately is a fictional concept
while keeping in mind the historically grounded unease that has inspired
such inventions, as well as the violence that has resulted from these not-so-
generous imaginings.[17]

Although I attempt to warn against investigations into "authentic Jewishness," I nonetheless believe that it is critical to consider the existence of real people who have lived as Jews—whether by religious observance, patrilineal descent, participation in Yiddish theater or Zionist socialism, or by having been victims of the Holocaust or other forms of anti-Semitic violence—without limiting the boundaries of this category. In other words, real people died in concentration camps because they were determined to be Jews. This is perhaps the most vivid example of the violent and unmistakably real consequences of symbolic constructions of "Jewishness." In addition to signaling the gap that exists between the real and imaginary "Jew," then, I would also acknowledge the complicated relationship that exists *between* these concepts. Garb underscores the tension between what she terms the textual "Jew" and the historical Jew: "The situating of the Jew in the text does not deny his or her experience in the world. Indeed, in so far as the text is of the world, in its material as well as its symbolic manifestations, to situate the Jew in the text is both a refusal of some preexisting known and uncontested Jewish identity, which we either accept or reject, and an assertion that it is in the world (and the symbolic systems through which we try to understand it, indeed articulate it at all) that identity is formed" (1995, 30). Garb's argument is useful in that it complicates the division between "text" and "world"; the textual "Jew" simultaneously transcends and affirms history. Writing or imagining "Jewishness" imposes a rupture with reality, while at the same time entering into an intertextual dialogue with each previous iteration of "Jewishness." In this sense the figurative "Jew" lives in both text and world, while "real" Jews are impacted by the fictions that define them (and that they themselves define).

Another issue to consider is the actual Jewish population in the place where a symbolic "Jew" has been constructed. The interpretation of a text written before many Jews lived in the country in which the text was written must differ from the reading of a text published during the height of a wave of Jewish immigration. On the one hand, "Jews" can be present in the imaginary of an individual or society that is wholly unfamiliar with "real" Jews, as the religious historian Norman Cohn has demonstrated: "'Regardless of the real situation of Jews . . . [anti-Semitism] can be found among people who have never set eyes on a Jew and in countries where there have been no Jews for centuries'" (quoted in Bauman 1991, 38–39). At the same time, anti-Semitism itself can be fueled by frustration resulting from the contradiction between the mythological "Jew" and the Jew next door as previously segregated groups begin to interact.[18] Bauman characterizes the inevitable confrontation of competing images of real and imaginary Jews as one consequence of modernity. "Their previously unnoted incompatibility had now become a problem and a challenge. Like everything else in the rapidly modernizing society, the problem had to be 'rationalized.' The contradiction had to be resolved; either by total rejection of inherited imagery, as hopelessly incongruent, or by rational argument providing new and acceptable grounds for the same incongruence" (ibid., 44). Thus, while encounters between these incompatible categories could potentially call into question prevailing stereotypes, allowing for the substitution of the figurative by the real, these contradictory realities more often than not inspire anxiety that leads to a desire for acute rationality. Such logic, characteristic of modernity, has produced ideological positions responsible for the violence of the Holocaust, according to Bauman.

A final issue has to do with the possibility of agency. Although it is not my objective to assess the possibility of Jewish agency, this is a problem that is central to the question of representing "Jewishness." "Jewishness" can operate on a symbolic level with or without the possibility of Jewish agency, as is evident in several texts by Jewish writers who utilize metaphors of "Jewishness" to articulate a secondary preoccupation, such as the problem of exile. In these cases, the rhetorical function of "Jewishness" does not depend on the existence or lack of Jewish agency. Rather, "Jewishness" is "used" on a symbolic level by both Jews and non-Jews—and by philo-Semitic and anti-Semitic writers alike—albeit toward differing ends.[19]

The writings of Cheyette and Marcus, Bauman, Silverman, Žižek, Boyarin and Boyarin, Garb, and Nochlin prove helpful in theorizing the symbolic presence of "Jewishness" within the European imaginary, but do not sufficiently account for this phenomenon in Latin American literature and culture. Though some of the questions postulated by these writers can contribute to an analysis of Latin American discourse on "Jewishness," particularly in light of the mobile nature of both real and symbolic "Jews," it is necessary to approach the problem from a culturally and historically specific perspective.

LATIN AMERICA'S OTHERS

In a 1951 lecture entitled "El escritor argentino y la tradición" (The Argentine writer and tradition) the essayist, poet, and short-story writer Jorge Luis Borges reflects on the place of the Argentine writer, as well as on the possibility of innovation within the peripheral cultural spaces of the West. Refuting the notion that *literatura gauchesca* (gauchesque literature) stands as the only example of genuine Argentine culture, Borges points out that the use of local color does not determine the authenticity of the cultural product. On the contrary, he insists, the presence of consciously sought out native terms and references in *poesía gauchesca* exposes the *inauthenticity* of the genre. In order to support this theory, he includes an apocryphal reference to the English historian Edward Gibbon's *The Decline and Fall of the Roman Empire*, which, Borges says, argues that the Koran does not contain a single reference to camels, and that this absence confirms that it was written by an Arab.

> Fue escrito por Mahoma, y Mahoma, como árabe no tenía por qué saber que los camellos eran especialmente árabes; eran para él parte de la realidad, no tenía por qué distinguirlos; en cambio, un falsario, un turista, un nacionalista árabe, lo primero que hubiera hecho es prodigar camellos, caravanas de camellos en cada página; pero Mahoma, como árabe, estaba tranquilo: sabía que podía ser árabe sin camellos. (Borges 1957, 132–33)

✵

> It was written by Mohammed, and Mohammed, as an Arab, had no way of knowing that camels were particularly Arab; they were for him a part of reality, he had no reason to draw attention to them; in contrast, a forger, a tourist, an Arab nationalist, the first thing he would have done would be to supply an abundance of camels, caravans of camels on every page; but Mohammed, as an Arab, remained calm: he knew that he could be Arab without camels.[20]

Instead of mimicking the gaucho, Borges suggests, the Argentine writer should concentrate on the whole of Western culture, which, while it may appear identical to the work of a non-Argentine, is approached from a distinctly Argentine position. This inversion of logic, typical of Borges, is used to support his contention that the Argentine, as a marginal citizen of the West, is actually more capable of innovation because of his simultaneous status as insider and outsider.

In order to substantiate his argument further, Borges turns to the figure of the "Jew" in Western culture.

> Recuerdo aquí un ensayo de Thorstein Veblen, sociólogo norteamericano, sobre la preeminencia de los judíos en la cultura occidental. Se pregunta si esta preeminencia permite conjeturar una superioridad innata de los judíos, y

contesta que no; dice que sobresalen en la cultura occidental, porque actúan dentro de esa cultura y al mismo tiempo no se sienten atados a ella por una devoción especial; "por eso"—dice—"a un judío siempre le será más fácil que a un occidental no judío innovar en la cultura occidental." (Borges 1957, 135–36)

ℬ

I recall here an essay by Thorstein Veblen, a North American sociologist, on the preeminence of Jews in Western culture. He wonders if this preeminence allows us to assume an innate superiority of Jews, and answers that it does not; he says that they stand out in Western culture because they act within that culture without feeling tied to it by a special devotion; "for that reason," he says, "it will always be easier for a Jew than a non-Jew to innovate within Western culture."

The Irish, Borges adds, have proven equally exceptional within English culture, and so, he suggests, can the Argentine—and the South American in general—handle European themes without superstitions but with a degree of irreverence that promises "consecuencias afortunadas" (fortunate consequences).

This essay—hardly the only reference to "Jews" in Borges's work—highlights the usefulness of the "Jew" within broader projects of subject formation, here, as part of an attempt to articulate the position of the Latin American intellectual within Occidental culture. The dynamic set up by Borges in "El escritor argentino y la tradición" suggests one of many possible explanations for the proliferation of Jewish figures in Latin American letters: if the "Jew" serves as a placeholder for Latin America's many controversial "others," so too does it codify the position of the Latin American intellectual himself or herself (and of the Latin American subject in general) within the unequal cultural terrain of the West.

While a substantial research corpus exists on representations of "Jewishness" in North American and European literature and culture, few studies have analyzed the symbolic "Jew" within the context of Latin America, despite the fact that texts such as Borges's are so widely read and analyzed. How can this gap be explained? Is it possible to theorize the problem of "Jewishness" from Latin America, taking into account the critical work realized by European and North American scholars without arbitrarily imposing its epistemological categories onto a radically distinct political, cultural, and racial context? Can an analysis of "Jewishness" in the Latin American imagi-

nary take historical difference into account while highlighting the relationship between currents of thought on both sides of the Atlantic?

Although there have been a number of attempts to study Jews in Latin
America, most research in the newly emergent field of Latin American Jewish studies has remained focused on isolating and clarifying Latin American
Jewish identity.[21] To be sure, there are a small number of studies that detail
the ways in which the idea of the "Jew" has been imagined. In her widely
read treatise on Latin American foundational fictions, the literary and cultural critic Doris Sommer examines the way that inassimilable "Jewishness"
stands for racial ambivalence in post-abolition Colombia in Jorge Isaacs's
María, while the Argentine literature scholar Josefina Ludmer undertakes a
broader analysis of "Jewish stories" in late nineteenth and early twentieth
century Argentine literature in a chapter of her recent book, The Corpus Delicti. The Borges scholars Evelyn Fishburn, Edna Aizenberg, Saúl Sosnowski,
and Jaime Alazraki have investigated the presence of Judaic and kabbalistic themes in the fiction of Argentina's preeminent writer, and the historian
Jeffrey Lesser has discussed the construction of Brazilian-Jewish ethnic identity, both by Brazilian Jews and by their non-Jewish compatriots. Yet the majority of research in the area of Latin American Jewish studies has as its goal
the delineation of a Latin American Jewish identity and tends to overlook the
imagined or constructed nature of "Jewishness," even when allowing for the
possibility of a hybrid or multivalent identity.

Sosnowski, for example, opens a recent essay on Jewish identity in Argentina with the commonly overheard question from Jewish schools in Argentina in the 1950s: "If there were a war between Argentina and Israel, for
which side would you fight?" (2000: 263). Despite the fact that Sosnowski
criticizes this question for ignoring the possibility that Jewish Argentines
might have double loyalties—he rightly argues for a defense of the "hyphen"
(1987, 297)—his retention of the military metaphor for identity is significant.
It reveals not only a dependence on nationalistic definitions of identity even
when one would like to subvert them, but also that the very attempt to define
a Latin American Jewish identity is riddled with problems. Sosnowski continues his discussion by citing Alberto Gerchunoff's Jewish gaucho as an example of a hybrid identity that synthesizes Jewish and Argentine qualities, but
he does so without problematizing the equally essentialist idea of hybridity,
disregarding that any Jewish figure in literature is just that: a figurative "Jew."
While Sosnowski's pioneering work has made a significant contribution

to the understanding of Jewish culture in Argentina, I move in a different direction by posing new questions about how "Jewishness" is imagined and represented in Latin American culture.

Given the lack of attention paid to symbolic "Jewishness" (in the minds of Jews and non-Jews alike), the relationship between real and imaginary "Jews" has yet to be explored in great detail within a Latin American context. It is my intention to highlight and explore this tension and to inquire into the usefulness or *functionality* of the rhetorical "Jew," even in instances in which the author herself identifies as Jewish. Of course, in order to address the symbolic presence of "Jewishness" in Latin American literature, it is necessary to consider the sociological and historical presence of Jews in the region. Maintaining an awareness of the historical and contemporary Jewish presence in Latin America highlights both the connection and the chasm between "figurative" and "real."

A number of the texts that I analyze come from Argentina and Brazil, which reflects the large number of Jews in these countries relative to the rest of Latin America. Yet I have also included texts from Mexico, Peru, and Colombia, countries that do not boast a significant Jewish population. Thus, to Cohn's contention that anti-Semitism can exist among people who have had no contact with Jews, I would add that the symbolic "Jew" can exist in countries whose Jewish population is negligible. The Jewish influence on a society or its cultural imaginary, moreover, is not directly related to the size of the population, as demonstrated in the Latin American Jewish historian Judith Laikin Elkin's argument that Jews disproportionately affect the cultural life of their countries.[22]

While the majority of contemporary Latin American Jews are descendants of late-nineteenth- and early-twentieth-century immigrants, the Jewish presence in Latin America dates back to the earliest explorers, following the expulsion of Jews from Spain and Portugal in 1492 and 1496, respectively. Though Jews were prohibited from traveling to the New World, many settled in the Caribbean and Brazil, particularly Portuguese *cristãos novos* (New Christians). These New Christians were Jews that had either forcibly or voluntarily converted to Christianity during the Inquisition, and while they outwardly professed Catholic faith, some continued to follow religious customs clandestinely. Temporary exceptions to this phenomenon include the brief Dutch occupation of Northeastern Brazil, during which time some cristãos novos began to openly practice Jewish religious traditions. When the Portuguese reconquered this region in 1654, these Jews either went back into hiding or left Brazil for Curaçao, New Amsterdam, and Holland (Elkin 1998, 15–16). Thus, early Jewish life in the Americas could be characterized as invisible, largely relegated to private rather than public spaces. Yet while ritual Judaism was largely hidden, the figurative "Jew" already occupied a significant place in the early colonial imaginary, due to the legacy of Sefarad, as well as the presence of New Christians in the Americas.

While small numbers of descendants of New Christian settlers from the colonial period remain in some Latin American countries (like Brazil), these have survived principally as Catholics. Elkin addresses this controversial issue in her discussion of modern Jewish communities in Latin America: "Folklore has it that Marranos who survived the colonial period were the progenitors of contemporary Jewish communities. This is not in fact the case. Descendants of those who were not killed may well have survived physically, some even with memories of Jewish tradition, however distorted by the secrecy imposed upon them. But they survived as Catholics" (1998, 21). Given this lack of openly Jewish continuity, the steady presence of "Jewishness" in Latin American culture occurs more dramatically on a symbolic level. Therefore, nineteenth-century texts such as the Mexican writer Justo Sierra O'Reilly's La hija del judío or the Brazilian poets Castro Alves's "Hebraia" and Machado de Assis's "A cristã nova," as well as the Colombian Jorge Isaacs's María, predate the existence of established Jewish communities in these countries. Instead, these texts draw heavily on biblical or Orientalist images, rather than on modern representations of "Jews" seen in European culture at the time, because Jews were not yet a significant part of a modernizing Latin America.

Several hundred years passed before Latin America saw the first significant wave of Jewish immigration, whose descendants comprise much of Latin America's Jewish communities today. These immigrants were met with varying degrees of acceptance and hostility, depending on the political moment and the country in question. This is at least partially attributable to the fact that the ideological and political conditions that allowed for the entrance of Jews and other immigrants beginning in the late nineteenth century were fraught with tension and contradiction. While the dominance of positivist social theory justified projects to bring Europeans to Latin America in order to whiten the population, these same ideas constituted the Jewish other as degenerate, creating a double bind for Jewish immigrants.[23] These Jews entered into a political, philosophical, and racial dynamic already in existence before their arrival. Ideology and discourse surrounding "Jewishness" did not originate with the presence of these immigrant groups; rather, theories

of religious and racial alterity were constantly being proposed and negotiated throughout colonial and modern Latin American societies, interacting
periodically with real and symbolic "Jews."

In addition to the historical Jewish communities to which some texts refer, there are a number of individual "real" Jews and conversos that enter this
study, either as authors or as fictionalized or "translated" versions of historical figures.[24] The Colombian novelist Jorge Isaacs's *María* represents an
interesting case of rewriting "Jewishness," given Isaacs's own complicated
affiliation with his Jewish roots. The son of a Jewish convert to Christianity, Isaacs oscillated between seemingly incongruous identities, exhibiting
political and religious ambivalence and entertaining loyalties as contradictory as conservativism, liberalism, Catholicism, and Freemasonry (Sommer
1991, 178–80).[25] These tensions are played out in his novel *María*, in which
María, Efraín, and his father occupy distinct points on a continuum between
"Jewish" and "Christian" identities. The Hungarian-Jewish psychiatrist Max
Nordau also exhibits a problematic relationship with his own Jewish background. As author of the idea of the "muscle Jew," a modern Jewish subject
that both appropriates and resists images of the degenerate Jew in fin de siècle European thought, Nordau was simultaneously a "Zionist" and an "anti-
Semite." Nordau enters the work of the Nicaraguan *modernista* Rubén Darío,
the Italian-Argentine positivist José Ingenieros, and the Colombian poet and
novelist José Asunción Silva, who engage with Nordau's ambivalent attitude
toward his own "Jewishness," translating him in much the same way that he
reinvented himself. Luisa Futoransky, a Paris-based Argentine poet, novelist,
and journalist, and Margo Glantz, a Mexican fiction writer and literary scholar,
exemplify the phenomenon of Jewish authors who utilize metaphors of "Jewishness" in their writing in much the same way as do their non-Jewish counterparts: in order to articulate preoccupations with secondary issues. While
Futoransky engages rhetoric surrounding "Jewishness" and disease in order
to construct a writing subject in exile, Glantz utilizes the deformed Jewish
body in order to talk about her semiautobiographical protagonist's condition as an outsider. Finally, the leftist playwright Alfredo Dias Gomes's *O
Santo Inquérito*, in which the Inquisition allegorizes the violence of the dictatorship in 1960s Brazil, is based on the life of Branca Dias, a Portuguese New
Christian who lived in Northeastern Brazil and was persecuted under the Inquisition. Dias Gomes "textually converts" the historical Branca into an "authentic" Christian in order to highlight her unjust suffering, constructing
Branca's character as an ideal "militant" subject.

Despite the presence of these "real" Jews in Latin American intellectual and aesthetic traditions, Latin America's "significant others," that is, those others who have regularly needed to be dealt with in order to attempt projects of nation building and consolidation, are not generally Jewish, but rather tend to be of indigenous and African descent.[26] Despite momentary focuses on (and reactions against) the Jewish population—for example, the anti-immigrant backlash in early-twentieth-century Argentine nationalist rhetoric, the anti-Semitism of the Vargas era in Brazil, and conflations of "Jews" with both rightist and leftist movements in many countries—Latin America has been primarily preoccupied with how to integrate the "non-white," subaltern communities of indigenous and African descent into the nation.[27] The "Jew" often comes to stand for these others in literature, either as an allegorical representation of a specific ethnic group or racial concern (as in Machado de Assis and Mario Vargas Llosa) or as a marker of a more generic form of alterity or marginality (as in Julián Martel, Rubén Darío, Ricardo Piglia, Margo Glantz, Rodolfo Enrique Fogwill, and Sergio Chejfec).

When exploring the treatment of Jewish difference in literature, one must also consider the way(s) in which modern Latin American societies have dealt with alterity, whether as part of official state rhetoric or within the broader cultural imaginary: methods that differ dramatically from rhetoric across the Atlantic, and which translate into original manipulations of the signifier "Jew" in order to address social realities unique to Latin America.[28] Latin American attempts to establish and consolidate national identities in the nineteenth and twentieth centuries ranged from politics of exclusion (Domingo Faustino Sarmiento's civilization versus barbarism) to inclusion (the most crystallized version of which can be found in Brazil's "myth of racial democracy").[29] Yet even the most explicitly racist attitudes have had to confront the social reality that the African, indigenous, and foreign "others" they fear are here to stay. This fatalism of difference plays a significant role in determining the symbolic significance of Jewish difference in Latin American letters. Put another way, the "Jew" enters the Latin American imaginary at distinct ideological and aesthetic moments precisely in order to address what is perceived as unavoidable heterogeneity.

In the infamously anti-Semitic Argentine classic La bolsa (1890), the "Jew" represents the destructive and undesirable, yet inevitable force of immigration, capitalism, and globalization, so that while the text might articulate a desire for national purity, this purity is—by definition—impossible. Fin-de-siècle "whitening" projects yielded to the necessary inclusion of darker, less-desirable others who, when bred with citizens of European descent, contributed to an overall whiter population. While these eugenic theories of racial engineering undoubtedly had as their objective the erasure of the African and indigenous influence, it was through mixing, not extermination or expulsion, that these goals were considered attainable.[30] Thus, nineteenth-century Brazilian abolitionist rhetoric advocates racial mixing based on the idea that "miscegenation would gradually and inexorably 'whiten' and thereby 'upgrade' the Brazilian population" (Skidmore 1990, 9). Needless to say, it was not out of love that miscegenation was advocated in these cases, but rather out of the pseudoscientific belief that whiteness could dilute blackness, that the dominant racial subject could absorb the dark other, or at the very least out of the pragmatic view that the racial "other" was an unavoidable element of the national body.

The 1920s and 1930s ushered in an era of nationalism grounded in a new affirmation of racial syncretism; here, the idea of mixing did not have as its ultimate objective the whitening of the population, but rather the postulation of a uniquely mestizo (or mestiço) culture as that which made Latin American national identities distinct from European identities and, therefore, original. During this period, the historian Thomas Skidmore argues, elite Brazilians began to take pride in what they claimed to be a lack of racism, which they contrasted with the systematic racism of the United States and Germany, and theories of racial mixing abounded across the region (1990, 27). While the philosopher José Vasconcelos's utopian La raza cósmica (The Cosmic Race), published in 1925, promotes a vision of a universal mestizo race in Mexico, the Brazilian sociologist and anthropologist Gilberto Freyre celebrates miscegenation as a positive national trait in his 1933 Casa-grande e senzala (The Masters and the Slaves). The Cuban anthropologist Fernando Ortiz postulates the idea of transculturation, a racially inflected theory of culture that is multidirectional and interactive, in his 1940 Contrapunteo cubano del tabaco y el azúcar (Cuban Counterpoint). Yet these ideas circulated predominantly on the level of rhetoric, and as the Latin American literary and cultural critic Joshua Lund has argued, the ostensible eroding of pseudoscientific classifications of race often depended on these very categories for their existence: "If hybridity is rooted in a notion of blending, these same roots are nourished by a concept that always returns to segregation. . . . An impasse arises: hybridity as the incessant process of mixing traces its condition of possibility to a discourse— race—that legitimates and institutionalizes separation" (2006, 5).

Even more recent attempts to "define" Latin American culture rely heavily on ideas of mixing and incorporation: in his 1982 book *Transculturación narrativa en América Latina* (Narrative transculturation in Latin America), the Uruguayan intellectual Angel Rama reworks Ortiz's theory of transculturation and brings it to the scene of the literary, while the Peruvian literary critic Antonio Cornejo Polar attempts a critical reevaluation of these terms, proposing the notion of heterogeneity in order to underscore, rather than erase, the violent and unequal power dynamics at work in these cultural and ethnic encounters and clashes.[31] Finally, the Mexican-based Argentine sociologist Néstor García Canclini's controversial *Culturas híbridas* (*Hybrid Cultures*) reframes the idea of hybridity within the context of globalization and border culture, a move that has inspired criticism among Latin American and Latin Americanist intellectuals for its romanticization of the "border" as well as its naïve emphasis on the market as a site of potential empowerment.[32]

Throughout several centuries of discourse and across national boundaries, theorizations of difference in Latin America have repeatedly turned to models of hybridity and syncretism, even when the conditions of possibility of these concepts remained linked to segregation and isolation. Despite the inevitable return to a politics of racial exclusion, then, a rhetoric of inclusion persists. Though differing by country and historical moment, these racial politics of integration and segregation can perhaps be explained by what Roberto González Echevarría describes as a Latin American obsession with the "Other Within." Beginning in the nineteenth century, he asserts, "Latin American narrative will deal obsessively with that Other Within who may be the source of all; that is, the violent origin of the difference that makes Latin America, distinct, and consequently original" (1998, 97).[33] This provocative notion begins to address the specifically Latin American modes of engaging alterity and helps one to understand the ways in which "Jewishness" is articulated. While it is possible to identify an impulse to expel the "stranger within" in pre-modern and modern Europe, the inclination to convert, assimilate, transculturate, or incorporate the racialized other into the nation prevails in Latin America.[34] If modern European notions of "Jewishness" (and, by extension, difference in general) often focus on a foreign invader that would corrupt the purity of the national corpus, Latin American representations of the "Jew" tend to recognize a primordial other that, symbolically or historically, forms a part of the individual or collective self, traceable to the traumatic and violent encounter of the Conquest. Thus, while in general the "Jew" appears as an anxiety-provoking figure from the perspective of the dominant subject, the construction of and reaction to this figure possesses diverse manifestations on both sides of the Atlantic.

Do Latin American representations of "Jewishness" generally reveal a broader preoccupation with ethnic or national alterity? Although I consider this question, I ultimately argue that the "Jew" does not simply represent another "other" (the immigrant, the slave, etc.), but rather functions as a powerful node onto which a fundamental anxiety toward difference can be projected and performed. Moreover, ideas of Jewish difference tend to appear embedded within other discourses of alterity, so that ideas about "Jewishness" often appear juxtaposed with complex constructions of gender— the most evident example being the hijas de judíos (Christian daughters of Jewish fathers)—but also surfacing in works by Jewish women themselves (Futoransky and Glantz both create semiautographical protagonists whose marginality has just as much to do with their "Jewishness" as with their "femaleness"). Representations of "Jewishness" then, must always be read within a broader constellation of social, sexual, and aesthetic disquiet. But if this book is ultimately about representation, it is equally concerned with the limits of representation: in writing the Jewish other, what is excluded from the text? What voices, ideas, or histories are suppressed in the constitution of new subjectivities vis-à-vis aesthetic creation? Is it possible to conceive of some extratextual element that could resist this totalizing effect?

THE ETHICS OF REPRESENTATION

In analyzing distinct figurations of "Jewishness" in the Latin American imaginary I raise the question of whether an ethical consideration of difference is a possibility when otherness is used rhetorically, when the other—here, the Jewish other—serves as a metaphor for a completely separate preoccupation. If "Jewishness" is thematized, turned into a rhetorical object, and is used as a means to an end—that of the construction of a national or aesthetic subjectivity—will this subject preclude ethics? Or will the subject simply absorb the other into itself: "Suppress[ing] alterity, subordinating it to the totality . . . reducing the absolutely other to the other of the same" (Robbins 1999, xiii)?

I focus primarily on the how of representation, that is, the multiple ways is which "Jewishness" is used rhetorically to articulate broader questions of difference, whether having to do with race, ideological dissidence, exile, or transculturation. At the same time, I address the broader problem of the ethics of representation, which, while not always treated explicitly in the close textual readings, has to do with the larger theoretical concerns that motivate this project. In order to address this issue, I turn to the work of Emmanuel Levinas, whose philosophical writings (relatively under-studied until very recently) detail the ethical relationship between same and Other.[35] His contention that the ethical subject is constituted through the face-to-face encounter with the Other seems, at first glance, to exclude the possibility of an ethics of literature, if literature is understood as a mediated relation to or an objectification of the Other. The idea of literary representation as a practice that violates the Other could certainly be supported by the majority of the texts I discuss in this book, which absorb Jewish alterity into the universe of the same. Yet I would problematize Levinas's repudiation of the written word as ontologically violent by asking the following questions: can "the face of the Other" enter the literary text, or does every attempt to characterize otherness within writing necessarily destroy or violate difference? Is an ethical treatment of the Other possible within literary discourse? Or, as Levinas would argue, does literature automatically fall into the category of rhetorical, as opposed to ethical, language? How do the mutually interdependent categories of the *saying* and the *said* help one to articulate what I will call the "double bind" of ethical representation? In codifying "Jewishness," is the Other always already thematized, or is it possible to identify the presence of something else, a remainder to the process of thematization that resists representation?

Levinas's unique contribution to the Western philosophical tradition—unprecedented at the time of his writing—has to do primarily with his focus on the demand of the Other as central in the constitution of the subject.[36] Rather than privileging an autonomous self (whose engagement with the Other is secondary to being), Levinas underscores the response to the Other's demand as that which makes subjectivity possible. He theorizes an Other that is prior to the self, though not in a temporal sense; the encounter between self and Other does not occur within history, but is rather "preliminary . . . prior to consciousness" (Levinas 1998, 82). The self does not exist without the Other; the Other is already present as the subject comes into being.[37] This Other stands before the same and demands a response: "The first word of the face is the 'Thou shalt not kill.' It is an order. There is a commandment in the appearance of the face, as if a master spoke to me. However, at the same time, the face of the Other is destitute; it is the poor for whom I can do all and to whom I owe all. And me, whoever I may be, but as a 'first person,' I am he who finds the resources to respond to the call" (Levinas 1982, 89). The response of this self—its *responsibility* toward the Other—founds the ethical relationship and, through it, establishes its own status as subject: "Responsibility [is] the essential, primary and fundamental structure of subjectivity" (ibid., 95).

One of the primary concepts that Levinas uses to articulate the encounter with the Other is that of the face, which he links to the idea of exposure: "The disclosing of a face is nudity, non-form, abandon of self, ageing, dying, more naked than nudity. It is poverty, skin with wrinkles, which are a trace of itself" (1998, 88). By exposing itself as destitute, the face of the Other demands responsibility in the same through the (figurative) commandment "Thou shalt not kill." The "listening eye" of the subject simultaneously sees this face and hears the order (ibid., 30, 37). As a result of this meeting of self and Other, the subject is constituted through its response to the Other's demand. Therefore, the intersubjective relationship stands at the heart of the problem of ethics; the encounter between same and Other is, by definition, an ethical one.

What are the implications of this relationship for an analysis of literary representation? It is vital to the question of literature because, as Levinas contends, language plays a constitutive role in the encounter between self and Other. Moreover, it adds a complicated dimension to the discussion, because while Levinas characterizes the intersubjective relationship as "wholly sign, signifying itself," language remains one of the most contentious issues in his work (1998, 15). The face of the Other disrupts the "imperialism of the same" through words, as in the reference to the Biblical injunction "Thou shalt not kill."[38] Though Levinas undoubtedly grounds the ethical demand in language, however, it is not clear whether this demand might be realized beyond orality. Can one think about the ethical relationship between the same and Other within the context of the *written* word? Is it possible to "hear" the face of the Other in literary discourse, particularly given Levinas's criticism of poetry as rhetoric, which he equates with violence and injustice?

In his 1974 *Otherwise than Being, or Beyond Essence* Levinas makes a critical distinction between ethical and rhetorical language, or the *saying* and the *said*. While the former pertains to a pre-original realm of language, the latter refers to a type of language that reduces the Other to a set of characteristics; rather than being experienced as a face, the Other is seen as merely eyes, nose, ears and mouth (Levinas 1982, 85).[39] In the second case, the saying is subordinated to the said: "The correlation of the saying and the said, that is, the subordination of the saying to the said, to the linguistic system and to ontology, is the price that manifestation demands. In language qua said everything is conveyed before us, be it at the price of a betrayal" (Levinas 1998, 6). The notion of betrayal implies a relationship in opposition to ethics; it signifies a refusal of relationship. Of course, there is a contradiction here if the response inherent to responsibility cannot be expressed within a linguistic system, if—as Levinas argues—the thematization of the Other will always come at the expense of the face. While Levinas does not clarify this paradox, which appears in his later work, he remains unambiguous in his treatment of aesthetic representation.

His division between rhetorical language as that which violates the Other's vulnerability, that which kills the Other, and ethical language as that which facilitates the encounter with the Other, is radical. "Thou shall not kill" instantiates ethical language, while any mode of representation that thematizes the Other, turns the Other into an object, exemplifies rhetorical language. Art—above all, literature—commits this discursive crime by making the Other a figure, an image. In his 1948 "Reality and Its Shadow," one of his earlier essays, published several years following the Nazi genocide that killed most of his family, he deems art potentially evil, like "feasting during a plague."[40] While his anti-aesthetic stance softens slightly in his 1961 *Totality and Infinity*, he nevertheless still equates art with rhetoric, which approaches the Other through "artifice."[41] In contrast, ethical language—God's "Thou shall not kill" or Abraham's "*hineni*" (here I am)—preserves the asymmetry between same and Other, and demands responsibility in the subject.

I would like to question this radical division between ethical and rhetorical language, and suggest that these categories might overlap and contaminate one another, following Jill Robbins's warning against dualistic readings of Levinas: "Can we be sure that [ethics and its opposite] do not communicate with each other, interpenetrate and contaminate each other, according to what Derrida calls a 'necessary general contamination' in order to be thought of as two distinct and irreducible poles of experience? That would be to say that there is also the possibility of thinking the ethicity of poetry, or of thinking the ethical and aesthetics together, of thinking *in a literary text* . . . the transcendence of the other in 'the proffered word,' the word of the other that *teaches* us" (1999, 90). Derrida, too, argues for a "misreading" of Levinas, suggesting the possibility of an ethical dimension of the written word: "The limit between violence and nonviolence is perhaps not *between* speech and writing but *within* each of them" (1978, 102, emphasis added). Indeed, does not Levinas himself rely on metaphor when he alludes to the ethical expressions "Thou shall not kill," "hineni," "après vous"?[42] Perhaps Levinas is speaking figuratively when he talks about language in the first place; the notion of the speaking face, after all, is rhetorical. And even if this is not what Levinas "means"—if one can presume to know what he "means"—isn't it one's duty as his reader, as his student, to misread him, to be ungrateful, to misunderstand?[43]

I would like to contribute to Derrida's and Robbins's interventions by suggesting that Levinas alludes to a relationship between ethical and rhetorical language when he acknowledges that "language permits us to utter, be it by betrayal, this *outside of being*, this *ex-ception* to being, as though being's other were an event of being" (1998, 6). His awe with respect to language is unmistakable in quotes such as the following: "Language issued from the verbalness of a verb would then not only consist in making being understood, but also in making its essence vibrate. *Language is thus not reducible to a system of signs doubling up beings and relations; that conception would be incumbent on us if words were nouns. Language seems rather to be an excrescence of the verb.* And qua verb it already bears sensible life—temporalization and being's essence" (1998, 35, emphasis added). Levinas attributes a redemptive potential to language through its "verbalness," which, in contrast with the reductive powers of the noun, opens rather than closes, vibrates rather than reproduces. The subordination of the saying (verb) to the said (noun), however, does not constitute a "fall of the saying": "Thematization, in which being's essence is conveyed before us, and theory and thought, its contemporaries . . . are motivated by the pre-original vocation of the saying, by responsibility itself" (ibid., 6). Here, there is an inextricable link—a motivation—between saying and said, a paradoxical bond in which thematization is both inspired by the ethical demand as well as that which renders it impossible. Language must thus play a role in recognizing being's Other, if only because it is all one has; the noun must accompany the verb.[44] Literature, as an art form that employs such linguistic performances and verbal play, adds a critical dimension to the problem of representing Otherness.

This necessary relationship between the saying and the said—the potential presence of ethical language within rhetorical discourse—leads one to the question of whether there might be an element of the literary text that resists the very signifying practices it employs. I am reminded of the English and American literary critic Elaine Scarry's provocative work on the possibility of resisting representation (1994), and I, too, search for that which does not enter the order of representation, as well as that which might resist it from within.[45]

Of course, Scarry is not the only thinker to consider experiences that exceed the order of representation. The French philosopher Jean-Luc Nancy posits the "surprise" as that which tests the limits of thinking: "The 'surprise' is not only an attribute . . . of the event, but the event itself. . . . What eventuates in the event is not only that which happens, but that which surprises" (1998, 91). He suggests that the surprise/event has everything to do with thinking, though thinking always runs the risk of turning the surprise/event into a category: "How is one to remain in the event? How can one hold oneself in it, if this can be said, without making an 'element' or a 'moment' out of it? Under what conditions can we keep thought in the surprise which thought has the task of thinking?" (ibid., 97).[46] Nancy sustains that the event remains excluded from the order of representation (ibid., 102), yet (paradoxically) is not "beyond the knowable and expressible" (ibid., 98–99). How is it possible to account for this aporia, this ostensible impasse between the surprise and thought, between the saying and the said, between the face of the Other and its thematization? Under what conditions might it be possible to bridge these conceptual divides? Can literary criticism, in signaling that which is absent from the text, enact a sort of presence?

It is crucial to consider these broader theoretical issues before embarking on a detailed analysis of literary texts in order to bear in mind the problem of the ethics of representation. The notion of the face of the Other described by Levinas, while not always mentioned directly hereafter, should be understood as that which has inspired this project. Just as the Other—understood as exteriority or as the Other within the same—interrupts, inspires, and transforms the subject, the ethical questions that I have elaborated should haunt the body of this study. By exploring the hysterical repetition of the signifier "Jew," in signaling the absence or presence of the Jewish other, I hope to excavate possible responses to Levinas's condemnation of literature from within the literary texts themselves.

❦ ❦ ❦

In chapters 1–3 I approach the problem of representing Jewishness through the analysis of three critical scenes: that of the diagnosis, that of the transaction, and that of the conversion. Rather than simply investigating the figure of the "Jew," I propose the idea of a scene in order to take into account the entire landscape within which "Jewishness" appears, so that it becomes possible to read not only figures but also context, discourse, images, desire—those potent elements that come into contact with one another to form a created object. Within these diverse scenes, I demonstrate the way in which the idea of "Jewishness" collides and interacts with other overdetermined metaphors—disease, medicine, money, prostitution, conversion—in order to produce ideological-aesthetic artifacts. Through the analysis of the three scenes, it becomes apparent that the diagnosis, the transaction (financial and sexual), and the conversion are more than mere objects of representation; they are also performative textual acts. That is, they appear not only as themes but also as literary devices through which meaning is constructed within the texts themselves. The diagnosis is thus not merely written about, but enacted as well; the financial or sexual transaction is not just narrated, but the negotiation also happens on the level of discourse; conversion not only appears as a motif, but the narrative *itself* realizes a textual conversion: it converts its object by assimilating it into the order of representation.

In chapter 1, I analyze texts in which the "Jew" appears as both contaminator and healer, highlighting the flexibility of the signifier "Jew." Taking as my point of departure the Latin American literary critic Sylvia Molloy's contention that the diagnosis is the means by which knowledge is organized, I sustain that the very *desire* to diagnose the other is symptomatic of anxiety surrounding the unknown, the uncharacterizable, the unfixable, all of which can be linked to, provoked by, and represented by "Jewishness." I propose the idea of the diagnostic scene in order to take into account a broader context, in which characters, language, and ideology interact to produce or *perform* diagnoses. In the texts I read the "Jew" does not remain limited to one side of the dichotomy between sickness and medicine, but rather straddles and questions this very divide. For this reason, I consider various *instances of "Jewishness"* as a part of diagnostic scenes in which the rhetorical "Jew" appears in diverse roles, never fully free of the diagnostic gaze.

In the second chapter of this study I analyze a number of texts in which cultural hierarchies and national identities are contested through the motif of the transaction. Drawing on references to capitalism and prostitution, debates over control of the subject, city, and/or nation play out as the "Jew" occupies these anxiety-ridden sites of exchange. Like the "Jew" herself, capitalism and prostitution possess "real" referents in early-twentieth-century urban centers of Brazil and Argentina. While a number of historical and sociological studies (Fonseca, Glickman, Guy, Kushnir, Rago) have attempted to analyze the presence of prostitution rings—some of them Jewish—in Buenos Aires, São Paulo, and Rio de Janeiro, the literary and cultural critic Julio Ramos has referred to the symbolic value that prostitution acquires: "In discourses about the city, the prostitute is a condensation . . . of the 'dangers' inherent in urban heterogeneity" (Ramos 2001, 136). Following Ramos, I explore the rhetorical linking of "Jewishness," money, and prostitution by focusing on discourses surrounding the "dangerous" spaces of the city and the nation. Once again, I insist on the notion of a critical scene: here, the scene of the transaction as a (nongeographical) space within which instances of "Jewishness" appear in order to negotiate the national and the foreign, gender and genre, "truth" and subjectivity.

In chapter 3, I focus on the motif of Jewish conversion as a model for racial assimilation, ideological engagement, and national consolidation. I propose the term textual conversion as a way to understand rhetorical acts in which difference is assimilated into the totalizing project of the text. By analyzing representations of Jewish conversion in Latin American literature, I argue that the notion of shifting identities is useful in thinking about the potential to erase difference, as well as the possibility of subverting this very erasure. On the one hand, conversion offers a vision of complete absorption of the other into the totality of the self. On the other hand, there is a particular anxiety provoked by the converso, which in some cases is stronger than toward the "Jew" himself. I argue that this is connected to the instability of this intermediate category; the question "Is the converso Jewish or not?" can ultimately never be satisfactorily answered.

While in chapters 1–3 I focus primarily on the how of the problem, that is, the ways in which "Jewishness" can be manipulated to talk about ideological, cultural, and aesthetic concerns, I return to the question of the ethics of representation in the final chapter. In chapter 4 I revisit the central theoretical question of this study: can the face of the Other be present within literary discourse, or is any attempt to represent the other by definition a violation of her alterity? What happens when "Jewishness" is used precisely to articulate the notion of the unsayable? What are the ethical and political implications of a poetics of unsaying? In order to address this preoccupation, I turn to Jorge Luis Borges's "Deutsches Requiem," Ricardo Piglia's Respiración artificial, and Sergio Chejfec's Los planetas, three Argentine works in which the scene of "Jewishness" is employed as part of postmodern aesthetic projects that challenge and expose the limits of representation.

ONE

Diagnosing "Jewishness"

During the latter part of the nineteenth century, the dominant Western epistemology of positivism, with its corresponding subtheories of race, degeneracy, eugenics, and hygiene, infiltrated the political and cultural landscape of newly independent Latin American nations. Across the region, *letrados*—politicians, doctors, intellectuals, religious leaders, and artists—began to appropriate these predominantly European concepts of corporality, relying on the belief in science as a principle resource in the constitution of collective subjectivities and national identities. Although principally found in the sectors of politics, religion, and science (sectors whose main objectives included the domestication or regeneration of the masses), the obsession with disease and health made its way into the aesthetic realm as well. Writers and other artists responded to the language of positivism, adopting and occasionally subverting the impulse to control the other through an aestheticization of scientific rhetoric. This phenomenon has been detailed by the Argentine literary and cultural critic Gabriela Nouzeilles, who, by investigating the "pact of meaning between literature, nationalism, and medical knowledge," has highlighted the process of fiction making inherent in both political and literary discourses at the end of the nineteenth century, underscoring the affiliation of the ideological and the cultural in the fashioning of national subjects through the rhetoric of science.[1]

Yet while the primary function of medical discourse has been to separate the "well" from the "sick," establishing, following Nouzeilles's argument, a boundary between the "healthy self" and the "infirmed other," there remains an implicit tension between these fields, a constant threat of the invasion of the dominion of the same by the contaminating force of the other. It is because of this intrinsic ambiguity in pathological discourse that the notion of "Jewishness" becomes a useful motif through which anxiety surrounding identity and alterity is articulated. The idea of "Jewishness" appears embedded in narratives of disease and medicine because of its status as wandering signifier, its ability to unsettle and seduce both writer and reader, simultaneously reifying and exploding the categories so vehemently fought for not only at the end of the nineteenth century but throughout the twentieth century as well.

By unpacking literary scenes in which the rhetorical "Jew" appears in diverse and often contradictory roles, never fully free of the diagnostic gaze, I address the following questions: in what way is the diseased "Jewish" body inscribed with larger social and aesthetic concerns? Why is the conjugation of "Jew" and "disease" present not only in nineteenth-century narratives of pathology but also in those of the twentieth century, well after positivism had lost its status as the dominant paradigm? In what way does the analysis of these scenes of "pathological Jewishness" help clarify the double bind of alterity proper to Latin American constructions of identity?

In order to expand the limiting conceptual framework of the dichotomous relationship between same and other, one must move beyond the figure of the "sick Jew" by considering the entire scene within which "disease" and "Jewishness" are juxtaposed. The idea of the diagnosis allows one to shift concern with the diseased body to the broader context within which subject and discourse are married. The diagnosis, as a discursive act whereby sickness is invented and defined, is the means by which knowledge is organized. In a Foucauldian analysis of fin-de-siècle diagnostic texts, Sylvia Molloy sustains that "el diagnóstico se vuelve . . . modo privilegiado de organizar el saber (represivo) del estado, la patología se convierte en 'forma general de regulación de (una sociedad)' que adjudica al diagnosticador incontrovertida autoridad" (the diagnosis becomes . . . a privileged way of organizing the [repressive] knowledge of the state, pathology turns into "the general form of regulating [society]" which attributes unquestionable authority to the diagnostician) (1996a, 174–75). Each scene of "pathological Jewishness" grants authority—whether aesthetic, social, narrative, or ideological—to the diagnosing subject, regardless of whether the object of diagnosis is doctor or patient, self or other. The diagnosed figure serves as a body upon which the values and preoccupations of the writer and the culture can be inscribed, as well as the means by which the diagnosing subject constructs his or her own discursive authority.

Three distinct but interrelated diagnoses of "Jewishness" are at play: as the nation's contaminating other; as the Jewish doctor; and as the pathological (writing) self. "Jewishness" does not remain restricted to one side of the dichotomy sickness-medicine, but rather straddles and questions this very divide. The act of assuming diverse positions within scenes of diagnosis appears as a fluid, often paradoxical activity: the "Jew" can appear as doctor or patient, self or other, even though "Jewishness" is always the object of diagnosis. Jorge Isaacs's *María* (Colombia, 1867) and Julián Martel's *La bolsa* (Argentina, 1891) exemplify the exclusionary politics of medical discourse by identifying a contaminating body that threatens the integrity of the nation. In Rodolfo Enrique Fogwill's *Vivir afuera* (Argentina, 1998), Rubén Darío's *Los raros* (Argentina, 1896), José Ingenieros's *Al margen de la ciencia* (Argentina, 1908), and José Asunción Silva's *De sobremesa* (Colombia, 1925), medical authorities—Max Nordau being the most fascinating example—also become fruitful objects of the diagnostic gaze. And the protagonists of Luisa Futoransky's *De pe a pa* (Spain, 1986) and Margo Glantz's "Zapatos" (Mexico, 1991) attempt a sort of "self-diagnosis," rendering the space of illness and deformity aesthetically productive. When unpacked, these rich textual scenes reveal the function of pathologized or medicalized "Jewishness" in a Latin American context—that is, what specific modes of anxiety surrounding otherness are at work within broader projects of imagining community.[2]

CONTAMI/NATION

> All aspects of the Jew, whether real or invented, are the
> locus of difference.—Sander Gilman, *The Jew's Body*

Every characterization of the "Jew" within the European imaginary highlights his otherness, claims the literary and cultural historian Sander Gilman, specifying that in the nineteenth century representations of "Jewishness" become intertwined with pathological discourse popular not only within scientific circles but throughout society: "The very analysis of the nature of the Jewish body, in the broader culture or within the culture of medicine, has always been linked to establishing the difference (and dangerousness) of the Jew. . . . In the nineteenth century [this analysis] is more strongly linked to the idea that some 'races' are inherently weaker, 'degenerate,' more at risk for certain types of disease than others" (1991, 39). As Latin American intellectuals produced their own positivist discourse during the second half of the nineteenth century, appropriating the connection between race and degeneration, representations of the Jewish body became entangled in broader attempts to imagine modern national and individual identities.

Jorge Isaacs's *María* (1867) and Julián Martel's *La bolsa* (1891) employ such literary politics of diagnosis, constructing "Jewishness" as pathologically other. In both novels, however, it is the *impossibility* of diagnosis—or the ambiguity of the other's disease—that is problematic within the context of national consolidation. Though the novels were published only twenty-four years apart, the economic, racial, and national landscapes from which each text emerges are quite distinct. While Isaacs's *María* conveys a Colombia (and an Isaacs, for that matter) in a crisis of identity, due in part to the recent abolition of slavery, Martel's *La bolsa* depicts a turn-of-the-century Argentina in the midst of a wave of European immigration that threatens the notion of national purity. Despite the fundamental differences between the two projects—Isaacs, himself the son of a Jewish convert to Christianity, expresses a deep ambivalence toward racial alterity, while Martel, at least on the surface, reproduces explicitly anti-Semitic clichés found in nineteenth-century European discourse—both writers employ the trope of contamination in order to articulate the place of the other within the evolving social landscape of the nation.

Described by the English and Latin American literary scholar David Musselwhite as "landowner, soldier, politician, editor, shop-keeper, litigant, bankrupt, explorer, prospector and, of course, writer" (2006, 42), Jorge Isaacs lived through and, to a certain degree, embodied the political turmoil of his generation in Colombia. The conflict between the Centralists and the Federalists as well as between the newly formed Liberal and Conservative Parties (in addition to the violent aftershock of slavery and the racial tensions that characterize the post-abolition period) did not, however, figure into the center of the Isaacs's romantic novel. While many critics have underscored what is "lost" or absent from the novel, it is worth noting the way in which that which is absent is strikingly present, that is, exclusions are also at the same time inclusions, both on the level of form and content.[3] The death that stands at the center of the novel thus serves as a reinforcement of that which cannot be part of the familial or national system, but which nevertheless cannot be symbolically eliminated.

Jorge Isaacs's lacrimogenous novel opens with a premonition.[4] As Efraín, the semiautobiographical protagonist and narrator, prepares to leave the family plantation in order to study medicine in Bogotá, everyone, it seems, is in tears. His father, mother, sister, and cousin María—after whom the tragic novel is named—are all distraught by his parting, and Efraín cries himself to sleep the night before his departure. Efraín confides to the reader that the sadness shared by the family that night had seemed to him a kind of foreshadowing of the suffering that was to come. Indeed, *María*'s readers should be prepared to mourn as well as *enjoy* the difficult events that follow. As terrible as it will be to witness María's mysterious illness and subsequent death, in addition to the sad fate of the tragic lovers, Efraín and María (who will never consummate their relationship), the highly sentimentalized plot—still popular among teenage girls and other lachrymose readers—produces pleasure in the readerly subject by establishing an economy of difference while preserving the ideal of romantic love. Isaacs draws on anxiety surrounding disease in order to create a family drama in which only the most assimilated members of the half-Jewish family thrive, allegorizing the impossibility of national consolidation in post-abolition Colombia.

While Efraín is portrayed as healthy, his father and cousin María, both of whom have converted from Judaism to Christianity, are stricken with unknown illnesses. María's body, the object of desire of Efraín and, indirectly, of the reader, is not characterized as repugnant (this is in contrast to the undesirable pathological "Jewishness" of Mackser in Martel's *La bolsa*, Saúl in Fogwill's *Vivir afuera*, Emma in Borges's "Emma Zunz," and Laura in Futoransky's *De pe a pa*). Rather, María is doubly marked as pure Christian and exotic Jewess. That her "Jewishness" is a source of attraction is not without precedent. Tamar Garb has noted the dissonant attitudes toward Jewish masculinity and femininity in the European cultural imaginary: "The physicality of the male Jew is generally an object of scorn and repulsion. Not so the image of the Jewess. If anything the sexualization of the female Jew involves an idealization that confers upon her an exotic otherness, a sensuality, and beauty, which make her an object of erotic fascination and protect her from some of the more virulent and overt animosity suffered by her male coreligionists" (1995, 26). This conflicting attitude toward Jewish physicality explains, in part, the exoticism with which María is regarded, the Orientalist gaze noted by Sylvia Molloy in her reflections on the construction of Isaacs's heroine (1984, 46). When Efraín's love interest is first introduced to the reader, she is characterized as unmistakably other: "Pude admirar en [sus ojos] la brillantez y hermosura de los de las mujeres de su raza" (I admired in [her eyes] the brightness and beauty of the women of her race) (Isaacs 1978, 5).[5] That the brilliance of her eyes and general desirability is linked to "her race" reveals not only the exoticism with which she is depicted but also that the articulation of her "Jewishness" depends on a racialized conception of identity. As a social invention of a biological category, ideas of race in the late nineteenth century are commonly linked to disease and degeneration: this is certainly not exclusive to Isaacs's text. What is interesting about María is the way in which anxiety surrounding racial difference is ambivalently played out through the family unit, a microcosm of the nation.

While María's body is represented as exotically other, she is simultaneously associated with a "Christian" innocence. Early in the novel, Efraín describes the dual quality of his attractive cousin: "Su paso ligero y digno revelaba todo el orgullo, no abatido, de nuestra raza, y el seductivo recato de la virgen cristiana" (Her light and dignified step revealed the undefeated pride of our race and the seductive modesty of the Christian virgin) (8). His narration reveals a contradiction: María is both proud as a Jew and modest like the Christian virgin after whom she is named. Moreover, the possessive "our" in reference to María's "race" represents a slippage from his earlier reference to "her race"; just as María's identity is marked as hybrid, so, too, does Efraín's religious affiliation appear as heterogeneous and conflicted.

Yet, while María's "Jewishness" is not explicitly deemed negative by the narrator, it is unquestionably tied to her mysterious illness, which ultimately keeps her from fully assimilating into the family. It is suggested that María has inherited this disease from her Jewish mother, Sara, who had died many years before, leading to the adoption and subsequent conversion of María, originally named Ester. Although this theory is later contested—María's team of doctors fails to agree on a diagnosis—a connection is irreversibly established between María's racial makeup and her mother's. (Sara, in turn, represents that which refuses to be converted; indeed, had she survived, she would not have allowed her daughter's baptism to take place). María's poor health is further associated with "Jewishness" in that it is described as a "nervous condition," recalling the dominant discourse that links hysteria to both women and Jews (Gilman 1985).

Only the fully assimilated, medically trained protagonist Efraín offers the potential for renewal within a post-abolition social order, where traditional divisions between black and white prove antiquated. Despite the fact that he is the son of a converted Jew, and even admits to this when he refers to "our race," he is ultimately more malleable than his cousin. María, by contrast, dies of her unidentifiable ailment, foreclosing any possibility of romantic consummation and national consolidation.[6] María's defective genes (read: "Jewishness") have no place in the new Colombia.

That the novel displays an ambivalent attitude toward difference—the exotic María is both an object of desire as well as that which does not fit into the family system—is hardly surprising, given the author's own oscillation between religious and political loyalties, as well as his hybrid family background. The author's father, George Henry Isaacs, was an English Jew who had converted to Christianity in order to marry Manuela Ferrer Scarpetta, the Catholic daughter of a Catalan official (Mejía 1978, 210). In addition to his father's status as a convert—which is recodified in the figure of Efraín's father—Isaacs himself exhibited "political ambivalence between nostalgic conservatism and New World liberalism," and mysteriously abandoned Catholicism to become a Freemason (Sommer 1991, 178–80). Without recurring to a biographical reading of María, which is limiting at best, it is crucial to note that Isaacs was already confronting the problem of difference and assimilation on a personal level when he wrote the novel.

Doris Sommer's well-known argument that "Jewishness" in María "is a figure for both sides of the unspeakable racial difference in the plantation society, the difference between black and white" rings true in my reading of the novel (1991, 173). I would expand this interpretation, however, and read Isaacs's "double bind" as an articulation of González Echevarría's notion of the "Other Within," a provocative concept that helps one to comprehend the specific modes of engaging with alterity in Latin American cultural production. While European notions of "Jewishness" (and, by extension, difference in general) tend to focus on a foreign "body" that threatens to contaminate the national corpus (a model to some degree echoed in Martel), Latin American literature codifies a primordial other that, symbolically or historically, appears inextricably linked to the collective or individual subject; that is, the

same is always necessarily other. That Isaacs elects to situate the pathological drama of María within the familial system underscores the notion that the
alterity that must be dealt with emerges from *within* the national body.

Perhaps this can begin to explain why it is that the tragic tone of Isaacs's
novel inspires both mourning and pleasure in the reader, why the loss that
resides at the core of the narrative is, in reality, a symbolic gain. The tragic
is, perhaps counterintuitively, a welcome option, considering the alternative:
the untethered existence outside of a symbolic network, as Gabriela Basterra
argues in *Seductions of Fate* (2004, 100). What is "meant to be" is reassuring
because it shields one from the other side of meaning ("meant") and being
("to be"). Tragic fate is what keeps one securely embedded in a universe of
meaning and sense, albeit at the expense of agency. Even death, if it is situated within the logic of tragedy, as it is in *María*, is preferable: María's death
not only preserves desire (between Efraín and María, between reader and
text), but also assures the integrity of the symbolic universe that has been
constructed around the central loss of the novel, a universe that, in failing
to assimilate difference, preserves it as such for the benefit of the national
subject.

A second textual example of ambivalence toward the infectious Jewish
other staged within the realm of the tragic is *La bolsa*, dubbed by Josefina
Ludmer as Argentina's "classic" anti-Semitic novel (2004, 46). Penned by Julián Martel (pseudonym of José María Miró), a journalist and poet in his early
twenties at the time, *La bolsa* was widely read during its initial serial publication in *La Nación* in 1891. The novel emerged during a crucial moment,
in which Argentina was in the midst of a great wave of European immigration as well as in a financial crisis following the stock-market crash of 1890.[7]
While "Jews" are not explicitly portrayed as ill in *La bolsa*, their effect on the
nation is construed as "contaminating," demonstrating that medical discourse reaches far beyond the more limiting realm of disease. By diagnosing
"Jewishness" as a contagious force that threatens the national body, *La bolsa*
also employs a tragic structure: here, to perform the impossibility of national
integrity, paradoxically creating the conditions of possibility for a collective
"national" identity.

In the opening scene of Martel's (in)famous novel the narrative voice describes a panoramic view of Buenos Aires, much like a camera panning the
city's architecture. The central metaphor of this scene is climatic; the wind
appears to be attacking the city and, by extension, the nation, threatening
the institutions that define it: "¡Qué viento aquél tan caprichoso! ¡Cómo se

metamorfoseaba! . . . Convertido de golpe en opositor intransigente, con qué empuje arremetía contra el palacio de Gobierno ante el cual un piquete de batallón se preparaba a saludar con el toque de orden la salida del presidente" (What a capricious wind it was! How it metamorphosed! . . . Abruptly transformed into an intransigent opposition, how strongly it charged against the government palace in front of which a regiment prepared to greet the president's approach with the call to attention) (Martel 1979, 5). The real threat to the palace—a synecdoche of the nation—is the invasion of the city by immigrants and foreign investors, in particular "Jews." But if the wind (specifically, a southeasterly) is identified as alien, the rain seems to have local allegiances; as it falls upon the stock exchange, it is likened to tears that cleanse the financial waste of the city: "¡Como si con las lágrimas que le hiciera derramar su pesquisa por los antros administrativos, intentase barrer y limpiar de una sola vez toda la escoria financiera!" (As if with the tears spilled due to its inquiry through administrative dens, it tried to sweep away and clean, at once, all the financial waste!) (5). The impulse to scour the polluted polis radicalizes the conflict initiated by the wind and rain, and the central tension of the text is thus established.

This visual then narrows in on the stock exchange, the heart of the city center.[8] Climatic motifs give way to the text's true preoccupation: the presence of immigrants. "A lo largo de la cuadra de la Bolsa y en la línea que la lluvia dejaba en seco, se veían esos parásitos de nuestra riqueza que la inmigración trae a nuestras playas desde las comarcas más remotas" (All along the block of the exchange, and on the line left dry by the rain, one could see the parasites of our wealth that immigration brings to our beaches from the most remote regions) (7). In this passage, the arrival of foreigners is compared to a parasitic infestation (an image not unlike those prevalent in Nazi propaganda), the only logical response to which is extermination.[9] Moreover, the narrative use of the first person plural ("nuestra") demarcates a limit between "us" and "them," a boundary which can nevertheless be read as arbitrary.

The corruption of Argentina's patrimony by cosmopolitanism and materialism is embodied by the protagonist Doctor Glow, whose well-being is threatened by the invasion of "Jews." As a successful lawyer who is seduced by the promise of easy earnings, Glow leaves his career in order to speculate on the stock market.[10] When the reader is introduced to Glow, he is surrounded both by native criollos and by foreigners who have come to Buenos Aires to take advantage of the financial explosion at the end of the nineteenth century, temporary "friends" who come together to invent shady schemes, the majority of which are illegal, based on fictitious businesses. Of this group, Luis Glow is presented as the moral voice, resisting the unlawful projects of his associates.

Although Glow's European business partners are hardly portrayed in a favorable light, it is the "Jews" who are described with explicit repugnance, as the most offensive of all (Fishburn 1981, 93–94). If Glow metonymically signals a decaying Argentine culture, the figure of the Barón de Mackser, a German Jew and the antithesis of Doctor Glow, personifies the rhetorical category of the "Jew." While Glow expresses disgust toward all Jews—"Me sublevan, me inspiran asco, horror" (they infuriate me, they disgust and horrify me) (100)—it is Mackser who serves as his antagonist within the overtly simplistic plot structure. Introducing Mackser to an ostensibly sympathetic reader, the narrator describes the Jewish businessman as the symbol of a degenerate cosmopolitanism.

> El que hablaba masticando las palabras francesas con dientes alemanes, y no de los más puros, por cierto, era un hombre pálido, rubio, linfático, de mediana estatura, y en cuya cara antipática y afeminada se observaba esa expresión de hipócrita humildad que la costumbre de un largo servilismo ha hecho como el sello típico de la raza judía. Tenía los ojos pequeños, estriados de filamentos rojos, que denuncian a los descendientes de la tribu de Zabulón, y la nariz encorvada propia de la tribu de Ephraim. (26)

❧

> The one who spoke chewing French words with German teeth—and not of the most pure kind, of course—was a pale, blond, lymphatic man of medium height, in whose unpleasant and effeminate face one could read the expression of hypocritical humility that the habit of a long servility has made into the typical stamp of the Jewish race. He had small eyes, run-through with red filaments that denounce the descendants of the tribe of Zebulon, and the curved nose of the tribe of Ephraim.

The "Jew," here, belongs to every nation and to no nation at all: he speaks French because he is unable to speak Spanish, he pronounces his words poorly because he is German, and yet he cannot even claim "pure" German status. His linguistic and cultural impurity is overshadowed only by his offensive physiognomy. The narrator highlights Mackser's insufficient masculinity— he is of medium build and has a feminine face—as well as his pale, sickly aspect and stereotypically "Jewish" nose. This overwhelmingly pejorative visual depiction makes the Jew's body a site on which fin-de-siècle positivist discourse—which compounds femininity, "Jewishness," and degeneracy—is projected.

While Mackser's cultural and physical deviance is not linked to a particular disease, the narrator employs a diagnostic discourse in order to posit him (and, by extension, all "Jews") as the enemy of a pure, healthy nation. Beyond his repellent physical body and degenerate cosmopolitanism, the most dangerous characteristic of the "Jew" is his ability to contaminate. Perhaps unexpectedly, the rhetoric of diagnosis is also applied to Doctor Glow, who announces his own infection: "¡Pobre patria, en qué manos has caído?—exclamó el doctor incorporándose—. . . Hasta yo me he contagiado" (Poor country, into whose hands have you fallen?—exclaimed the doctor while rising—. . . Even I have become infected) (26). Equating his own body with the national corpus, Doctor Glow simultaneously performs the roles of medical authority and patient. When the stock market crashes and Glow loses his mind, the tragic hero is again diagnosed, this time by the narrator, who exclaims, "¡Cómo había cambiado la fisonomía del buen doctor!" (How the good doctor's physiognomy had changed!) (237). At the end of the novel, Glow ends up deliriously ill, hallucinating a seductive woman who turns into a horrific monster. The monster announces, "Soy la bolsa" (I am the stock market) (237), at which point the plot comes to a tragic close and Argentina's fate is sealed as a nation contaminated by "Jewishness" and global capitalism. That disease and health coexist within the same body reveals the precarious state of the Argentine subject.

Although it is tempting to adhere to a dualistic reading of La bolsa in which the "Jew" serves as the other against which the national subject is defined, I would propose a second interpretation as well. It is certainly true that Glow conceives of the relationship between "Jews" and the nation as oppositional—he maintains that "asociarse a [los judíos alemanes] es ir contra la patria, contra la raza, contra todo lo que haya de bueno y honrado en el mundo" (associating with [German Jews] is to go against the country, the race, against everything that is good and honest in the world) (105)—yet a closer look reveals a subtler dynamic. The problem resides in the fact that the text does not succeed in completely separating "immigrants" from "natives," because the national is already profoundly foreign. The corruption of Glow by gold and cosmopolitanism is not a simple narrative of the healthy Argentine contaminated by the Jewish foreigner—although this clichéd version is rhetorically powerful due to its familiarity—because of the simple fact that Glow, too, is the son of immigrants. In an early scene he recalls his "infancia miserable, cuando su padre, un inglés muy severo, venido a América en persecución de una fortuna que no logró alcanzar jamás . . . le obligaba a estudiar noche y día, queriendo sacar de él un hombre de provecho" (miserable childhood, when his father, a very severe Englishman come to America in pursuit of a fortune he never obtained . . . forced him to study day and night, trying to make of him a hardworking man) (Martel 1946, 76). Of course, the fact that "the national" appears as a hybrid category does not exclude the possibility of performing the contamination by the foreign other. Through Glow's downfall, the text creates the illusion of a threat that emanates from outside. The tragic structure of the novel contributes to the elaboration of a xenophobic discourse, in which the impossibility of purity, the loss of something that never existed, emerges as a void around which a threatened national identity is constituted. "Jewishness"—understood as the corruption of purity, the destruction of borders, and the perversion of values—becomes a convenient rhetorical tool which serves to announce the crisis of nationality that other foreigners, with their fixed national identities, cannot corroborate.

As in *María*, the ambiguous disease associated with "Jewishness" cannot be properly diagnosed: one never learns the precise nature of the threat. It is, rather, the *desire* for diagnosis that informs the structure of both plots, in which the undefined source of contamination must be either assimilated or expelled, as in *María*, or passively accepted, as in *La bolsa*. Moreover, both Isaacs and Martel draw on the genre of the tragedy: the terrible conclusions of both novels appear not as the fault of the principal characters, but rather as an inevitable disaster resulting from forces outside their control. Though agency is sacrificed here, it is for a lofty cause: that of establishing a symbolic order within which alterity is clearly identified, even when it cannot be wholly eradicated.

The most pronounced contrast between the two texts is that while in *María* difference must be absorbed into or aborted from within the national corpus (and then only partially), *La bolsa* serves as a warning against the invasion of foreignness, which threatens to attack from the outside, though a critical reading reveals its inevitable presence within. This difference is at least partially attributable to the ideological disparity between Isaacs and Martel, in addition to their divergent religious backgrounds: if Isaacs is dealing with the Jewish other within himself, Martel is writing from a traditionally anti-Semitic position that posits "Jewishness" as wholly other.

In order to better understand Martel's project, it is useful to consider Josefina Ludmer's contention that "the 'story' of 'the Jews' (a place of margin, alterity, and exclusion) is a story of the Latin American modernity which appears at the end of the nineteenth century to link economic, political, and then pseudo-scientific racial elements in a cultural constellation" (2004, 154). Ludmer characterizes these texts as fictions of exclusion, in which the "Jew" always plays the role of the other within national and racial politics.[11] While Isaacs's text operates on the margins of this definition—"Jewishness" cannot be wholly purged from the family or the nation—Martel's novel seems to fit quite snugly into Ludmer's subgenre. In La bolsa, after all, it is "Jewishness" that, while destroying Doctor Glow, assures that his symbolic identification remains intact. As Žižek explains, "Without the reference to the Jew who is corroding the social fabric, the social fabric itself would be dissolved" (1989, 176). That is, society—in this case represented by Doctor Glow—must preserve the threatening presence of the "Jew" so that, paradoxically, it can retain definition, at least on a figurative level. Yet the boundaries drawn between self and other in La bolsa prove to be porous, in that while the threat ostensibly emanates from "outside," once contamination has occurred, the inside becomes irreversibly adulterated. Alterity, thus, alters the notion of autochthony, which of course was always already impossible.

JEWISH DOCTORS

The ambivalent attitude toward the diseased Jewish body in Isaacs and Martel reveals the complex way in which discourse surrounding "Jewishness" entered the Latin American imaginary in the second half of the nineteenth century. In addition to these already paradoxical associations between "Jewishness" and pathology, there exist further examples of textual "Jews" that represent medicine, rather than being identified solely with illness. Perhaps unexpectedly, one finds that in some cases, sickness, medicine, and "Jewishness" can populate the very same body. This dynamic is not restricted to the nineteenth century, but has its roots in medieval Christian culture: "Through their close association with illness [Jews] were also perceived as the best healers. For healing was magic, and the Jews, since they could cause illness, must also be able to affect cures" (Gilman 1985, 151). Moreover, this phenomenon continues well into the twentieth century: Isaacs's María and Rodolfo Enrique Fogwill's Vivir afuera both establish connections between

"Jewishness" and medicine that complicate the overdetermined pairing of "Jewishness" and disease.

In Isaacs's *María* it is the unavoidably "Jewish" nature of María's genes that ultimately excludes her from the nation. The depiction of Jewish physicality as diseased presumes a medical authority free from the contaminating qualities of Jewish identity. It is therefore surprising to realize that the two physicians in the novel can also be read as "Jews." Doctor Mayn—"whose profession and surname practically give him away as Jewish" (Sommer 1991, 198)—as well as the protagonist and medical student Efraín are both associated with "Jewishness." To what can one attribute this blurring of boundaries between the subject and object of diagnosis? Can disease and medicine emanate from the very same source? If so, how does the overlapping of categories or, if you will, the *contamination* of roles contribute to resolving the larger preoccupations of the novel?

While María represents that which is inassimilable to the family—and, by extension, to the nation—Efraín appears to stand as a potential model for national consolidation. The fact that Efraín would not be considered a Jew by Orthodox and Conservative Jewish law (because he was born to a Christian mother) only adds to the ambivalence surrounding his identity. Moreover, his name alludes to one of the lost tribes of Israel, the descendants of which have continually had to defend their Jewish "authenticity."[12] The protagonist's family, a microcosm of the nation, must transform or expel sickness in order to enter modernity. By becoming a doctor, Efraín embodies this modernizing move: in sending him to London to study medicine, the family attempts to complete the final stages of the father's conversion.[13] The son of a converted Jew, Efraín personifies the possibility of curing "Jewishness"—as well as, potentially, other forms of racial difference—from within.

This ambivalence or double signification with respect to "Jewishness" serves a number of purposes. First, Isaacs himself writes from a hybrid locus of enunciation. As the son of a convert, the author was particularly concerned with the possibility of assimilation as well as the potential of leaving "Jewishness" behind: a simultaneous inclusion and exclusion. Moreover, the post-abolition sociohistorical moment in Colombia demanded a vision that absorbed or appropriated difference. As the institution of slavery disintegrated, it became necessary to imagine a system that recognized otherness while simultaneously keeping it at bay. That "Jewishness" functions—and functions *well*—as a sign of ambivalence is not uncommon; the juxtaposition of desire and repulsion, of course, appears in numerous examples of rhetoric surrounding the Jewish figure. Perhaps it is Zygmunt Bauman who explains this phenomenon best through the notion of allosemitism, the mixed reaction to "Jewishness" as both attractive and hateful.

In *María* this ambivalence is performed, both by the narrator and by his ideal reader, through tears. Just as Efraín mourns his beloved, whom he will never be able to marry, so, too, do his readers lament the impossible romance between the two cousins. The characterization of María's death as tragic assures the survival of a remainder of otherness—a traumatic, inassimilable kernel, to use Žižek's words—within the broader context of racial integration.[14] The Other Within is symbolically expelled, but remains present through the assimilated Efraín and his highly sentimentalized memory of María. By killing María, the text assures the preservation of desire for the other, which, with its object absent, can never be fulfilled.

In Fogwill's *Vivir afuera* (1998), a curious text that radicalizes the possibility of the Other Within, sickness and medicine also overlap in an ambivalent relationship of interdependence, and it becomes unclear who is being diagnosed: the patient or the doctor. Despite the historical and cultural distance from rhetoric surrounding pathology at the turn of the nineteenth century, one finds that "Jewishness," disease, and medicine continue to interact discursively in this late-twentieth-century novel penned by the sociologist, essayist, and fiction writer known simply as "Fogwill." This is not altogether unsurprising; as the intellectual and activist Susan Sontag points out in *Illness as Metaphor* and *AIDS and Its Metaphors*, the use of disease as a receptacle for social and moral concerns is not restricted to the nineteenth century, but can be found in contexts as diverse as medieval European discourse on leprosy and the plague, fin-de-siècle anti-Semitic rhetoric connecting Jews and syphilis, as well as late-twentieth-century representations of AIDS, which attempt to link sexual difference with pathology. Yet if the use of illness as metaphor is seen by Sontag as consistently negative, Fogwill explodes the opposition between center and periphery, between disease and medicine, rendering such divisions obsolete.

Set in contemporary Argentina, *Vivir afuera* takes place on the margins of Buenos Aires; the plot's action unfolds outside the center, so much so that the very notion of "center" becomes irrelevant or meaningless. As in many of Fogwill's fictional works, *Vivir afuera* is concerned with the marginal subjects who populate the turn-of-the-millennium Argentine capital. The cast of characters includes every sort of outsider: "Jews," HIV-positive patients, drug addicts, prostitutes, and impoverished artists. Rather than valuing difference, however, this site of alterity blurs that which would make each figure *other*. Momentary attempts to form a hierarchy of otherness—"¿Vos sos judío? . . . Él dijo que no, que era pobre y que pensaba que eso era algo mucho peor que ser judío" (Are you Jewish? . . . He answered that he was not, that he was poor, and that he thought that that was much worse than being Jewish) (Fogwill 1998, 73)—turn out to be reflections of anti-Semitism from within the margins of society. Each element of alterity ends up in a relationship of equivalence with the others.

Saúl, a Jewish doctor, remains just as excluded from mainstream, anti-Semitic Argentine society as the HIV-patients he treats. His Jewish body is diagnosed as abject by his lover Diana, despite the fact that his is a "medical" body, and despite the fact that she, too, is Jewish.

> "Asco," podía haber dicho pensando en la ropa de Saúl. . . . Asco a la imagen de Saúl escuchando sus cassettes ruidosos de jazz antiguo. . . . Y otro asco distinto: asco a sus madrugones, a la rutina del hospital, al olor de la sala de espera, a . . . sus pacientes. Y—también distinto—asco a la imagen del cuerpo desnudo de Saúl, frente al espejo de su baño mal iluminado . . . desnudo, con la cara cubierta de espuma de afeitar, parecía un judío ortodoxo, de barbas grasientas y enruladas, vestido con un traje negro y cubierto con un gorrito kipá bajo un sol de verano, a mediodía, en la esquina más triste del barrio de Once. (76)

⌘

> "Revulsion," she could have said when thinking of Saúl's clothes. . . . Revulsion toward Saúl's image, listening to his tapes of noisy old jazz. . . . And a different type of revulsion: revulsion toward his early mornings, the hospital routine, the smell of the waiting rooms, . . . his patients. And—also different—revulsion toward the figure of Saúl's nude body, in front of the mirror of his badly lit bathroom . . . naked, face covered with shaving cream, he looked like an Orthodox Jew, with a greasy and curly beard, dressed in a black suit and covered with a kippah under the midday summer sun, on the saddest corner of the Once neighborhood.

In this voyeuristic scene, the feminine gaze exposes Saúl's physicality as the personification of disgust. The revulsion Diana feels as she regards his body emanates from its "Jewishness"; her likening of his nakedness to an Orthodox man characterizes him as even more *other* than the secular, assimilated Jew that he is. Interestingly, however, it is both the Jewish and the medical as-

pects of Saúl that make him repugnant to his lover. The image of Saúl conjures up the smell of a hospital waiting room, of his daily medical routine,
and, most dramatically, of his HIV-positive patients. In this scene medicine
joins "Jewishness" as that which provokes disgust and, therefore, demands
diagnosis.

The presence of drugs—legal and illegal—serves to complicate the notion of a possible "cure" to the various forms of illness in this novel. While
illegal drugs are generally regarded as a corrosive force in society, here their
presence serves to highlight the impossibility of the division between disease and medicine. Mariana, Saúl's patient, further subverts this opposition
by commenting that she is more afraid of doctors than she is of AIDS (127).
The novel does not attempt to resolve this contradiction, but rather equates
these seemingly opposite forces. *Vivir afuera* ends with Saúl suggesting that
a utopian world would exclude both sickness and medicine, because in the
end "son la misma cosa" (they're one and the same) (289). "Jewishness," together with viruses and cures, functions as a mechanism to blur distinctions
between center and periphery, self and other. While successfully deconstructing the mythical nation (Anderson's imagined community), Fogwill reimag-
ines "Jewishness" without de-essentializing it. He thematizes "Jewishness"
together with every other mark of difference, erasing what Levinas terms
the face of the Other, that remainder of human alterity. The marginalized
Jewish doctor portrayed in *Vivir afuera* serves a rhetorical function: he represents a postmodern aesthetic authority within an end-of-the-millennium
Buenos Aires.

READING MAX NORDAU: A CASE STUDY

While many of the "Jews" discussed in this book are fictional, it is crucial to
point out that "real" Jews, too, can be imagined. In a sense, the idea of "Jewishness" as an aesthetic construct becomes more nuanced if one considers
the codification of historical Jews, that is, the presence of "real" Jews within
literary discourse. The consideration of "real" Jews is helpful in two significant ways. First, the engagement with living, breathing Jewish bodies crystallizes, to a certain degree, what is both attractive and repellent about the
Jewish other. At the same time, it exposes Jewish identity for what it is: the
product of a process of fictionalization, even when one is speaking about
the "real" world. The Hungarian Jew Max Nordau, the well-known doctor
and Zionist who reinvented himself and was then reinvented by his Latin

American readers, is a useful "case" that allows one to understand more fully the creative process at work in the act of imagining "Jewishness," as well as the role of the figurative "Jew" in the invention of original Latin American subjectivities.

The articulation of national, cultural, and aesthetic subjectivities in nineteenth-century Latin America has often involved significant negotiation with ideas from abroad, whether ideological movements, artistic trends, or the figures behind these very innovations. Sylvia Molloy has explored this phenomenon of intertextual (or interauthorial) appropriation in the Cuban writer and independence fighter José Martí's reading of Walt Whitman, proposing the term *scene of translation* to characterize moments in which "Latin America encounters its influential cultural others and, depending on the sense attributed to the encounter, reads itself into, or reads itself away from, those others, for specific ideological reasons" (1996b, 370).[15] While the figure of Whitman exemplifies this dynamic within the field of literature (for Martí, the Nicaraguan modernist Rubén Darío, and even the Spanish poet and playwright Federico García Lorca), a second instance can be found in the Latin American reception of Max Nordau, a prominent participant in the debates over pathology and degeneration in fin-de-siècle Europe.

At the same time that newly independent Latin American nations employed positivist discourse to structure and justify projects of consolidation, Max Nordau entered into the imaginary of the Latin American cultural elite as a figure through which both scientific and aesthetic issues could be articulated. If Whitman is "translated" by Martí for a Latin American public according to his own ideological objectives, so, too, is Nordau treated as a blank slate—an empty signifier—upon which Rubén Darío, José Ingenieros, and José Asunción Silva inscribe their own intellectual concerns. By exploring the representations of Nordau in Darío's *Los raros*, Ingenieros's *Al margen de la ciencia*, and Silva's *De sobremesa*, I propose that Nordau, as a Jew and as a scientist who dabbled in both literature and politics, represents the possibility of liminal subjectivity for all three writers, who read and misread the doctor according to their respective ideological and aesthetic preoccupations. While Nordau's "Jewishness" is only mentioned explicitly in Ingenieros's text, it enters each work as part of a broader reference to Nordau's unsettling—and often unspoken—difference, which serves significant, albeit diverse, functions for each writer.

A disciple of the French neurologist Jean-Martin Charcot and the Italian criminologist of Jewish origin Cesare Lombroso, Max Nordau stood out as one of the principal theorists of pathology in the late nineteenth century. He attracted great attention—in Europe as well as in the Americas—due to the 1892 publication of his book *Entartung* (*Degeneration*), in which he develops a theory of disease that he applies to art and artists, among them the Parnassians, Symbolists, Decadents, and Pre-Raphaelites (not to mention "mystics" and "Ibsenists").[16] He became a controversial figure on publishing this book, in which he constructs unfavourable images of artists such as the French poet Paul Verlaine, whom he characterizes as "a repulsive degenerate subject with asymmetric skull and Mongolian face," adding that "in lunatic asylums there are many patients whose disease is less deep-seated and incurable than is that of this irresponsible *circulaire* at large" (1895, 128). In adopting such a radical stance against creative personalities, Nordau situates himself at the center of debates on the relationship between art and science. This is a particularly crucial theme among turn-of-the-century Latin American intellectuals, who are increasingly preoccupied with the articulation of literature as an autonomous discipline, despite its fundamental interdependence with the sciences.[17] Nordau's diagnosis of the artist as incurable lunatic, as well as his pathological rhetoric in general, underscores the radical anxiety toward the realm of the aesthetic from the perspective of science.

In addition to his controversial work on degeneration, Nordau also figured among the most prominent Zionists at the beginning of the twentieth century; indeed, some scholars have identified him as the second most important leader of the movement after Theodor Herzl. Although this crucial aspect of Nordau's career is generally overlooked by his Latin American readers, it is important to consider given that his ideas on Zionism are intrinsically connected to his theories of pathology, and the lectures and essays he published on the political topic coincide structurally with the theoretical assumptions developed in *Degeneration*. Nordau, whose given name was Simcha Meir Südfeld, was raised in an orthodox community against which he violently rebelled. Like many Zionists of his generation, Nordau regarded the traditional Jewish community—as well as religion in general—with disdain; before becoming a Zionist, he refused to acknowledge his Jewish roots in public or in private (Stanislawski 2001, 27). Even after he had joined the Zionist party, he married a Protestant woman, joking to an anti-Semitic friend that he had converted her: "I must guard myself, lest she convert me to Judaism after she's embraced it. In any event, she would be the only believing Jew in the household" (ibid., 67).[18] But perhaps the most dramatic sign of Nordau's ambivalent attitude toward his "Jewishness" can be found in his effort to alter his very identity: he changed his family name Südfeld (southern field) to Nordau (northern prairie), a decision that elicits, for the twenty-first-century reader, the overdetermined, hierarchical relationship between "North" and "South."[19] Nordau's attempt to manipulate his own identity is replayed in the works of Darío, Ingenieros, and Silva, all of whom reinvent and rename the Jewish doctor: while Darío refers to Nordau as "Max Simon," Ingenieros includes him, despite his Hungarian origin, in the section of his book entitled "Cuatro psicólogos franceses" (Four French Psychologists), and Silva calls him "el médico alemán" (the German doctor), revealing the radical translatability of the Jewish doctor.

After reinventing his own identity by changing his name, Nordau continues his attempt to redefine the Jewish subject by postulating an original vision of the Jewish body based on German ideals of physicality. The "muscle Jew" alludes to a figure whose vigorous body reflects a healthy mind. This novel yet problematic interpretation of Jewish identity is conceived in contrast with the diseased Jew of the European shtetl: "Nordau's call for a 'new muscle Jew' is premised on the belief that the Jew had degenerated 'in the narrow confines of the ghetto'" (Gilman 1985, 158). The new, physically robust Jew becomes the model Zionist subject; the creation of a Jewish state requires, according to Nordau, a capable body. Todd Samuel Presner has elaborated on this marriage of physical subject and political citizen in Nordau's work, asserting that "the goal of the muscle Jew discourse was not simply the rejuvenation of the individual body but rather the creation of a modern body politic through the aesthetics of corporeal regeneracy" (2003, 292). It therefore becomes possible to trace a correlation between science and identity formation, positivism and politics, degeneration and Zionism. Nordau's ambivalence toward "Jewishness" and subsequent invention of a new Jewish body signal a broader context, a motivation for his commitment to discourse surrounding degeneration. By occupying the position of the scientific authority that diagnoses degenerate artists, he is able to figuratively treat his own diseased Jewish body. Nordau's internalization of the anti-Semitic ideas of his intellectual generation—which defines the Jewish body as nervous, feminine, cowardly, and decadent—as well as his subsequent postulation of a hygienic, muscle Jew in an apparent attempt to compensate for this perceived degeneracy of the Jewish body, makes him a particularly translatable figure.[20] It is precisely this Nordau—the one in constant negotiation with the symbolic value of the Jewish body—who becomes a productive object of study within late-nineteenth-century Latin American thought.

Nordau as Raro

Rubén Darío's *Los raros* (1896), a collection of essays written on artists and intellectual figures from Europe and the Americas, emphasizes the "rare" or exotic characteristics celebrated by Spanish-American *modernistas*. In a sense, it can be thought of as a counter-reading of *Degeneration*, in that it valorizes precisely that which is pathologized by Max Nordau. It is thus surprising that Darío chooses to include the Jewish doctor among his cohort of *raros*. Given that Darío would not have been familiar with Nordau's Zionist activities (*Los raros* was published one year before the First Zionist Congress in Basle, Switzerland, at which time Nordau presented his secular vision of a Jewish state), it is to be expected that "Jewishness" does not explicitly enter the portrait of the Jewish doctor painted by the Nicaraguan poet. Nordau himself repeatedly suppressed this aspect of his identity when speaking of himself. In Darío, then, he is not marked as Jewish, but rather appears as yet another *raro* among many, despite the fact that Nordau represents for Darío that which *attacks* the rare. It thus becomes necessary to ask what, precisely, determines Nordau's strangeness for Darío. If Nordau falls on the "other" side of the opposition between literature and science, how does the Jewish doctor—whom Darío nicknames "Max Simon"—end up portrayed as a *raro* himself? Is it, perhaps, his unspoken "Jewishness" that accounts for Nordau's membership in the club of the strange?

Darío's book of essays reflects a broader desire to explore *lo raro*, not only in the sense of the foreign or the strange, but also in terms of the singular, the unique. This impulse to enter the terrain of the strange—by collecting exotic objects or being seduced by the Oriental—can be found in European symbolist and decadent poetry as well as Spanish-American *modernismo* in general. Darío's preoccupation with singularity, the roots of which can be traced to his early poetry, finds its most pronounced expression in this book, which is dedicated to the depiction of eccentric intellectual and artistic figures. The excessive traits of these "characters" are celebrated, rather than judged, complicating the diagnostic impulse of *Degeneration*. In the chapter dedicated to Verlaine, for example, Darío valorizes and appropriates that which Nordau has termed degenerate in his own work. He subverts Nordau's diagnosis by privileging the space of the hospital, the site in which Verlaine is able to access the poetic. In this scene Darío directs himself to Verlaine as his ideal interlocutor: "Mueres seguramente en uno de los hospitales que has hecho amar a tus discípulos, tus 'palacios de invierno,' los lugares de descanso que tuvieron tus huesos vagabundos" (You will surely die in one of the hospitals that you taught your students to love, your "winter palaces," the places where your vagabond bones had found rest) (1972, 41). The "winter palace" alluded to here reminds the reader of Darío's notion of the *reino interior*, the privileged space within which the work of art is conceived.[21] The construction of the hospital room as a winter palace reveals an attempt on the part of Darío to aestheticize the space of the pathological (as opposed to Nordau, who pathologizes the space of the aesthetic).

Nordau appears in *Los raros* as the enemy of Verlaine and, by extension, of Darío's poetic space. The opposition Nordau-Verlaine serves, according to Oscar Montero, as one of the central tensions of the text: "On the one hand, Verlaine, the 'magic father and master' of the 'Response [to Verlaine]'; on the other, Nordau, who calls Verlaine 'the most famous leader of the symbolists' in order to conclude that he is also a 'repulsive degenerate'" (1996, 823).[22] Darío affirms the position that Nordau has created for himself, that of the scientist in dialectical opposition to the artist.

> Cuando el doctor Nordau publicó la obra célebre . . . la figura de Verlaine, casi desconocida para la generalidad . . . surgió por la primera vez en el más curiosamente abominable de los retratos. El poeta . . . estaba señalado como uno de los más patentes casos demostrativos de la afirmación seudocientífica de que los modos estéticos contemporáneos son formas de descomposición intelectual. (45)

℘

> When Doctor Nordau published his celebrated work . . . the figure of Verlaine, almost unknown by the majority . . . arose for the first time in the most curiously abominable of portraits. The poet . . . was pointed to as one of the most patented cases to demonstrate the pseudoscientific affirmation that contemporary aesthetic modes are forms of intellectual degeneration.

Apart from the prefix "seudo," which relativizes the adjective "científica," Darío does not problematize the line drawn by Nordau between sickness and medicine. It is not until the chapter dedicated to Nordau himself that one sees a more complicated interpretation of Nordau's rhetoric and, by extension, of Darío's. Here, Darío begins to deconstruct the oppositions Verlaine-Nordau, sickness-medicine, degeneration-progress, literature-science, despite the fact that these are the very divisions that have helped to define Darío's poetic authority.

The chapter opens with a metaphorical scene in which Nordau is speaking to an audience of modern artists, diagnosing each one. Addressing "todos los convidados al banquete del arte moderno" (all the guests of the modern-art banquet), Nordau enumerates the symptoms of each artist, classifying them individually as "imbécil" (imbecile), "idiota" (idiot), "degenerado" (degenerate), and "loco peligroso" (dangerous madman) (184). The reader witnesses the same Nordau as in the chapter on Verlaine: Nordau appears as the antithesis of the aesthetic, the nemesis of Verlaine, and, above all, as a figure that allows the division between art and science to exist without complications. At the same time, Darío begins to question this opposition, referring to examples of relationships between the two fields: "Cuando la literatura ha hecho suyo el campo de la fisiología, la medicina ha tendido sus brazos a la región oscura del misterio" (When literature has made the field of physiology its own, medicine has opened its arms to the dark regions of mystery), and later, "En tanto que la literatura investiga y se deja arrastrar por el impulso científico, la medicina penetra en el reino de las letras: se escriben libros de clínica tan a menos como una novela. La psiquiatría pone su lente práctica en regiones donde solamente antes había visto claro la pupila ideal de la poesía" (as long as literature investigates and allows itself to be dragged by a scientific impulse, medicine penetrates the realm of letters: clinical books are written as easily as a novel. Psychiatry points its practical lens to regions that, previously, only the ideal pupil of poetry had seen clearly) (185–86). One must question the motive that leads Darío to explore such interdisciplinary space: how does it serve him and his work? It would seem that Darío intends to appropriate that which he terms the "practical lens" of psychiatry in order—ironically—to endow *himself* with scientific authority; after all, isn't it Darío who diagnoses in this work?[23]

It is helpful here to return to Montero's argument that Darío wishes to situate himself among los raros and, at the same time, distinguish himself from them in order to attract and please "two publics."[24] One way in which Darío distances himself from Verlaine is by approaching Nordau: "No hay que negarle mucha razón a Nordau cuando trata de Verlaine, con quien—en cuanto al poeta—es justo" (one must not disagree overmuch with Nordau when it comes to Verlaine as a poet, with whom he is—at least in these terms—fair) (191). I would extend this logic and suggest that it is Nordau, in addition to Verlaine, who allows Darío to represent himself in such a manner. Nordau, as an intellectual who travels seamlessly between the disciplines of art criticism, psychiatry, and political theory—as a Jew who, paradoxically, diagnoses "Jewishness"—serves as a model of liminal subjectivity for Darío. The Nicaraguan poet requires the discursive flexibility exemplified by Nordau so that he may identify with the Parisian decadent poets and, at the same time, appeal to the Latin American bourgeoisie. Darío's construction of his own authority depends precisely on the inversion of roles between Nordau and himself. Through the *rarización*—the "making strange"—of Nordau, Darío is able to create a narrative voice that straddles art and science, thus constituting his own diagnostic discourse.

"He's Something Else": Nordau's Vigorous Paradoxes

In *Al margen de la ciencia* (1908) José Ingenieros, too, "translates" the figure of Nordau, this time from the sciences. As a psychologist, Ingenieros travels to Europe to meet and dialogue with his contemporaries in the fields of medicine and psychology.[25] Nevertheless, as the title implies, Ingenieros does not construct his locus of enunciation in the center of the discipline, but rather delineates his position "on the margin," revealing from the outset a desire to stray from the bounds of disciplinarity. Ingenieros dedicates a section of his book, which he titles "Max Nordau," to the portrayal of the Jewish doctor, echoing Darío's title chapter in *Los raros*. This likeness to Darío's book is probably not a coincidence; it is very likely that Ingenieros had read *Los raros* by the time he wrote *Al margen de la ciencia*, and that he was responding to this text. The intellectual relationship between the two men has been documented by Sylvia Molloy, who notes the men's shared interest in lo raro: "The scientist Ingenieros sees in the poet Darío . . . 'a partner in the observation of anomalies and rarities.'"[26] One thus sees that Ingenieros does not remain relegated to one discipline—specifically, psychology—but rather flirts with several at the same time. The seductiveness of multiple disciplines parallels Ingenieros's attraction to Nordau himself, who titillated the Argentine during their Paris meeting. Ingenieros underscores the paradoxical traits of the Jewish doctor, seemingly because it is Nordau's contradictory heterogeneity that appeals to the Argentine visitor.

Although Ingenieros does not describe his encounter with Nordau as explicitly erotic, he confesses the "girlish" excitement he feels while waiting for Nordau to arrive: "La primera vez que le visitamos, los breves minutos de espera fueron de curiosidad femenina, casi infantil" (The first time we visited him, the brief minutes of waiting were of feminine, almost childlike, curiosity) (1908, 171). Here, Ingenieros depicts himself as feminine and childlike, giddy almost, in anticipation of Nordau's presence. He confesses an attraction—though an intellectual one—to Nordau: "Frequentar á este hombre, es uno de los mayores atractivos intelectuales que nos ha ofrecido París" (Frequenting this man is one of the greatest intellectual attractions Paris has offered us) (171). While the construction of a male subject as nervous and feminine is not without precedent in turn-of-the-century Latin American letters—indeed, Silva's José Fernández finds an alter ego in the hysterical Marie Bashkirtseff in De sobremesa—it is more surprising to find such a sentiment expressed by the less eccentric scientist and socialist Ingenieros. At the same time, his voyage to Paris and visit to Nordau mark a crossing of boundaries for the Argentine: the thrilling encounter between the two men represents a significant departure for Ingenieros, who expresses delight at the Jewish scientist's ability to straddle distinct disciplines, even while he articulates a certain discomfort with respect to Nordau's "Jewishness."

Molloy's contention that "the intersection of disciplines and discourses within which Ingenieros realizes his diagnoses, and within which literature plays a vital role" encounters a solid foundation in Al margen de la ciencia.[27] Ingenieros's portrait of Nordau reflects a longing to mix distinct disciplines, to enter into a space riddled with paradox. He writes that if Nordau "fuera loco podría escribir poemas filosóficos dignos de Schopenhauer y de Nietzsche; si poeta, odas de Carducci . . . si fuera superficial, escribiría libros dignos de Tarde. Pero es otra cosa" ([if he] were crazy, he could write philosophical poetry worthy of Schopenhauer and Nietzsche; if he were a poet, odes worthy of Carducci . . . if he were superficial, he would write books worthy of Tarde. But he is something else) (170, emphasis added). Ingenieros exaggerates Nordau's excesses; he depicts him as a man who surpasses clearly defined limits. In addition to the flattering description of Nordau as a potential philosopher and poet, he also alludes to him as "otra cosa"—something else. What does this otherness signify? Is it the same singularity that Darío alludes to when he depicts him as raro?

Ingenieros continues his portrait of Nordau by focusing on his physicality: "Las canas rodean completamente su fisonomía, como un halo: es una característica astral. Podría deducirse que tener talento equivale á ser un astro. Las canas parecen una revancha del tiempo contra su organismo que no envejece; Nordau está joven como sus ideas, sonriente como sus ironías, vigoroso como sus paradojas" (White hair completely surrounds his physiognomy, like a halo: it is a heavenly characteristic. You could conclude that having talent is equivalent to being a star. The white hair seems like a vengeance of time against an organism that does not age; Nordau is young like his ideas, smiling like his ironies, vigorous like his paradoxes) (170). In this illustration one sees a Nordau whose talent is conveyed through a vital body, despite his age. Ingenieros seems particularly interested in highlighting the doctor's contradictions: he is simultaneously old and young, he appears transcendent in his angelic quality—he even seems to wear a halo!—and, at the same time, robust in his "vigor." The almost dialectical codification of the doctor mirrors the contradictory, multidisciplinary nature of his work, as well as the malleability of his very identity. Nordau's vigorous paradoxes—he is ancient and youthful, spiritual and physical, "Northern" and "Southern"—prove appealing and useful to Ingenieros, who arrives in Paris in search of an interaction between the scientific and the aesthetic.

The notion of "Jewishness" enters the text in a curious manner; while Ingenieros and his colleagues await Nordau in his house, there appear two other men, "al parecer judíos" (seemingly Jewish), whom Ingenieros feels compelled to report to the reader. The physical appearance of the two seems to make an impression on Ingenieros, who interprets their racially marked bodies: "La raza les desbordaba por todos los ángulos y curvas de la fisonomía; no emanaba ningún olor étnico, no obstante la especie difundida por Drumont" (Their race exceeded the angles and curves of their physiognomy; no ethnic odor emanated from them, despite the species disseminated by Drumont) (172). The idea of "desborde," of excessive "Jewishness," collaborates with the representation of Nordau as "otra cosa," as someone who pushes and destroys limits, even the very limits of the Jewish body. The "angles and curves" are suggestive of the stereotypically Jewish nose, as well as other parts of the body that are constructed to mark otherness. Although Ingenieros feels disappointed by the absence of "ethnic odor"—as if he lacked proof of their racial status—he does not doubt that he is face to face with several of the "Jews" so repudiated by the infamous French anti-Semite Edouard Drumont.

The first Jew is characterized as the incarnation of the stereotype; his body is constructed as wholly other, and this physical alterity is then extended to his hypothetical identity. His face is marked as ethnically other: "Lucia uno de esos perfiles que ilustran los libros idiotas . . . muy leídos por los analfabetos durante la crisis de judiofobia que complicó la cuestión Dreyfus" (He had one of those profiles illustrated in those idiot books . . . read by illiterates during the crisis of Judeophobia that complicated the Dreyfus Affair)

(172). It is interesting that Ingenieros simultaneously critiques and reproduces the anti-Semitic discourse of Drumont and his "illiterate" followers, as if his own diagnosis of "Jewishness" possessed an enlightened foundation. He exposes his own approach as universalizing and, in its own way, illiterate, when he comments that the man "merecía llamarse Moisés ó Salomón" (deserved to be called Moses or Solomon), as if the Jewish body were to grant the observer the right to name it. Ingenieros continues to hypothesize about the man's profession based on his body: "Su fisonomía denunciaba que era copista á máquina, sin empleo; ello no impedía ser estudiante—pues todos lo son" (His physiognomy denounced him as an unemployed typist; this did not impede him from being a student—since they all are) (173). The idea that one's physicality could reveal one's occupation exposes the naïve determinism that informs Ingenieros's analysis: the (pseudo)scientific belief that biology determines identity. His reference to "todos" (all "Jews" are students) implicitly condemns Nordau to a sentence of "Jewishness"; if they are all alike, Nordau could not possibly be an anomaly. At the same time, Nordau's "Jewishness" does not have to be justified by Ingenieros, because it is understood as the exception to his talent.

The second Jew confirms and clarifies the "other" side of Nordau's persona. Ingenieros comments that "el otro se nos figuró . . . presidente de algún lejano comité sionista, venido á París á fin de consultar al sabio sobre un milésimocuarto proyecto de reorganizar la nacionalidad" (the other, we imagined to be . . . the president of some faraway Zionist committee, come to Paris to seek the wise man's advice on project number one thousand and four to reorganize nationality) (173). Nordau's Jewish affiliation is finally named as that which is unattractive about the otherwise fascinating figure. But Ingenieros justifies Nordau's Zionism by explaining that it is his sole deficiency: "Nordau, como todos los hombres, tiene su laguna mental: cree en el sionismo, es decir, en un 'ismo' de tantos" (Nordau, like all men, has his mental shortcomings: he believes in Zionism, that is, in one of so many "isms") (173). It is left unclear whether Nordau's flaw is due to his commitment to a trivial political project, to his belief in an "-ism," to the fact that he is Jewish, or to a combination of the three. What is significant about this fragment is that it is the sole moment in all three texts in which Nordau is explicitly linked to his "Jewishness," a detail that demands further exploration. Why would Ingenieros associate Nordau with his Zionism only to immediately qualify the accusation? "Su sionismo es una simple actitud" (His Zionism is a mere attitude) (174), Ingenieros concludes, as if trying to save the reputation of the man so attacked by the public. While he attempts to paint an attractive portrait of Nordau, he cannot help but include his one "weak" characteristic, his Zionism. Since Ingenieros did not have to include a reference to this "other face" of Nordau, one must ask what it contributes to his essay: how does Nordau's "Jewishness" form a part of Ingenieros's rhetoric? Do Nordau's Zionist tendencies—a flaw on his otherwise impressive intellectual record—serve as the most dramatic example of the doctor's "vigorous paradoxes"? Might not this uncontainable difference add to Nordau's attractiveness? Can one think about "Jewishness"—mentioned and promptly dismissed in this text—as a necessary contradiction that aids Ingenieros in his articulation of his own position "on the margins of science"? Once again, as in Darío, Nordau's alterity serves a function, rather than possessing any positive value of its own.

When the famous doctor finally appears, he is described as "una delicadísima figura, que igual podría tener diez y ocho ó veinte años . . . ojos . . . capaces de hacer abjurar de su fe al católico más convencido" (a delicate figure, that could equally be eighteen or twenty years old . . . eyes . . . capable of making the most devout catholic renounce his faith) (173). The same narrator that has described himself as "feminine" while waiting for Nordau, now transfers his femininity to the very man who has inspired his own transgression of gender boundaries. He moreover claims that the Jewish doctor has the power to convert a Catholic, again associating him with the crossing of boundaries, here religious boundaries. Ingenieros seems at once intrigued and threatened by this possibility of conversion, just as he is simultaneously attracted to and repulsed by Nordau and his coreligionists. Although Ingenieros is speaking metaphorically when he refers to Nordau's power to "convert the Catholic," I see another semantic level at work, one in which the anxiety caused by Nordau begins to surface. This tension, although nameless, appears in Darío, too: it is the dangerous, as well as the fascinating, quality in Nordau. Nordau's unspeakable difference—which could be related to what Robert van der Laarse calls his "hidden Jewishness"—is represented as both unsettling and functional for his Latin American interlocutors. Just as Nordau has reinvented his own identity and constructed a discourse on degeneration in response to anxiety surrounding the diseased Jewish body, he serves as a blank slate on which the desires and obsessions of Darío and Ingenieros can be articulated. In this sense, the figure of Nordau serves as a malleable signifier, one that is infused with meaning according to the necessities of the text, a dynamic that will be repeated in Silva's novel De sobremesa.

The Practical and the Horrific: Silva Diagnoses the Doctor

Written in the 1880s, then reconstructed in the 1890s after being destroyed in a shipwreck, De sobremesa was not published until 1925, almost three decades after the author's suicide. In this fascinating novel, which could be characterized as a catalog of modernista preoccupations—sickness, hysteria, the rare, cosmopolitanism, and an almost obsessive focus on form— Max Nordau reappears, again as the enemy of artists revered by the protagonist, José Fernández. The role played by Nordau en De sobremesa resembles that of Los raros; in both texts, he represents the other against which the modernista writer invents himself.

Nordau's presence in Silva's novel is of a textual nature; he appears mediated by his book Degeneration, which Fernández reads together with Marie Bashkirtseff's diary.

> La lectura de dos libros que son como una perfecta antítesis de comprensión intuitiva y de incomprensión sistemática del Arte y de la vida, me ha absorbido en estos días: forman el primero mil páginas de pedantescas elucubraciones seudocientíficas, que intituló Degeneración un doctor alemán, Max Nordau, y el segundo, los dos volúmenes del diario . . . de María Bashkirtseff, la dulcísima rusa muerta en París, de genio y de tisis, a los veinticuatro años. (1996, 47)
>
> ✳
>
> The reading of two books that are like a perfect antithesis of intuitive comprehension and systematic incomprehension of Art and life, have absorbed me in recent days: the first made up of a thousand pages of pedantic, pseudoscientific lucubration which a German doctor, Max Nordau, titled Degeneration, and the other, the two-volume diary . . . of Marie Bashkirtseff, the incomparably gentle Russian girl dead in Paris of genius and of consumption, at age twenty-four. (Silva 2005, translation modified by Martínez)

Here one sees a dynamic similar to that of Los raros; while Darío attempts to read Nordau against Verlaine, Silva juxtaposes Nordau with Bashkirtseff, "like a perfect antithesis."[28] The young Russian writer—whose failing health mirrors Fernández's own undiagnosed disease—serves as the aesthetic ideal against which Nordau's diagnostic discourse is constructed. It is also significant that Nordau's presence is mediated by his book Degeneration, creating a complex dynamic in which the reader reads José Fernández, who in turn reads Nordau reading "degenerate" artists. These multiple textual layers make transparent the translated nature of the figure of Nordau, who appears always as a *version* of himself, not only in this work but in that of Darío and Ingenieros as well.

The author of *Degeneration* is characterized as the enemy of beauty, imagination, and artistic mastery. In the first scene in which he appears, the reader sees him—through José Fernández's readerly imagination—strolling through an art museum, diagnosing every work that, according to the protagonist, should be considered beautiful and transcendent: "Nordau se pasea por entre las obras maestras que ha producido el espíritu humano en los últimos cincuenta años. . . . Detiénese al pie de la obra maestra, compara las líneas de ésta con las de su propio ideal de belleza, la encuentra deforme, escoge un nombre que dar a la supuesta enfermedad del artista que la produjo" (Nordau wanders among the masterpieces the human spirit has produced in the last fifty years. . . . He lingers at the foot of the masterpiece, compares its lines with those of his own ideal of beauty, finds it deformed, [and] chooses a name to give to the artist's imagined disease that produced it [2005, 64]) (1996, 47). This diagnostic scene establishes Nordau's position as a destroyer of the beautiful and questions the science he employs. The word "enfermedad" appears modified by the adjective "supuesta," which—in the same way that Darío describes Nordau's "ciencia" as "seudo"—deconstructs Nordau's medical authority. Further, the notion that this imaginary Nordau "chooses" the name to signify the illness in question denaturalizes the diagnostic and creates a space of resistance against discourse surrounding degeneration.

At the same time, the act of diagnosing does not remain wholly outside the discursive subjectivity desired by the protagonist, or perhaps by Silva when he invents the protagonist. Although the aesthetic discourse postulated in this text is constituted in contrast to, or in the shadow of, scientific discourse, it could also be argued that Nordau is the one who is diagnosed in this work, and that his presence allows José Fernández to mimic the diagnostic authority of positivists like Nordau. Consider another moment within the same scene, in which their roles are inverted, complicating the division between subject and object, art and science, disease and medicine.

¡Vuelve tus manos rudas hacia el fondo de los siglos y distribuye tiquetes de clasificación patológica a esos que sintieron y expresaron lo que sienten los hombres de hoy! ¡Oh, grotesco doctor alemán . . . tu oscuro nombre está salvado del olvido! . . . Tus rudas manos tudescas no alcanzaron a coger en su vuelo la mariposa de luz que fue el alma de la Bashkirtseff. (48)

❦

Plumb the depths of the centuries with your coarse hands and stick your pathological classification tags on each of those who felt and express what the men of today feel. Oh, grotesque German doctor . . . your obscure name is rescued from oblivion! . . . Your coarse German hands could not catch in flight the butterfly of light that was Bashkirtseff's soul. (65)

The association of Nordau with that which is "rudo" (coarse), "grotesco" (grotesque), "oscuro" (obscure), and later with that which is "asqueroso" (disgusting) and "horroroso" (horrible), introduces a new discursive hierarchy, in which José Fernández writes Nordau's physicality as repugnant.[29] In a reversal of roles, it is the *artist* who assumes the authority to diagnose the body of the other, while Nordau's body becomes the object of diagnosis. Nordau is again linked rhetorically to the idea of an unsettling difference that cannot be named directly—if not the "hidden Jewishness" of van der Laarse, then a more general alterity, which provokes horror. Nordau's hands, after all, could not in themselves be sufficiently hideous to have inspired such aversion; rather, they metonymically point to some other, unnameable, object of disgust.

Although Nordau is not explicitly represented as Jewish in this text, the presence of a second "functional Jew" fills the empty space that surrounds the first. A certain unspeakable difference comes into play with relation to Nordau, in Darío as well as in Silva, and is expressed more by that which is not named or, in this case, by that which is named in another moment of the same text: his "Jewishness." Nordau's foreignness—which is signaled by his title "German doctor" in De sobremesa—is mirrored and exaggerated in the figure of another German Jew, the wealthy businessman Nathaniel Cassares. This anxious transference parallels that which is undertaken in Al margen de la ciencia: just as Ingenieros assigns the undesirable aspects of Nordau to his "seemingly Jewish" visitors, so, too, does Silva associate Nordau's undesirable "Germanness" (read: "Jewishness") with Nathaniel Cassares. This "Jew" embodies all of the stereotypes that are not mentioned in connection with Nordau—he is a banker, he is physically recognizable as a "Jew" (he has a "nariz de águila," an eagle nose), and he speaks with a strong German accent: "¿A qué depemos el fonor de per al señor Fernández en esta su casa?" (To vat to ve owe ze honah of zeeing Mr. Fernández here at his home? [170]) (172). His distorted language and excessively Jewish characteristics serve to remind the reader of that which is objectionable about the other "German" in the novel, Nordau.

What is interesting is that Cassares's role in the novel resembles Nordau's; both men represent the functionality or usefulness that José Fernández simultaneously seeks and attempts to purge from his life, keeping in mind that lo útil—that which serves a purpose, that which has a practical use—is posited in opposition to lo estético within the modernista imaginary. Reacting against Nordau's position in relation to modern art, Fernández complains, "¡La realidad! ¡La vida real! ¡Los hombres prácticos! . . . ¡Horror!" (Reality! Real life! Practical men! . . . Horrors! [141]) (139). Cassares appears later in the text to confirm and elaborate the association between "Jewishness" and usefulness; after consulting the Jewish banker about the whereabouts of his obsession, Helena, Fernández comments, "Un banquero judío sirve para todo" (A Jewish banker is useful for everything [169]) (172). On the one hand, that which is useful—as is evident in the work of Darío as well as of José Enrique Rodó—serves as the other against which a modernista aesthetic subject position can be constituted. On the other hand, the notion of the practical is something with which Fernández is constantly negotiating in this novel; it is his Other Within.[30] In this sense, it seems appropriate—if ironic—that Jewish characters should represent functionality, because it is clear that "Jewishness" in general as well as Nordau in particular serve functions in Darío, Ingenieros, and Silva.

Nordau's status as functional citizen—a figure who becomes useful even as part of a critique of "usefulness"—plays a central role in the constitution of new subjectivities in Los raros, Al margen de la ciencia, and De sobremesa. By deconstructing the numerous reformulations of Nordau's identity, one witnesses the flexibility not only of this fascinating fin-de-siècle figure but also of the signifier "Jew" within the Latin American imaginary. Within Spanish American modernismo, there is a particularly aporetic relationship between the attraction to spaces of alterity as desirable places from which to write, on the one hand, and the distancing from the pathological other characteristic of scientific discourse. Exploring the simultaneous fascination with and disgust toward Max Nordau allows one to better understand the paradoxical, interdisciplinary subjects so prominent in turn-of-the-century Latin American letters. By translating the figure of Max Nordau, Darío is able to situate himself between the decadent poets and the Latin American bourgeoisie, Ingenieros flirts with the otherness of literature, and Silva appropriates diagnostic discourse in order to construct a pathological aesthetic subject. The unspeakable difference associated with Nordau in all three works, and the anxiety provoked by this unsettling alterity, is productive for Darío, Ingenieros, and Silva: through the reading and misreading of the complex figure of Max Nordau, an interdisciplinary rhetoric is fashioned within which new intellectual subjectivities can be imagined. By highlighting and hiding Jewish difference, Darío, Ingenieros, and Silva succeed in articulating hybrid sites of enunciation in the face of modernity.

PATHOLOGICAL SUBJECTS

> Degenerates are not always criminals, prostitutes,
> anarchists, and pronounced lunatics; they are often
> authors and artists.—Max Nordau, *Degeneration*

The malleability of the signifier "Jew," which oscillates between sickness and medicine, complicating the discursive attempts to keep these categories discrete, is clear. In both cases, however, "Jewishness" remains the object of representation, with discursive authority reserved for the diagnosing subject. What happens when the infirmed Jewish body enters the text not as the other, but as an element that aids in the construction of the aesthetic subject? Does the incorporation, rather than the exclusion, of pathological "Jewishness" prove any less violent from an ethical perspective? These questions merit consideration in conjunction with the reading of the Argentine poet and novelist Luisa Futoransky's *De pe a pa: De Pekín a París* (1986) and the Mexican writer Margo Glantz's "Zapatos: Andante con variaciones" (1991), in which the site of illness is constructed as aesthetically productive. In both texts, whose female Jewish protagonists bear autobiographical links to the authors, disease still (re)presents a problem, but without a direct cure or consequence. Rather, illness is utilized to construct an original locus of enunciation, a new "writing self."

De pe a pa and "Zapatos" appeared in the last two decades of the twentieth century, during which time disease in particular and marginality in general enjoyed an afterlife as productive factors in the construction of aesthetic subjectivity. Like Fogwill's *Vivir afuera*, Futoransky's and Glantz's texts draw on the space of pathology not as a means of distancing the subject from such contamination, but rather as a way of positing alternative modalities of narrative authority. Futoransky and Glantz (both of whom identify as Jewish, albeit in nontraditional ways) internalize the image of the diseased or deformed "Jew," appropriating the scene of diagnosis in order to propose a new writing subject. The protagonists of De pe a pa and "Zapatos" both exhibit symptoms that serve as metaphors for their general status as outsiders, whether due to their religious, artistic, sexual, or national identities.[31]

Futoransky's semiautobiographical novel opens with an epigraph defining *abracadabra* as a "palabra cabalística a la cual se atribuía la propiedad de curar las enfermedades" (kabbalistic word that was attributed the property of curing illnesses) (1986, 9). Literally translated from Hebrew, *abracadabra* means "I will create as I say," alluding to the metaphysical properties of language. In addition to signaling the magical aspect of linguistic creation, the epigraph also hints at the idea of illness as that which requires a cure through the creative act of "saying." This textual opening reveals a triangular relationship between "Jewishness," illness, and writing that collaborate to form a poetics of displacement in Futoransky's work. That is, "Jewishness" appears as one of several central motifs that participate in the articulation of a secondary concern: that of political and existential exile.

As the novel begins, the reader witnesses the protagonist, Laura Kaplansky, characterized as "argentina, cuarentona, judía, pobre y poeta" (Argentinean, forty-something, Jewish, poor, and a poet) (123), arriving in Paris after living in China for many years, like Futoransky. The sequel to Son cuentos chinos, which recounts Laura's experiences in Beijing, De pe a pa narrates Laura's arrival in France and attempt to establish a place for herself. While China marks a locus of total alterity in Son cuentos chinos—"Pekín a veces me da nauseas" (Beijing gives me nausea sometimes) (Futoransky 1999, 23)—Paris represents a potential site of identification. In the first novel, Beijing is represented as a temporary place, in which Laura never expects to settle: "Debido a mi precariedad todos mis cuartos han tenido y tienen todavía cosas en la pared clavadas con chinches, nada de marcos, clavos ni clavitos, nada de permanente ni de permanecer, al menos por ahora. La inseguridad de no tener derecho (real) a estar en el lugar donde se está. De paso, marginal o casi fuera de la ley" (Due to my precariousness, all my rooms have had, and still have, things nailed to the wall with thumbtacks; no frames, no large or small nails, nothing permanent or meant to remain, at least for now. The insecurity of not having any (real) rights to remain in the place you are in. Passing by, marginal or almost outside of the law) (ibid., 13). By situating herself on the other side of the law, Laura articulates a position of extreme alterity, or exclusion. Both the language ("los enigmáticos y sombríos caracteres chinos" [the enigmatic and somber Chinese characters]) and the religion ("Tengo una foto del Buda de Kamakura; le miro larga . . . por si alguna vez aprendo" [I have a picture of the Kamakura Buddha; I look at it at length . . . in case I learn sometime]) elude Laura; their meaning remains wholly inaccessible to the exiled Argentine (ibid., 13–14).

In *De pe a pa* Laura also identifies as exiled; although she has not been forced out of her country of birth, she chooses not to return to Argentina, wishing to avoid the repressive dictatorship of the 1980s: "Entre volver a una Argentina aterrorizadora, carcomida por el videlismo y de consecuencias imprevisibles para alguien con un pasaporte tachonado por las muchas estrellas de una residencia en una Patria Socialista y volverse a París, no había en verdad mucho para pensar" (Between returning to a terrifying Argentina, eaten away by Videla's dictatorship and with unforeseeable consequences for someone with a passport crisscrossed by the many stars of a residence in a Socialist Country and returning to Paris, there was not really much to think about) (15). The narrator reflects on her various national loyalties characterizing them as physical traumas, wounds, illnesses, disasters, and poisonings. While China remains Laura's most recent corporal obsession ("La tiene demasiado cerca, en carne viva" [She has it too close, too raw]), Argentina echoes through her body like an asthmatic wheeze ("Su país es una herida crónica; como fumar desde los quince. Algún día uno intentará dejar de fumar. Algún día" [Her country is a chronic wound, like smoking since the age of fifteen. Some day you'll try to quit. Some day]) (11).[37] At first glance, it would appear that the narrator distinguishes between a temporary relationship ("Laura todavía está en el período de no poder leer ni tampoco dejar de leer nada referente a China" [Laura is still in the phase in which she cannot read or keep herself from reading anything regarding China]) and a more permanent one ("una herida crónica" [a chronic wound]) (11). Yet, on further examination, it becomes clear that this is a false dichotomy within the logic of the novel. The promise that "algún día," one will quit smoking, suggests that Laura's native affiliation is also unstable; the reiteration of this promise makes leaving her country behind an infinitely postponed possibility.

The novel does not limit the potential of national identification to one's country of origin nor to one's place of residence. Rather, the narrator constructs an alternative map of identification that goes beyond ideas of citizenship and residency. The significance of these places for Laura is measured by their impact, or potential impact, on the body.

Claro que también existen las zonas de electrificación temporaria. Si uno pasa las vacaciones en Portugal, por un tiempo, todo cuanto ocurre en ese país le interesa . . . (si a los pocos días del regreso se produce por caso una epidemia de salmonella en Algarbe, secretamente uno se inquieta: "mis mejillones, mis almejas, ¿estarían contaminados?"). . . .

Después están las zonas de electrificación semipermanentes; si se tienen parientes en Israel—quién que se apellide Kaplansky no los tendría—y se reciben noticias de un nuevo atentado, se piensa en seguida que gran parte de los pasajeros del autobús dinamitado eran íntimos carnales. (11–12)

ℬ

Of course, there are also temporarily electrified zones. If one spends one's vacations in Portugal, for a time, everything that goes on in that country is of interest . . . (if a couple of days after one's return there is a breakout of salmonella in Algarbe, one is secretly worried: "my mussels, my clams, could they have been contaminated?"). . . .

Then there are the semipermanent electrified zones; if you have relatives in Israel—who wouldn't with the last name Kaplansky—and you receive news of a new attack, one immediately thinks that a great part of the bus's passengers were intimate friends.

In this fragment, it becomes evident that even places where Laura has never lived offer the possibility of symbolic identification. Laura's multiple geographical affiliations go beyond mere status of residency or citizenship; instead, they expand to include the home of hypothetical relatives as well as vacation destinations. Further, each national relationship presented bears a pathological quality, recalling the *abracadabra* of the epigraph. The potential for contamination after a salmonella epidemic together with the threat of harm to "íntimos carnales," while exaggerated and ironic, ultimately establish a relationship of equivalence between identity and disease. Each space of encounter between self and nation appears as a threat to the integrity of the body, as if each experience of identification emerged from a body in crisis. The emergencies named here—a chronic wound, an epidemic, political violence—culminate in Laura's hospitalization.

"Jewishness" thus enters the text for the second time. If the first mention of "Jewishness" (the *abracadabra*) signifies the potential to cure the illness of geographical displacement, thereby linking language with Judaism, the second mention (hypothetical relatives in Israel) suggests that Judaism forms part of Laura's multilayered identity. Yet perhaps the most significant aspect of her "Jewishness" has to do with the impossibility of a fixed, pure identity. On recalling her childhood, the narrator describes Laura's "kaplanskidad" as that which always separated her from mainstream Argentine society, suggesting that she never felt a homogeneous identification with her country of origin. Nor, however, does she experience an affinity to the Jewish community; her own family ostracizes her for marrying a goy, a non-Jew. If "Jewishness" enters the text to illustrate one of Laura's many affiliations, it also serves to complicate the very notion of identity. The rhetorical function of "Jewishness" in this novel consists of formulating a concept of identity as ever elusive, and of belonging as always impossible.

While "Jewishness" has historically kept Laura from integrating into any community, Frenchness has always existed in her imagination as an ideal nationality. As a young girl, Laura imbued the notion of Frenchness with a certain literary authority; she even invented a pseudonym for herself, Ruth París, "para abrazar, incluyéndose geográficamente, la cosmogonía de lo mítico literario" (to embrace, including geographically, the cosmogony of literary myth) (14).[33] However, Laura's idealism begins to disintegrate when France exposes its xenophobic side. As she tries to establish herself, each attempt at finding an apartment—an activity with overdetermined significance—is rejected with explanations such as "que a extranjeros no porque el dueño tuvo ya la experiencia con unos argelinos y ahora sólo quiere alquilar su casa a . . . nativos" (not to foreigners because the owner already had the experience with some Algerians and now only wants to rent his house to . . . natives) (35). France, which had existed in Laura's imagination as a potential site of belonging, reveals itself as xenophobic, echoing her experiences in China. Thus, the person who had conceived of herself as cosmopolitan and mobile in every way finds herself playing the role of the foreigner in need of hospitality.[34]

Rather than discovering hospitality, however, Laura finds herself in the hospital. Her hospitalization follows a long segment of automatic writing, in which language begins to deconstruct, along with the disintegration of Laura's mental and physical state. Her symptoms include swollen ears and "boca nariz clítoris inflamados" (swollen mouth nose clitoris) (117, 120). It is interesting to note that each part of her body that exhibits inflammation marks a point of entry; the ears, nose, mouth, genitals, and skin all designate borderlands, where fluids enter and leave the body.[35] The image of an inflamed body, a body in flames, provokes the sensation of fire; the border territories of the body are places of emergences and emergencies.

The chapter in which Laura is hospitalized, almost at the end of the short novel, opens with a dictionary definition of hospital as an "establecimiento donde se recogen pobres y peregrinos por tiempo limitado" (establishment where the poor and drifters are sheltered for a limited time) (115). The reading of hospital as a temporary shelter for wanderers follows the logic of the book thus far in its equation of illness with displacement. The hospital offers potential protection to Laura as nomad, as well as a possible remedy to her mysterious symptoms. Yet the hospital does not "cure" Laura; none of her multiple physicians can successfully diagnose her ailment. What significance can one draw from Laura's stay in the hospital if it does not satisfy the traditional requirements of the medical profession or offer a more figurative antidote to the problem of exile?

The site of the hospital is important because it is the space within which Laura is finally able to articulate a poetics of displacement and, paradoxically, where the possibility of representation is called into question. *De pe a pa* ends after Laura leaves the hospital, without having found a cure. The plot, which at no point could be characterized as linear, is suddenly interrupted, and abruptly ends in a footnote. This amputated narrative simultaneously affirms and questions the redemptive potential of writing, of the *abracadabra* with which the book opens. Further, Laura's very character is deconstructed in the final pages of the text, in which the narrator reveals an autobiographical pact with the protagonist at the same time that it confirms her status as invented.

> Laura (Falena) Kaplansky fue un personaje que creé con parte de mi melancolía, mi mirada, mis alegrías, dolores y tristezas. A través de Laura, una especie de apasionada cándida y a veces lúcida, traté de explicar qué es ser poeta suelto en el mundo, con sus particulares agravantes; mujer mayor, pobre, judía, argentina y sola. . . . Hoy me levanté y me di cuenta, Laura, que ya basta. (123–24)

↪

> Laura (Falena) Kaplansky was a character that I created with part of my melancholy, my gaze, my joys, pains and sorrows. Through Laura, a sort of passionate, and sometimes lucid, naïf, I attempted to explain what it is to be a poet loose in the world (with particular aggravating factors); an aging woman, poor, Jewish, Argentine and alone. . . . Today I woke up and realized, Laura, that enough is enough.

In this final footnote—in which the narrator takes her leave from both text and protagonist—exile, gender, poverty, "Jewishness," and solitude combine to form a layered, semiautobiographical, displaced subject: a subject who writes and a subject who is written, a subject whose status as fictional object grants her both substance and artifice.

After the decomposition of narrative, health, and of Laura herself, the narrator mentions poetry as the only surviving element: "Escribe poemas, si no qué haría" (She writes poems, if not, what would she do) (124). If the hospital serves as the site within which a poetics of displacement is formulated, Laura's only option on leaving the hospital is to put such poetics into practice. "Jewishness" makes a final appearance, though indirectly, in the figurative enunciation of the *abracadabra*, the kabbalistic word that cures illnesses. The interaction of "Jewishness," disease, and writing produces a survival mechanism, as well as a space within which an alternative to national identity is realized.

Margo Glantz's "Zapatos: Andante con variaciones," originally published in 1991 in the Mexican journal *Debate Feminista*, reappeared in the 2001 *Zona de derrumbe*, a collection of Glantz's stories that, despite having been written at different times, all feature Nora García as the protagonist. Like Futoransky's Laura, Nora also struggles with an aberrant body that precludes her successful integration into mainstream Mexican society. Nora's one goal—to walk the road of life in designer shoes—is frustrated by her deviant physiognomy, a deformed foot. While Glantz's 1981 family memoir, *Las genealogías*, underscores the cultural and religious Jewish aspects of the author's family, "Jewishness" in "Zapatos" appears as one of several characteristics that marginalize the protagonist. Nora's status as an outsider, represented synecdochally by the misshapen foot, is linked rhetorically to her family, Russian-Jewish immigrants who own a shoe store in a lower-middle-class district of Mexico City.

In "Zapatos" the narrator refers to Nora by alternating between first and third person, recalling the autobiographical play of Futoransky in *De pe a pa*. The autobiographical pact, announced in the joking manner typical of Glantz's fiction—"Es hora de confesar que esta historia es autobiográfica, y por tanto profundamente sincera" (It's time to confess that this story is autobiographical and, therefore, profoundly sincere [1999, 198]) (2001, 74)—is neither serious nor uncomplicated. Nora's "Jewishness," like Glantz's, is not represented in a straightforward manner, which is unsurprising given the author's unorthodox relationship with Judaism (she is a particular devotee of

Mexican saints, to which she keeps a shrine in her home). Despite the designation of Nora's parents as Jewish—like Glantz's own Eastern European immigrant family, who were also shopkeepers in Mexico City—the author opts to Mexicanize her protagonist with the last name García. This ambivalent relationship with identity echoes the complicated Jewish identity apparent in *Genealogías*, in which Glantz situates herself both inside and outside the Jewish community: "Me atraen esos niños de *jeider* (escuela judía) que van acompañando a un abuelo, el niño sin zapatos y el abuelo con la mirada gastada y la barba blanca, pero no les pertenezco, apenas desde una parte aletargada de mí misma" (I also feel drawn to those children at the *heder* [Jewish school] walking beside their grandfather, the boy with no shoes and the old man with his tired expression and his white beard. But I don't belong to them, except for one distant part of me [1991a, 2]) (1997, 18). Her sense of alienation stems from being a woman and from having been born in Mexico, both of which have prevented her from being given a traditional Jewish education: "A mí no puede acusárseme, como a Isaac Bábel, de preciosismo o de biblismo, pues a diferencia de él (y de mi padre) no estudié ni el hebreo ni la Biblia ni el Talmud (porque no nací en Rusia y porque no soy varón)" (I can't be accused like Isaac Babel of being precocious or bookish, since unlike him [or my father] I never studied Hebrew or the Bible or the Talmud [because I wasn't born in Russia and I'm not a male] [1991a, 1]) (1997, 17). The relationship she traces with her Jewish heritage is represented as interrupted, dislocated, complicated by both gender and nationality: she is excluded from her own status as a Jewish outsider by her other marginal traits.

Like Glantz's portrayal of herself in *Genealogías*, as well as Futoransky's Laura, Nora finds herself not only in an ambivalent relationship with her "Jewishness," but in a situation of multiple displacement in general. As a Mexican writer, her exile can never measure up to Nabokov's; as a woman desperately in love, her suffering pales in comparison with heroines like Anna Karenina or Madame Bovary (Glantz 2001, 75–76). As if Nora's being a second-generation Jewish immigrant were not enough, the narrator comments, her parents had had to emigrate to Mexico, rather than to the more prestigious option north of the Rio Bravo: "Mis padres eran ya de por sí inferiores (judíos-rusos). . . . Ni siquiera fueron a América, la verdadera, sino a México, al sur del Río Bravo, donde los habitantes somos despreciables" (My parents were already underlings in their own right [Russian Jews]. . . . [They] didn't even go to America, the real one, but to Mexico, south of the Rio Grande, where we're all deemed worthless" [1999, 199]) (2001, 76). The daughter of immigrants, Nora works in the family shoe store selling copies of high-market brands. The opposition drawn between original and copy refers to the status of Mexico in the shadow of the "real" America, and is parodically codified in the image of the shoe store, the trivial economic parallel to the national situation: "Vendía modelos (imitaciones) del centro a precios accesibles" ([They] sold city styles, that is, imitations or copies, at reasonable prices [198]) (74). Just as Latin Americans, to the narrator, appear as imitations of the "true" Americans, Nora sells copies of designer shoes while dreaming of the real thing. Moreover, the fact that she works in a shoe store on the outskirts of the city ("una zapatería de provincia") alludes to her marginal position within the Mexico City class hierarchy. Hence, Nora's status as Mexican, Jew, and working class reveals a triply marginalized condition.

As if all this were not enough, her dream to "walk the road of life in designer shoes" is complicated by the fact that she has a deformed foot:

> Su tragedia consiste en una paulatina deformación del pie izquierdo que le produce un dolor continuo y mediocre (opacado por analgésicos) como el de un callo o una muela inflamada, dolores nada comparables con el dolor lacerante que les producía a las santas mártires del Cristianismo la amputación de un seno, la mutilación de un miembro, el desollamiento o la crucifixión. (76)

%

> [Her] tragedy consists of a slowly evolving deformation of the left foot, which produced a persistent but middling pain, lessened by analgesics. It's like the pain of a callous or an infected molar, pains wholly incomparable to the lacerating pain inflicted on Christendom's holy martyrs: the amputation of a breast, the mutilation of a limb, flaying, crucifixion. (198–99)

Her mediocre tragedy, like the shoe store full of copies, pales in comparison to the suffering of Christian martyrs. Nora's is a Jewish suffering that, unlike the self-inflicted pain of the saints, is unintended; further, it excludes her from that which she desires to experience, in contrast to the martyrs' fortunate mystical initiation.

Perhaps because of her unheroic disability, the narrator embarks on the task of recounting the etymology of the shoe—"¿Quién recuerda que la palabra zapato en español proviene del turco?" (Who remembers that the Spanish word zapato comes from the Turkish? [197, emphasis added]) (73)—as well as the history of the shoe-wearing subject. The barefoot subject also plays a heroic role in the history of the shoe: "Los grandes colosos egipcios llevan

los pies desnudos. Los héroes homéricos también" (The great Egyptian co-
lossi are barefoot. The Homeric heroes, too [197]) (73). The notion that the
act of wearing shoes—or not wearing them—could be heroic constitutes
a space of resistance against the unfortunate situation of the deformed protagonist and creates a need for the narrator to "escribir la historia de una mu-
jer cuya máxima ambición fue caminar el camino de la vida con zapatos de
diseñador" (write the story of a woman whose greatest ambition was to walk
life's road wearing a pair of designer shoes [197]) (74).

Nora's deformed foot, in addition to preventing her from walking around
town in designer shoes, recalls a long tradition of representing the Jewish
foot as other. The myth of the malformed Jewish foot likely has its roots in
the medieval representation of the "Jew" as devil-like: "The idea that the
Jew's foot is unique has analogies with the hidden sign of difference attributed to the cloven-footed devil of the middle ages. That the shape of the foot,
hidden within the shoe (a sign of the primitive and corrupt masked by the
cloak of civilization and higher culture) could reveal the difference of the
devil, was assumed in early modern European culture" (Gilman 1991, 39).
This medieval codification of the Jewish foot evolves into a more secular discourse in the nineteenth century. Rather than alluding to the cloven-footed
devil, the deformed foot becomes that which excludes the Jew from being
a "foot" soldier, and therefore from complete citizenship: "The Jew's foot
marked him . . . as congenitally unable and, therefore, unworthy of being
completely integrated into the social fabric of the modern state" (ibid., 39–
40).[36] So, too, does Nora's foot metaphorically exclude her from the cosmopolitan centers of London (Bond Street) and Dallas (Neiman Marcus).
Although Nora's deformity is not a catastrophe (she is neither considered
devil-like nor excluded from complete citizenship), the narrator does suggest that it might be the result of her marginal position: "¿No tendrá ella los
pies deformados y adoloridos porque no solía comprarse zapatos de diseñador?" (Wouldn't her feet be pinched and sore because she never wore designer shoes until now? [203]) (85).[37] By parodying Nora's situation, Glantz
continues the tradition of the symbolic exclusion of the Jewish foot from the
cultural paradigms of each era: medieval Christianity, modern citizenship,
and postmodern fashion.

In response to this podiatric problem that transcends historical and geographical distance, Nora makes a promise to Santa Teresa de Jesús—a Catholic cure to a Jewish ailment!—that she will only wear her new Ferragamos
(her dream shoes) while writing. In fact, she justifies her extravagant pur-

chase in the name of her prose: "Sabe que la novela que quiere escribir no po-drá escribirse cabalmente si no se compra el calzado ideal, de Ferragamo, su ábrete sésamo, su zapatilla de cristal, su hada madrina" (She also knows that the novel she wants to write can't be written if she doesn't decide to buy the Ferragamo shoes; they are her open sesame, the glass slipper from her fairy godmother [205]) (88). Like Laura, Nora utilizes her pathology to further her art; Nora's "ábrete sésamo" recalls Laura's *abracadabra*. Though Nora's deformity does not allow her to walk around town in her new Ferragamos, wearing these shoes at her desk enables her to write prose.

> Con los zapatos puestos . . . sentada como franciscano seráfico a la máquina de escribir o frente a la computadora, fumándose un cigarrillo, oyendo a Bach, comiendo turrón de yema y bebiendo un oporto, comienza el acto más heroico de su vida; escribir *la historia de la mujer que caminó por la vida con zapatos de diseñador*. (91–92)

⅋

> With her shoes on . . . seated like a seraphic Franciscan before the typewriter or at the computer, smoking a cigarette, listening to Bach, eating turrón de yema candy and drinking a glass of port, she begins the most heroic act of her existence: to write The Story of the Woman Who Walked Through Life Wearing Designer Shoes. (206)

This final scene of writing proves quite revealing: not only has Nora over-come the contradiction between her physical limitation and her Ferragamo fantasy, but she has consequently utilized it to her own advantage as a writer, and has constructed a heroic subject as well. It is through her (Jewish) disease that Nora acquires the status of hero and sits down to write her own story.

In each of the examples discussed, a curious dynamic is at work. While Laura and Nora both suffer from various unidentifiable diseases or deformi-ties, they retain a certain discursive authority based on the fact that they have diagnosed themselves. If this seems paradoxical, it is because the discourses of science and pathology are not contradictory, but rather interdependent and logically consistent with one another. In fact, Barbara Spackman sug-gests, an oppositional relationship between sickness and health is not neces-sarily what the Decadent writers aimed to construct in every case. Baudelaire and D'Annunzio seem to have favored what Spackman terms the scene of convalescence which, she argues, represents a space "in-between, a hazy yet paradoxically crystal-clear state between sickness and health" (1989, 42).

The Jew possesses a similar flexibility, or in-betweenness, depending on the ideological, intellectual, or aesthetic goals of the writer. By announcing their own symptoms and subsequently constructing a space from which to write, the narrative subjects appropriate the privileged position of the diagnostician. At the same time, both Futoransky and Glantz utilize parody and self-deprecating humor as a way to diminish the protagonist's heroic qualities (or to highlight the lack of such qualities) while positing an alternative locus of enunciation. Here, the opposition diagnostician-patient no longer works as a theoretical construct: this model is completely collapsed in Futoransky's and Glantz's texts. "Jewishness," which simultaneously signifies science and disease, does not remain on the margins of literary discourse, but rather occupies a central position in the negotiation of aesthetic subjectivity.

❧ ❧ ❧

Within the diagnostic scene, "Jewishness" represents a force that threatens to contaminate boundaries, be they physical, pathological, national, religious, racial, economic, or sexual. Whether desirable or undesirable, whether the face of the abject or a model for alternative identities, the presence of "Jewishness" unfailingly plays a role in the constitution of original subjectivities. While in *María* and *La bolsa* Isaacs and Martel invent a contagious Jewish other through which the notion of (contami)nation can be imagined, Futoransky and Glantz utilize the figure of the "Jew" in juxtaposition with disease and deformation to articulate the experiences of exile and marginality. In the case of Fogwill "Jewishness" is thematized practically to the point of extinction; the identification of "Jewishness" with AIDS, poverty, medicine, and prostitution erases any "real" form of difference (the absolute Other).

It is important to accentuate the *performative* quality of the diagnosis: after all, it is only by writing, by pronouncing the diagnosis, by "sentencing" the diseased body to its marginalized status that the diagnostic subject is born. This subject belongs to a flexible category; s/he enters and leaves the position of diagnostician at will, so that one witnesses Silva or even Darío, normally "allies" of pathology, condemning the "grotesque" and "strange" aspects of Max Nordau. Futoransky's and Glantz's semiautobiographical protagonists appropriate the diagnostic position—despite the fact that they are "self"-diagnosing—in order to assume aesthetic authority. "Jewishness" enters the picture as an equally flexible entity, a manipulable category that aids in the construction of the diagnostic subject.

The case study of Nordau crystallizes the distinct modalities of reading "Jewishness" in the texts considered in this chapter, readings that imply translation, invention, interpretation, that simultaneously imagine "Jewishness" and react to a perceived Jewish presence. Nordau's case also highlights the double functionality of rhetorical "Jewishness," that is, how "Jewishness" can be invented from the outside, as well as from within (by Jewish writers themselves). What I have termed "misreadings" in Nordau (Silva calls him the "German doctor" while Ingenieros lumps him into the category "Four French Psychologists") finds an unexpected parallel in Futoransky, whose fragmented protagonist refuses or is unable to be categorized as merely one thing: Jewish, Argentine, French. Moreover, the fact that Simcha Meir Südfeld renames himself Max Nordau allows one to rethink the process of self-representation or invention involved in Isaacs's, Futoransky's, and Glantz's creation of semiautobiographical characters. In Futoransky and Glantz the narrative "I" becomes blurred with the protagonist, as well as with the author herself, revealing the artifice implicit in character, narrative voice, and in "Jewishness" itself. The malleability of the figure of Nordau affirms the very same dynamic at work in Martel and Fogwill, in which imagined "Jews" (or hypothetical real Jews) are recodified to fit the needs of each text.

Of course, the opposition between "imagined" and "real" is misleading at best, if not outright false; therefore the "case study" of Max Nordau is no more (or less) relevant to the discussion of imagining "Jewishness" than the other texts discussed in this chapter. While I would certainly draw a distinction between historical Jews and fictional "Jews," an analysis of the representations of "Jewishness" reveals the constructed nature of both groups. Although a Jew named Max Nordau did exist (and irreversibly altered modern Jewish history), one sees that the inventions of Nordau as Jewish (Nordau's inventions of himself as well as the translations by his Latin American readers) carry more weight, culturally or intellectually speaking, than any "authentic" Jewish characteristic. This last idea is of course irrelevant to my discussion, and yet the possibility of an identifiable Jewishness has been central to numerous studies of so-called Jewish literature.[38]

I would thus suggest that the way in which "Jewishness" is imagined serves as a litmus test for each text's broader concerns. That is, by critically revisiting textual representations of "Jewishness," one can learn more about the cultural context of the work, as well as its aesthetic concerns, than about "Jewishness" itself. If one does learn anything about "Jewishness," it has more to do with its rhetorical power and flexibility, its unique status as wandering signifier.

℘ TWO

The Scene of the Transaction

Having unpacked the rhetorical coupling of
"Jewishness" and disease within diagnostic
scenes in nineteenth- and twentieth-century
Latin American literature, I now investigate the scene
of the transaction, in which "Jewishness," money, and
prostitution are textually linked as part of projects of
imagining the self, the nation, modernity, and fiction.
By considering the juxtaposition of three concepts
with such fertile symbolic presence—both in Europe
and the Americas—I address the following questions:
what kinds of social anxieties are addressed through
metaphors of "Jewishness," money, and prostitution?
What role do the concepts of value and promiscuity play within textual attempts to fashion individual
and national subjects? How are problems of globalization, modernity, subjectivity, and difference played out
through the "Jew," the dollar sign, and the prostitute?

Is it possible to identify a remainder, a surplus of difference that survives these symbolic transactions?

In nineteenth-century Europe and turn-of-the-century Latin America, cities in the process of modernization and industrialization became influenced and populated by capitalism and prostitution on a cultural, economic, and rhetorical level. During this period, the "transaction" emerged as a dominant mode of social interaction, and the "Jew" became a convenient figure through which political, financial, and cultural shifts could be debated. Yet the discursive linking of "Jewishness," money, and prostitution was not a new phenomenon: the relationship between these three elements within the Western cultural imaginary can be found in medieval Christian society, in particular in the writings of the philosopher and theologian St. Thomas Aquinas (Gilman 1991, 124). The canonical prohibition of interest taking—which limited the profession of money lending to the Jews—was deduced from money's status as an object. Since money was not alive, reasoned Aquinas, it should not be able to reproduce. Thus, the taking of interest by Jews was understood by Christian society as the *reproduction or sexualization* of money: "Jews, in taking money, treated money as if it were alive, as if it were a sexualized object. The Jew takes money as does the prostitute, as a substitute for higher values, for love and beauty. . . . But the image of the Jew as prostitute is not merely one that draws an economic parallel between the sexuality of the Jew and that of the prostitute. It also reveals the nature of the sexuality of both Jew and prostitute as diseased, as polluting" (ibid., 124). The association between "Jews" and money is not a neutral judgment, but rather is construed as an intrinsically perverse relationship, in which money is distorted from its true function. In the same way, the prostitute contaminates ideals of spiritual love, femininity, the family, the nation. Thus, both "Jew" and prostitute actively participate in the commodification of sex and the sexualization of money.

The triad "Jewishness"-money-prostitution has also been linked to discourse surrounding disease in the Western imaginary. Within the violently anti-Semitic ideological apparatus of Nazi Germany, for example, Jews, prostitutes, and money were linked to the spread of syphilis in Germany: "Jews were the arch-pimps; Jews ran the brothels; but Jews also infected their prostitutes and caused the weakening of the German national fiber" (ibid., 97). Yet while the radical implications of such discursive associations can be located within Nazi rhetoric, less fascist versions of this phenomenon continuously resurface throughout the cultural imaginaries of Europe and the Americas.

Narratives of "Jewishness" are narratives of difference, of immigration, exile, travel, and, in many cases, of negotiation. Thus it is no coincidence that many literary texts and other cultural products utilize figures of "Jewishness" within scenes of transactions. These scenes, in which everything can be negotiated—value, identity, alterity—establish an economy of difference. Alterity is simultaneously invented and evaluated using metaphors of exchange. The "Jewish transactions" that appear in these texts often go beyond hackneyed stereotypes of Jews being "wealthy," "cheap," "bankers," or "moneylenders," though they depend on these recycled ideas for verisimilitude, strength, success. The scene of the transaction is "successful"—convincing—on a rhetorical level because metaphors of "Jewishness," money, and prostitution function well together; a long historical trajectory of associations between these symbolic elements compound and are reaffirmed with every new invention. They work well together because each motif represents that which travels from country to country, body to body, contaminating all involved and threatening to destroy that which would keep these systems discrete.

In addition to existing on the limits of body, family, and nation, "Jewishness," money, and prostitution traditionally reside on the margins of the law. Of course, prostitution has historically vacillated between the realms of the legal and the illegal, and even during periods of legalized prostitution, one finds strict regulations governing the trade. In *Sex and Danger in Buenos Aires* the historian Donna Guy writes that "like many other nineteenth-century cities in the throes of modernization and industrialization, Buenos Aires legalized prostitution to isolate and, it hoped, control the social and medical consequences of commercial sex" (1991, 47). Across the Atlantic, an 1830 police edict in Paris banned prostitution in the public space of the arcades, limiting it to the more enclosed, and controlled, space of licensed brothels (Benjamin 1999, 499). Managing prostitution in this way reserves for the state the power to legitimize, while consigning prostitutes and their clients to the border between legality and illegality. Financial transactions, too, offer an inherent possibility of transgression, and Jewish transactions in particular bear traces of suspicion, originating perhaps in the practice of usury condemned by the church and thus relegated to the margins of morality.

What does the limit of the "legal" and "illegal" signify? Josefina Ludmer details the importance of the "crime" in her book *The Corpus Delicti*, in which she argues that the crime represents a powerful, oft-used motif in literature due to its ability to distinguish "culture" from "nonculture": "From the very beginning of literature, crime appears as one of the instruments most utilized to define and found a culture: to separate it from nonculture and to mark what culture excludes" (2004, 4). While the power of differentiation referred to by Ludmer is relevant to my analysis—indeed, many of the texts I analyze in this chapter can be read from this perspective—in some texts "Jewishness," prostitution, and money are used not simply to separate culture and nonculture— same and other—but to address the tension inherent in the space in *between* these spheres.

What is the site of the in-between? Within what cultural terrain or psychic landscape can the in-between be "located"? In his writings on the Parisian arcades the German-Jewish philosopher and literary and cultural critic Walter Benjamin proposes the *passagen* (arcades) together with the bordello and the casino as sites of transaction, situated "within as well as outside the marketplace, between the worlds of money and magic" (Eiland and McLaughlin 1999, xii). Within these passagen, these spaces of passage from one realm to the other, these *thresholds*, can be found the figures privileged by Benjamin: the prostitute, the gambler, the flâneur, the collector.[1] In modern life, he argues, "we have grown very poor in threshold experiences," with the possible exceptions of falling asleep and waking up (1999, 494). The threshold, a half-dreamlike state between two levels of consciousness, is distinct from the concept of a border in that it designates a zone, rather than a line. While he mourns the loss of such spaces within urban modernity, he maintains that prostitutes (and, by extension, gamblers) "love the thresholds of these gates of dream."[2] For Benjamin, the liminal experience of semiconsciousness parallels the more tangible "borderline" practices of gambling and prostitution.

By situating both financial and sexual impropriety within the space of the threshold, Benjamin outlines the theoretical framework necessary to see thresholds within modernity. Perhaps Benjamin has mourned too early, for it is precisely in these liminal zones that the "Jew" resides: if not in "reality," then in its figurative representations. While modern life may not be characterized by the threshold experience that Benjamin describes, one nevertheless finds echoes of the threshold in the margins of modernity. The idea of the in-between is particularly relevant to a discussion of cultural products from Latin America, where the idea of modernity has been characterized as unequal, incomplete, and even impossible (Beverley and Oviedo 1995; Brunner 1992; Ramos 1989). This intermediate site of experience bears a resemblance to the notion of liminal space, which comes into play in each of the scenes I discuss in this book. The diagnosis, the transaction, and conversion all involve negotiations between bodies, subjects, nations, and religions. The idea of "Jewishness," due to its status as wandering signifier, is able to bridge these diverse spaces, simultaneously reifying and exploding the categories it delineates.

Although rhetoric surrounding "Jewishness" and money is inseparable from rhetoric linking "Jewishness" and prostitution, for the sake of organization, this chapter addresses each in turn. First, I explore how the texts in question establish a corrupt relationship between "Jewishness" and money in an attempt to negotiate national and aesthetic "values": identity and authenticity, the national and the foreign, "truth" and meaning. I revisit Julián Martel's *La bolsa*, as well as analyze the songwriter Noel Rosa's samba "Quem dá mais?" (Brazil, 1930) and Jorge Luis Borges's short story "Emma Zunz" (Argentina, 1948). I then turn to Hilário Tácito's *Madame Pommery* (Brazil, 1920), Clara Beter's *Versos de una . . .* (Argentina, 1926), Borges's "Emma Zunz," and Rodolfo Enrique Fogwill's *Vivir afuera*, investigating how the conjugation of "Jewishness" and prostitution enacts a kind of promiscuous textuality that disrupts the boundaries between nations and subjects, genres and genders.

VALUE AND REPRESENTATION

If one follows Ludmer's theory of "the 'story' of the 'the Jews'" within late nineteenth- and early twentieth-century Argentine narratives, one sees that rhetorical connections between money and "Jewishness" have not only to do with stereotypes about Jewish moneylenders but also with the *symbolic* function of both "Jews" and money. By linking the idea of "the 'story' of 'the Jews'" with the "economic story," Ludmer demonstrates the way in which the signifier "Jew" joins the signifier money to create an exponential form of representation.

> "The Jews" are always the representatives of money, and the narrative that includes them is an economic narrative: banks, stock exchanges, and gold. "The Jews" are the sign of the money sign: a sort of representation squared. Or better yet, "the Jews" are the representatives of money, which is itself *an apparatus of representation.*
>
> For money is a symbolic substance, a pure abstraction that reduces everything to a common denominator; it is at once material and immaterial, it is mental but it is also a mental "thing," it is a mediator of social relations, and it represents social interaction. Money creates "reality" and reduces everything

to merchandise; everything can be bought, everything has its price, above all that which is priceless. (2004, 155)

Although I would take issue with Ludmer's insistence that "Jews" are *always* representative of money, it is worthwhile to consider her explanation of the symbolic relationship between "Jews" and money. The "story" (which Ludmer defines loosely as "a moment, a scene in a story or a novel, a quote, a dialogue, but also a long 'history' encompassing many novels") that includes "Jews" is not always an economic tale, as Ludmer would have it, yet "Jews" and money both function as symbols, as representatives of broader ideas, as abstractions (ibid., 6). While I would question the causality of this relationship—do "Jews" signify money or does money signify "Jewishness"?—I would affirm that one is dealing primarily with a matter of representation, and that both "Jews" and money serve as mediating forces in social relations.

In *La bolsa*, a text that Ludmer rightly places in the category of the "economic story," "Jewishness" and gold together threaten the concept of national integrity. While Martel employs a medicalized rhetoric in order to construe "Jewishness" as that which threatens to contaminate Argentina, he also links the motif of illness to the problem of money, a rhetorical move that is not unprecedented: the belief that disease can be spread through economic relations echoes throughout the Western cultural imaginary (Gilman 1991, 97). I will now explore the perverse, threatening relationship between "Jews" and money in Martel's work, asking how the idea of the nation is constructed in relation to this paranoia.

La bolsa, which responds to the drastic fluctuations of Argentina's economy at the end of the nineteenth century, is part of a broader genre that one could call, following the nineteenth-century French literature scholar Halina Suwala, the "novel of the stock exchange" (quoted in Wasserman 2001, 193). These "financial fictions," to borrow the comparatist Renata Wasserman's term, include such works as Emile Zola's *L'argent* (France, 1891), Alfredo de Taunay's *O encilhamento* (Brazil, 1894), and Frank Norris's *The Pit* (United States, 1903), all of which "focus on stock or commodities operations, that is, on forms of using or defining 'money,' [and whose] plots turn on 'speculation'" (ibid.). As characterized by Wasserman, as well as by the German sociologist Georg Simmel in *The Philosophy of Money* and Slavoj Žižek in his reflections on Marx and the fetish of the commodity, "money"—both historically as well as in its literary representations—appears as a fictitious object, the value of which is not innate, but rather determined by its users. The novel

of the stock exchange could be understood as a *fiction of an object of fiction.*
Narratives that juxtapose "Jewishness" with "money" contribute yet another
symbolic operation to this formula, creating a complex web of signification
in which ostensibly a priori concepts are subject to invention.

In the opening scene of *La bolsa* the narrator figuratively alludes to the invasion of Buenos Aires by foreign investors, blaming cosmopolitanism and
materialism for the decay of Argentine society. Invoking a climatic motif,
Martel refers to the rain which cleanses the *escoria* (waste) of the financial district. The "financial waste" referred to in this scene is highly suggestive—the
characterization of the financial sector as the dregs of society invokes the
idea of surplus, of leftovers. This surplus is generated by foreign involvement
in the national economy and represents an element of difference that must
be eliminated in order to preserve the integrity of the state.

What is the role of "Jewishness" within the (here, problematic) connection
between cosmopolitanism and materialism? Do "Jews" represent foreignness in general, or is the parasitic immigrant a generalization of an anti-
Semitic stereotype? *La bolsa* seems to regard foreignness with ambivalence,
as evidenced by the distinction between different types of immigrants. This
difference is elucidated by Doctor Glow's runner, who confides in him that
"los ingleses que tan buen ojo tienen para descubrir filones, están trayendo
sus capitales con una confianza que nos honra" (the British, who have such
a good eye for discovering good deals, are bringing their capital with a confidence that honors us), while "los judíos . . . empiezan a invadirnos sorda-
mente. . . . Si nos descuidamos acabarán por monopolizarlo todo" (the Jews
. . . are beginning to surreptitiously invade us. . . . If we don't look out they
will end up monopolizing everything) (Martel 1979, 18). If English investment in the Argentine stock market is linked to the notion of "honor," Jewish involvement in the country's economic affairs, in contrast, is regarded
with suspicion. Glow himself is the son of English immigrants, revealing a
stratified attitude toward foreignness; a generalized group of immigrants is
not sufficient to articulate the fear of losing control over the national marketplace and, by extension, the nation itself.[3] Instead, the text focuses on "Jews"
as those leading the invasion of Argentina.

Doctor Glow becomes the mouthpiece for hackneyed, paranoid opinions
about "Jews," appropriating anti-Semitic discourse nearly verbatim from
Edouard Drumont (Fishburn 1981, 99). Glow, whose paranoia is channeled
through a fear of financial takeover, complains that "iya son dueños de los

mercados europeos, y si se empeñan lo serán de los nuestros, completando así la conquista del mundo!" (they already own the European markets, and if they persist they will own ours too, completing their world conquest) (18). He describes the Jewish community as a homogeneous entity, as an "ejército israelita lanzado sobre la América para conquistarla con el dinero" (Israelite army attacking America, conquering it with money) (Martel 1946, 119). This idea, of course, does not originate with Martel; it is not an Argentine or even a Latin American invention. The idea of a Jewish conspiracy to take over the world finds expression in European thought since the Middle Ages, so that the fear articulated here has to do, more specifically, with the impossibility of national purity.[4] That Glow employs a military metaphor (an "Israelite army") to talk about "Jews" is significant, for it underscores and compensates for the lack of a Jewish national identity. As a people without a state (at that time), "Jews" present a threat not only due to their alleged financial activities but also because they subvert the concept of "the national" as an essential determinant of identity.

This dual danger is detailed by Glow, who links gold to cosmopolitanism, insisting that money destroys national identity: "Pero el oro es corruptor. Allí donde el dinero abunda, rara vez el patriotismo existe. Además de eso, el cosmopolitismo, que tan grandes proporciones va tomando entre nosotros, hasta el punto de que ya no sabemos lo que somos, si franceses o españoles, o italianos o ingleses, nos trae, junto con el engrandecimiento material, el indiferentismo político. . . . se nos ha contagiado este culpable egoísmo importado" (But gold corrupts. Wherever money abounds, rarely does patriotism exist. Moreover, cosmopolitanism—which is taking on such great proportions among us, to the point that we no longer know what we are, whether French or Spanish, Italian or English—brings us, along with material growth, political indifference. . . . we have become infected with this imported guilt-ridden selfishness) (1979, 103). The opposition of gold and foreignness on the one hand and patriotism on the other, locates economic agency within the realm of the global, reserving cultural purity (and passivity) for the local. The idea that "we don't know who we are anymore" is a nostalgic construction that posits nationality as an ideal belonging to the past.

Yet attitudes toward cosmopolitanism and "Jewishness" are not wholly conflated in the text, or in the culture in general. Thus it is critical to bear in mind the distinction drawn between a positive cosmopolitanism, through which Argentine culture can better itself, and the xenophobia typified by anti-

Semitic representations of foreignness. Glow conveys his anxiety toward alterity by repeating stereotypical myths about "Jews," insisting that, through interest taking, "Jews" steal money from legitimate businessmen. The Jewish moneylender is referred to by Glow as "ese pájaro negro del comerciante honrado" (bane of the honest businessman) (110). He elucidates the perverse relationship between ("honest") businessman and ("dishonest") usurer by turning to the idea of "Jew" as vampire: "Vampiro de la sociedad moderna, su oficio es chuparle la sangre. . . . Banquero, prestamista, especulador, nunca ha sobresalido en las letras, en las ciencias, en las artes, porque carece de la nobleza de alma necesaria, porque le falta el ideal generoso que alienta al poeta, al artista, al sabio" (Modern society's vampire, his trade is sucking blood. . . . Banker, moneylender, speculator, he has never excelled in letters, in science, in the arts, because he lacks the necessary nobility of spirit, the generous ideal that inspires the poet, the artist, the sage) (110). The relegation of the "Jew" to the financial sector is justified by the contention that he lacks any true talent—he possesses no transcendent value. The prevalence of this belief can be found in German culture beginning with the Enlightenment: "It was the superficiality of the Jew, the Jew's mimicry of a world which he could never truly enter, which produced works which were felt to be creative but, in fact, were mere copies of the products of truly creative individuals" (Gilman 1991, 129). Incapable of producing a work of transcendent value, the "Jew" must occupy himself with "false" value (money) and extract more "false" value from this money in the form of interest. This goes back to the idea of the sexualization of money: because "Jews" cannot produce anything of true value, they must reproduce inanimate objects, casting a perverse spell on society as a whole.

Though the "Jew" can only join culture through falsifications and dubious financial dealings—remember that Mackser buys his title of "Baron" in order to appear more honorable than he "really" is—the notion of "being Argentine" appears as a similarly manipulable identitary category. A critical reading of La bolsa reveals that, on a discursive level, Martel invents national identity through an equally questionable rhetorical negotiation. The idea of the autochthonous is paradoxically embodied in the figure of Glow, the son of an Englishman. Anxiety toward the "Jewish transaction" has to do with an already existent unease toward foreignness that is inextricably linked to what it means to be criollo. It is only through a fictional transaction—in which Glow comes to represent Argentina through literary discourse—that the impossible nation comes into existence.

In "Quem dá mais?" a song composed by Brazil's leading *sambista* Noel Rosa in 1930 and recorded in 1932, "Jewishness" reappears as that which threatens to destroy the nation through financial dealings. Instead of participating in the stock market, however, the "Jew" appears in a new scene of transaction: that of the auction. While "Jewishness" is juxtaposed with money in both examples, Rosa displays a less vehemently anti-Semitic, more ambivalent attitude toward "Jewishness" in particular and hybridity in general. The "Jew" is at once identified as participating in the "selling out" of Brazilian culture as well as—in an indirect and perhaps unexpected way—in its preservation. By situating the "Jew" within the scene of the auction, Rosa utilizes "Jewishness" as part of a broader attempt to imagine a heterogeneous Brazilian identity.

"Quem dá mais?"—as well as Rosa's short-lived but prolific career as sambista—appeared during a moment in Brazilian history in which samba was, to use the words of the anthropologist Hermano Vianna, "invented" and converted into a symbol of Brazilian national identity. This was a curious point in time and space, a moment of encounter—between "white" and "black," elite and popular, center and margin—in which a musical tradition that was already the result of a series of encounters between different sectors of society began to be widely consumed by the dominant classes. What is perhaps most fascinating about this encounter—transculturative, to be sure—is not only the way in which samba came to be widely listened to (thanks in part to its diffusion by a rapidly exploding radio industry), but also the way in which it came to signify Brazil's national essence. Indeed, at the same time that the Brazilian sociologist and anthropologist Gilberto Freyre was writing about *mestiçagem* (miscegenation) as the defining characteristic of Brazilian culture, Brazilianness—or *brasilidade*—was being actively invented by intellectuals, politicians, and artists.

What role would the notion of foreignness play in the constitution of an authentic national subject? To what extent was the presence of the foreign necessary to realize this project? During a time in which the division between "black" and "white" was being blurred in order to imagine a collective autochthonous subjectivity, who would mark the limit between self and other? "Quem dá mais?"—in which typically Brazilian artifacts (a *mulata*, a guitar, and a samba) are sold to foreign buyers at an auction—offers some possible answers to these questions. While for Rosa, as the historian Bryan McCann contends, foreigners pose a threat to the culturally rich world of samba by selling out the Brazilian soul, a more ambivalent, paradoxical relationship between foreignness and Brazilianness is imagined through the figure of the "Jew."

Composed at nearly the same moment as Getúlio Vargas's rise to power as a result of the Revolution of 1930, Rosa's samba emerged as nationalism was on the rise, and as an increasing number of Jewish immigrants were arriving in Brazil (Lesser 1995, 28).[5] While the fictional horizon of the lyrics is not unrelated to the presence of "real" Jews in the country, the idea of "Jewishness" serves a rhetorical function in the invention of brasilidade. Rosa's samba depicts a fictional auction, in which Brazilian cultural artifacts are sold off one by one to willing buyers. The scene of the auction is unique in that value is not predetermined by the seller, but rather is negotiated between the auctioneer and potential buyers. Likewise, the notion of Brazilianness is undetermined, open, ready for definition by both native and foreign actors. As each article is called out by the auctioneer, as each potential buyer is addressed, the notion of brasilidade is offered as a sacrifice and, paradoxically, constituted through the very threat of its loss.

The first item for sale is a mulata, a stereotypical figure used to represent the notion of Brazilian sensuality and racial hybridity. In Brazil the rise in popularity of the samba in the 1930s coincided with a growing acceptance—and romanticization—of Afro-Brazilian culture by the whiter elites. As Vianna demonstrates, samba served as one of the key tools in the "invention of Brazil's national essence" as specifically Afro-Brazilian (1999, xvii). That the figure for sale in "Quem dá mais?" is a mulata, in particular, represents an erotic yet safe solution to the problem of race: her whiteness promises assimilation into the dominant classes, her blackness stimulates desire for that which is other (to a white consumer of music), while her gender assures a lack of political agency. The North American and Caribbean literary scholar Vera Kutzinski, whose work traces the power dynamics at play within discourse on mestizaje in Cuba, explains that the mulata "is a symbolic container for all the tricky questions about how race, gender, and sexuality inflect the power relations . . . in colonial and postcolonial Cuba" (1993, 7). It is therefore unsurprising that the mulata should appear at the auction, a site of economic and cultural negotiation. In Rosa's lyrics she is described by the auctioneer as a "moça formosa / fiteira, vaidosa e muito mentirosa" (beautiful lady / flirtatious, vain, and very false), at once inspiring attraction and suspicion.[6] She is finally sold to Vasco da Gama, a popular Brazilian football club that, as McCann points out, was "founded by and strongly associated with Portuguese immigrants" (2001, 7). The club purchases her, in place of a car, as a gift for their star player, Russinho (literally, "the little Russian"): "O Vasco paga o lote na batata . . . / E em vez de barata / Oferece ao Russinho uma mulata" (Vasco pays the lot . . . / and instead of a car / offers Russinho a mulata).[7] From the outset, there is a complex dynamic at play between the national and the foreign. On the one hand, it is implied, brasilidade—through the figure of the mulata—is sold, or sold out, to Vasco to be given to Russinho, both of whose names simultaneously connote foreignness and Brazilianness.[8] Yet each agent in the transaction participates in a complicit relationship, and in the end any attempt on the part of the lyrical subject to rhetorically separate self and other is thwarted, because the mulata remains within the space of the national: soccer, after all, rivals samba as the ultimate emblem of Brazilianness.

The second item up for auction is a guitar, a symbol of Brazil's rich musical tradition. Like its country of origin, this instrument possesses colonial roots: "Pertenceu a Dom Pedro, morou no palácio / Foi posto no prego por José Bonifácio" (It belonged to Dom Pedro, it lived in the palace / It was put in a pawn shop by José Bonifácio). That the guitar was placed in a pawnshop by Bonifácio—an intellectual who as Dom Pedro I's counselor participated in the fight for Brazil's independence—establishes an inextricable link with Brazil's status as an autonomous country. Yet by recalling Bonifácio's act, the samba seems to suggest a betrayal at the heart of Brazil's existence; even the moment of independence is marked by the selling or selling out of a precious national commodity. The guitar, which is characterized as an incomplete object—"só não tem braço, fundo e cavalete" (it's missing an arm, base, and stand)—signifies an inherent imperfection, or lack, at the center of brasilidade. This authentic yet flawed artifact is bought by a Jew, who threatens Brazilian authenticity not only through his foreignness but also because he complicates the very idea of national identity by not belonging to any nation.

The final item for sale is a samba, a metalyrical reference that reveals one of the song's principal objectives: to announce its own centrality within the landscape of Brazilian culture. By juxtaposing the samba with the mulata and guitar, Rosa performatively establishes its status as an emblem of brasilidade. Like the two other items for sale, the samba is a vulnerable, partial object: it has only a refrain, and is missing the introduction and second part. Yet while the mulata and guitar are both purchased, there is no reply to the auctioneer's offer of the samba, which could be interpreted in a number of ways. It is not that there is no buyer, but rather that the lyrics of "Quem dá mais?" trail off before the sale can be completed, designating the samba as an open text whose meaning is only fully determined through its reception. Moreover, it is as if the listener of Rosa's song were to function as a potential buyer, who does not answer, but is nevertheless implicated in the selling out of Brazil simply by consuming one of its products. An alternative reading might be that Rosa proposes the samba as that which cannot be sold, an object that refuses to be converted into a commodity, that transcends the market and the value assigned to items within the scene of the transaction. While "Quem dá mais?" ends before the price of the samba can be determined, its objective has been fulfilled: it has warned the Brazilian public about the threat to their national patrimony.

The auction thus stands for that which disrupts a stable, albeit hybrid, national subject. One by one, various figures of Brazilianness—a mulata, a guitar, and a samba—are put on the auction block, awaiting the highest bidder. Yet the announcement of the loss of Brazilianness actually serves to reify the very possibility of its existence: the mulata, the guitar, and the samba are stereotypes that, one could argue, surface especially during times of crisis. That is, the overdetermined items on the auction block are infused with the responsibility to represent the nation precisely at the moment when it is endangered; the condition of possibility of brasilidade is the very threat of its destruction.

The figure of the "Jew" is important because, although he is not the only one to purchase a relic of Brazil's uniqueness, it is he who, according to the lyrical subject, will probably resell his lot to a museum for double the price: "Quem arremata o lote é um judeu/ . . . Para vendê-lo pelo dobro no museu" (The one who picks up the lot is a Jew/ . . . who'll sell it for double to a museum). Not only is the Jewish figure depicted as the most cunning, indeed the most entrepreneurial of the buyers; through this hypothetical transaction with the museum, he extracts a supplementary value from the national artifact. In a sense, he profits from this deal in a manner analogous to the auctioneer; by becoming the salesman, he participates in the selling (or the selling out) of Brazil. At the same time, by returning the guitar to a museum, the Jewish buyer is restoring this symbol of Brazilianness to its rightful owner: the Brazilian people. Rosa thus constructs the "Jew" in a more ambivalent manner than is understood by McCann; in a perverse way, Rosa's "Jew" could be understood as a productive figure for the nation.

Thus the "Jew" possesses contrasting qualities, fulfilling multiple functions at once. As both buyer and seller, he is not only a flexible figure; he becomes, more specifically, a middleman, occupying the intermediary space Benjamin terms the threshold. The middleman possesses an in-between status that, though it destroys the possibility of Brazilianness (both by selling it out and because the very idea of a middleman interrupts the categories it straddles), could also offer a distinct mode of conceiving of national identity. The fact that the auctioneer, the one who has sold Brazil to foreigners, is himself Brazilian—"Quanto é que vai ganhar o leiloeiro / Que é também brasileiro / E em três lotes vendem o Brasil inteiro" (How much will the auctioneer earn / He's also Brazilian / and in three lots he sells all of Brazil)— suggests that what is really being talked about here is the question of Brazilian subjectivity itself. The middleman signals a struggle in Brazilian culture to articulate a concept of identity that incorporates heterogeneity, a notion that Gilberto Freyre termed hybridity in the 1930s, and that the Brazilian novelist and cultural critic Silviano Santiago would call "the space in between" decades later.[9]

Or maybe the subject in question is the *sambista* himself, who, as Vianna notes, acts as a mediating force between different sectors of society: "The samba composers of the 1920s and 1930s . . . connect the elite and middle class to the world of popular street festivals like carnival" (1999, 84). Noel Rosa, as one of the first white samba composers, takes his role as middleman to a new level. He embarks on ethnographic-like research visits to favelas in order to learn as much as possible about the popular classes whose music he appropriates and sells to middle- and upper-class Brazilians. His task, to a certain degree, resembles that of the auctioneer's: selling "authentic" (read: popular, mixed-race) cultural artifacts to willing buyers. At the same time, the sambista aids in the construction of an autochthonous cultural product, paralleling the Jewish buyer's conservation of the Brazilian guitar in a museum. Both "Jew" and sambista, then, indirectly work to preserve Brazilian music for the nation.

I therefore both agree and disagree with McCann's argument that Rosa "perceived Brazilianness as an endangered quality, threatened by the encroachments of foreigners and squandered by bad Brazilians" (2001, 3). I see in Rosa's samba a slightly more nuanced vision of national identity politics, an aporia of sorts in which brasilidade is simultaneously threatened and made possible through perverse transactions between foreigners and natives. While Rosa unquestionably blames both the "Jew" and the Brazilian auctioneer for the buying and selling of the nation, the hidden actor within this scene is the sambista himself, a transcultural subject who, through his lyrics and musical production, asserts his own role at the same time that he announces the loss of brasilidade. By simultaneously appropriating and popularizing samba, Rosa himself participates in the buying and selling of Brazil, establishing a locus of enunciation for the lyrical subject of samba, while revealing a double bind at the heart of the Brazilian subject.

Like Noel Rosa's samba, composed during the rise of Getúlio Vargas and the spread of nationalism in Brazil, Jorge Luis Borges's "Emma Zunz"— published in the intellectual periodical Sur in 1948 and included in the short-story collection El Aleph in 1949—emerged at the height of Peronist populism in Argentina (as well as three years after the end of World War II).[10] Although Borges's political loyalties have been debated by many, it is evident that he represents a critical position vis-à-vis populist nationalism: while the Paris-based Argentine literary critic Annick Louis discusses the political nature of Borges's work during this period, arguing that the ideologically complex writer "propone una lectura del pasaje entre la militancia contra el nazismo y la oposición al peronismo" (proposes a reading of the passage from anti-Nazism to anti-Peronism) (1997, 199), the Borges scholar Edna Aizenberg identifies the writer as the "founder of literature after Auschwitz" (1997, 141). In "Emma Zunz" Borges exposes the problematic link between violence and "truth." He does so by flirting with stereotypes linking "Jews" to money while simultaneously deconstructing these very notions, employing a Jewish thematic that, although not entirely new in his oeuvre, engages the sociohistorical, rather than mystical, aspects of Judaism.[11] The story reproduces familiar images of "Jews" from within the Western imaginary (the Jewish bourgeois owner, the Jewish murderer, the religious Jew), always taking care to provide their opposites (the Jewish worker, the Jewish victim, the secular Jew).[12] The slippery roles of the characters in "Emma Zunz" serve to undermine fixed notions of "Jewishness" in the Argentine cultural imaginary of the 1940s; at the same time, however, it is the flexibility of the signifier "Jew" that allows Borges to create such malleable figures.[13]

In a conversation with the Argentine writer Raquel Ángel, Borges describes the genesis of the plot of "Emma Zunz."

> Yo estaba enamorado de Cecilia Ingenieros y ella inventó ese argumento. Y yo así, como una especie de bajo soborno que resultó inútil, lo escribí. Y ella me dijo que había sido un error que los personajes fuesen judíos, que debían haberse llamado López y González. Y yo le dije que no, puesto que como el argumento es raro y ocurre en Buenos Aires, el lector acepta con más facilidad

algo que es raro si le dicen que ocurre entre judíos. Si le dijese que ocurre entre argentinos, no lo aceptaría. (Bravo and Paoletti 1999, 143)

✿

I was in love with Cecilia Ingenieros, and it was she who came up with the plot. I, under a sort of useless coercion, wrote it. She then told me that it was a mistake that the characters be Jewish, that they should be called López and González. I told her no; because the plot is strange and takes place in Buenos Aires, it is easier for the reader to accept such strangeness if he is told that it happens among Jews. If he were told that it takes place among Argentines, he would not accept it.

This amusing anecdote is revealing on a number of levels: first, it conveys a sense of literary creation that is collaborative, or multiple (Cecilia Ingenieros invented the plot while Borges "revised" it); second, it elucidates a particular motive for "Judaizing" the characters (who would believe that something so "rare" could occur among Argentines, that is, non-Jewish criollos?); finally, it emphasizes the role of the reader as central to the construction of meaning. That is, if the "origin" of the story is difficult to pinpoint, its meaning is only fully realized in the moment of reading. The (non-Jewish?) reader's expectations of Jews, or of "strangeness" in general, are what lend verisimilitude to the text.

The question of the story's "credibility" is thus addressed both paratextually and diegetically: the events of the story, as well as the events that frame these events, reside not only on the limits of legality but in a hazy hermeneutic space as well. Alleged robbery, possible framing, suspected suicide, false prostitution, staged rape, and veiled murder are all subject to interpretation, and the agent of each of these ambiguous acts is a Jew: Emma Zunz; Emanuel Zunz, her father; and Aarón Loewenthal, their boss. The sequence of events commences in 1916, when Emanuel Zunz is accused of stealing from the factory in which he works. On his departure to exile in Brazil, he swears to his daughter that he has been framed by the true thief, Loewenthal. After her father's suicide, which she learns of through a letter, Emma decides to avenge his death by confronting Loewenthal and bringing him to justice.[14] Emma becomes the protagonist of this story as she responds to the events that precede her status as an agent. By gathering, organizing, and finally acting on the facts of her father's history, she constitutes herself as a subject.[15]

In "Emma Zunz" everything appears debatable, negotiable. The act of remembering is narrated as a delicate balance between recall and amnesia:

"Recordó veraneos en una chacra . . . recordó (trató de recordar) a su madre, re-cordó la casita . . . recordó (pero eso jamás lo olvidaba) que su padre . . . le había jurado que el ladrón era Loewenthal" (She recalled family outings to a small farm . . . she recalled [or tried to recall] her mother, she recalled the family's little house . . . recalled [and this she would never forget] that . . . her father had sworn that the thief was Loewenthal [2004b, 45]) (1999b, 59–60). The notion of truth, too, is called into question. The narrator acknowledges a chasm be-tween signifier and signified, admitting the difficulty of making unreal events believable: "Referir con alguna realidad los hechos de esa tarde sería difícil y quizá improcedente. Un atributo de lo infernal es la irrealidad . . .¿Cómo hacer verosímil una acción en la que casi no creyó quien la ejecutaba . . . ?" (To recount with some degree of reality the events of that evening would be difficult, and perhaps inappropriate. One characteristic of hell is its un-reality. . . . How to make plausible an act in which even she who was to commit it scarcely believed? [46]) (61). The narrator further exposes the precarious quality of "truth" when he alludes to the relationship between the story and the events it means to represent: "Verdadero era el tono de Emma Zunz, verdadero el pudor, verdadero el odio. Verdadero también era el ultraje que había padecido; solo eran falsas las circunstancias, la hora y uno o dos nombres propios" (Emma Zunz's tone of voice was real, her shame was real, her hatred was real. The outrage that had been done to her was real, as well; all that was false were the circumstances, the time, and one or two proper names [50]) (66). The linear nature of time and narrative is rearranged as well: "Los hechos graves están fuera del tiempo, ya porque en ellos el pasado inmedi-ato queda como tronchado del porvenir, ya porque no parecen consecutivas las partes que los forman" (The most solemn of events are outside time—whether because in the most solemn of events the immediate past is severed, as it were, from the future or because the elements that compose those events seem not to be consecutive [47]) (61). The validity of memory, the referential-ity of narrative, and the possibility of truth are all called into question at the very moment that they are asserted as options within the story.

Even Emma's Jewish identity can be doubted, if one is to follow Lud-mer's rationale: "Was Emma Jewish, or rather, was her dead mother Jew-ish?" (2004, 147). While it is true that Emma's mother is never named, her father does seem to be represented as Jewish through his name. For the pur-poses of the literary construction of identity, it is of relative unimportance, I believe, whether or not her mother was Jewish, that is, whether or not Jewish law would consider Emma to be a Jew. She has a direct bloodline to a Jew, she is associated with "Jewishness," and therefore even if she is not technically a Jew, she is, in the eyes of the text, Jew-"ish."

Yet Ludmer's point should not be wholly disregarded; Emma's lack of religiosity is indeed apparent in the story. She swims at the gymnasium on Friday afternoon with her Jewish friends, Urstein and Kronfuss, rather than preparing for Shabbat. Hers is a cultural Jewish identity, if anything. The "real" Jew in the story is Aarón Loewenthal, who, the narrator says, "era muy religioso" (was quite religious [48]) (65). Further, it is Loewenthal—with his unmistakably Jewish name—who is associated with the stereotypical characteristics of greed: "El dinero era su verdadera pasión" (Money was his true passion [48]) (65). He has a transgressive relationship with money: he has robbed from the company in which he serves as manager and has blamed the robbery on someone else. He even profanes his relationship with God by praying for financial success: "Creía tener con el Señor un pacto secreto, que lo eximía de obrar bien, a trueque de oraciones y devociones" (He believed he had a secret pact with the Lord—in return for prayers and devotions, he was exempted from doing good works [48]) (65). Emma confirms this interpretation of Loewenthal as an observant Jew by waiting to meet with him until sundown on Saturday, when he can ostensibly resume the work he has abandoned during the Sabbath.

If Loewenthal is the "real" Jew, then one could argue that "Emma Zunz" is a "real" example of anti-Semitism. The murder of Aarón Loewenthal certainly fulfills the Nazi fantasy of extermination, and Borges is fully aware of the context in which his story is being read in 1948. Yet Borges would never write anything so simple. This text questions "Jewishness" (through Emma's character, in particular) far more than it affirms any such idea. At best, the story exterminates that aspect of "Jewishness" that is associated with capitalism, greed, perverse piety, and false witness, while heroizing the more flexible, difficult-to-identify "Jew." Of course, the story is not actually *about* "Jewishness" at all; rather, it utilizes "Jewishness"—as do the other texts analyzed here—in order to address a secondary problem: the fixedness of truth. Perhaps Loewenthal's real crime was being a stereotype; as such, he had to be eliminated in order to realize a Borgesian, postmodern justice.

The concluding words of the story—"La historia era increíble . . . pero . . . sustancialmente era cierta. . . . sólo eran falsas las circunstancias, la hora y uno o dos nombres propios" (The story was unbelievable . . . yet . . . in substance it was true. . . . all that was false were the circumstances, the time, and one or two proper names [49–50]) (66)—acquire added significance when read from the perspective of Borges's (perhaps equally fictional) account of the work's conception. If the story, within the microcosm of Argentine culture, codifies "universal" experience (remember that Borges characterizes *pudor* as a distinctly Argentine trait), it does so only through the particular, or eccentric, actions of Jews, that is, through characters whose "nombres propios" have been marked as "raros."

If, as Ludmer argues, one is dealing with "a sort of representation squared" in stories of "Jewishness" and money, one might ask what this exponential form of representation excludes. Following the idea that "'The Jews' are the sign of the money sign" in which a sign is squared, one is left with an excess of signifiers. The surplus of value created by this rhetorical equation implies a remainder, an element of difference that cannot be fully digested by any one text, or by any culture, any nation. Could such leftovers indicate an aspect of the text that cannot be contained, a quality of the other than cannot be absorbed by the totality of the self?

SIGNIFYING PROMISCUITY

> Promiscuous: adj. 1. consisting of different elements mixed together or mingled without discrimination 2. characterized by a lack of discrimination; specif., engaging in sexual intercourse indiscriminately or with many persons
> —*Webster's New World Dictionary of the American Language*

> Jews trafficked in their own daughters until Moses prohibited this custom.—Cesare Lombroso, *Criminal Woman, the Prostitute, and the Normal Woman*

Unlike the invention of money, and the ambivalent values constructed in relation to it, prostitution almost always represents a marginal aspect of society, an activity that is confined to subaltern spaces, that, even when rampant, is often hidden, denied, or repressed. Although both financial and sexual transactions can oscillate between legality and illegality, morality and immorality, prostitution remains the more charged of the two categories. While prostitution and prostitutes are less often imbued with positive values from the perspective of dominant social norms, they are nevertheless inscribed with the ideological, sexual, and moral preoccupations of society. For this reason, the literary representation of prostitution engages a sphere whose meaning is already overdetermined, casting a positive, negative, or ambivalent light on the commodification of sex.

Promiscuity, while generally used in reference to loose women, alludes to an entire field of behavior that falls outside of the realm of morality (while, of course, sustaining the very morality it is thought to destroy). Yet promiscuity is not simply a slackening of sexual mores, but rather a broader corruption of borders, of the very limits that are established as part of attempts to construct the nation. There is a problematic of "visibility" at work, an exhibition and an exhibitionism of alterity. If, as Sylvia Molloy suggests in her essay on the politics of posing, "countries are read like bodies" and "bodies, in turn, are read (and are offered up for reading) as cultural statements," then the literary representation of a promiscuous body would seem to denote a corruption of the distinction between the realms of the public and the private (1998, 142).

Taken in this broader context, promiscuity would serve as a characteristic associated with prostitutes, but also, in a more indirect way, with "Jewishness." Like promiscuity, "Jewishness" as a constructed concept represents that which does not remain restricted to designated categories. Both ideas allude to a sort of transgression of boundaries, whether literal or figurative, whether sexual, religious, cultural, or national. Promiscuous "Jewishness" would be that element of difference that, instead of remaining relegated to its own discrete and discreet realm, bleeds into the public space, the site of the collective or the national.

This is not to say that the texts I will read do not also refer specifically to the historical phenomenon of Jewish prostitution. Hilário Tácito's *Madame Pommery*, Clara Beter's *Versos de una . . .* , Borges's "Emma Zunz," and Fogwill's *Vivir afuera*, while ranging historically from the end of the nineteenth to the end of the twentieth century, all take place in the cosmopolitan centers of Argentina and Brazil and, as such, are inseparable from the wave of Eastern European Jewish prostitutes of the early twentieth century that entered the broader cultural imaginary of both societies. The Zwi Migdal criminal organization trafficked in "white slaves," bringing Polish-Jewish women (*polacas*, as they came to be known in Argentina and Brazil) to the urban centers of Buenos Aires, São Paulo, Rio de Janeiro, and Porto Alegre at the beginning of the twentieth century, under the false pretext of marriage. Nora Glickman explains that "the *polacas* were deceived by Jews of good economic standing that came to their native villages to ask for their hand in marriage. Sometimes the girls were visited by suppliers who made 'contracts' which were in fact stratagems to raise the hopes of the parents, whose wish was that their virgin daughters would keep their religion and marry men who would provide them with a respectable life—even if it was in such a remote place as Buenos Aires" (2000, 7). Yet "Jewishness" and prostitution move beyond the historical because they function well together on a rhetorical plane. An analysis of their relationship is a logical progression from the discussion of symbolic associations between "Jews" and money, because "Jews" are thought to sexualize money and commodify sexuality.

A discussion of the symbolic value of prostitution must also take the issue of gender into account. As the Spanish literature scholar Georgina Dopico Black comments in *Perfect Wives, Other Women*, the female body (not unlike the Jewish body) has served as a site of manipulation both in literary and broader cultural contexts: "The female body has regularly been appropriated as an object of reading, a site on which to project—and contest—interpretations" (2001, 24). The prostitution (and feigned prostitution) of Madame Pommery, Clara Beter, and Emma Zunz serves as a means to an end—even when this consists of establishing the protagonism of each woman within her own story. In *Vivir afuera* the prostitute and the "Jew" come together to constitute the outside, the *afuera*, of Fogwill's fictional universe.

In the texts that I discuss here, promiscuity and "Jewishness" are juxtaposed in order to signify new ways of conceiving of identity. While in *Madame Pommery* "elegant" prostitution serves as a model for a rapidly modernizing São Paulo, César Tiempo invents a prostitute alter ego through the figure of Clara Beter in order to write the popular. Borges uses the idea of the Jewish prostitute-as-simulacrum in order to articulate a deconstructed version of "reality" in "Emma Zunz" and, finally, Fogwill in *Vivir afuera* creates an alternative social space in which "Jews" and prostitutes coexist in a postmodern realm of marginality.

In his work on the fin-de-siècle Spanish American modernista chronicle, the Latin American literary and cultural critic Julio Ramos remarks on the treatment of the prostitute, which he describes as embodying the dangerousness of the modern city within the broader cultural imaginary. Early-twentieth-century chroniclers, among them Rubén Darío and the Guatemalan novelist Enrique Gómez Carillo, go out to the street in order to register this newfound urban promiscuity. Ramos affirms a connection between the chronicler and the prostitute, both representative of a mercantilization of the private, the interior, the sexual, the aesthetic. In the chronicle, he suggests, there is a constant slippage between the idea of prostitution and the mercantilization of art, which "forces us to at once suspect the chronicler's introjection of the prostitute's condition into his own practice. For is not the chronicle precisely an incorporation of art into the market, into the emergent culture industry? And was not mercantilization, following the idealism professed by many modernists, a form of prostitution?" (2001, 139). But if Ramos's analysis focuses on the dangerousness of the prostitute—and, by extension, of the modern city—it is because he wishes to emphasize the socioeconomic character of both, that is, their working-class status. What happens when that which is represented in the chronicle is so-called elegant prostitution, when the action is situated within the bordello and not on the streets, when the prostitute is Jewish, and when the very genre of the chronicle appears unstable?[16] In *Madame Pommery*, a satirical chronicle-novel penned in 1919, one sees a dynamic similar to the one that Ramos details, but in an altered context.

Written on the eve of São Paulo's *Semana de Arte Moderna* and the inauguration of Brazilian modernism (avant-garde) in 1922, *Madame Pommery* marks the limits of Brazilian pre-modernism.[17] José Maria de Toledo Malta published the text in *Revista do Brasil* in 1920 under the pseudonym Hilário Tácito. This fictitious name reveals a simultaneous attempt to parody (the hilarious) and to document (after the Latin historian Tacitus); moreover, the notion of the "tacit" also alludes to that which does not require verbal communication, that which is beyond or before language.[18] The text, which bears characteristics of the novel and, at the same time, is defined as a "crônica muito verídica" (very truthful chronicle) by the author himself, plays on the border between poetic and scientific discourses, fiction and biography, pre-modernism and modernism, realism and parody, public and private, in addition to complicating notions of class, nation, and modernity. It is the figure of the Jewish prostitute, I argue, that allows for the creation of a flexible space within which it is possible to negotiate the fixity of these concepts.

In the preface to the fifth edition of the text, published by the Fundação Casa de Rui Barbosa, Francisco Foot Hardman, a historian who studies ideas of progress in Brazil, describes the story of Madame Pommery as "uma historia do progresso da cidade de São Paulo" (a history of the progress of São Paulo) (1997, 9).[19] The first decades of the twentieth century represent a moment of transition for São Paulo, which was experiencing rapid urbanization and industrialization at the time. The prostitute in general played a central role within the city in the process of modernization, on both empirical and symbolic levels. Historically, prostitution grew in popularity as the white slave trade brought poor European women—many of them Jewish—to Latin

America (specifically to Buenos Aires and the Brazilian cities of Rio de Janeiro, São Paulo, and Porto Alegre) under the pretense that they would marry
men, who later turned out to work for the mafias (such as the infamous Zwi
Migdal).[20] While Madame Pommery's history follows a different trajectory, in
which a prostitute comes to the Americas alone and becomes her own boss,
the connection between prostitution and "Jewishness" was already well established in the urban Latin American imaginary at the time of the chronicle's
publication. Further, these elements were linked to money, because both the
"Jew" and the prostitute were perceived as elements of a foreign, capitalist
modernity. Ludmer details the paranoia that surfaced in response to the presence of these elements in late-nineteenth-century Argentina: "'Jews' as usu-
rers, simulators, madmen, effeminate men, who sexualize money and power
(and who are linked to prostitution) hide in the shadows, in the caves, and
from there they carry out a clandestine invasion of society, a conspiracy against
'the nation'" (2004, 155). The connection between "Jewishness" and promiscuity works on a rhetorical level because of the flexibility of both concepts—
both destabilize boundaries between bodies, nations, subjects, and families,
threatening the existence of these systems. It is worthwhile to ask how this relationship is appropriated in Tácito's text and to what rhetorical ends.

The narrator—also named Hilário Tácito—admits that Madame Pommery possesses a metaphorical weight while simultaneously defending the
text as "truthful." He addresses the issue of the protagonist's historicity, an-
ticipating possible criticism by the reader.

> Mme. Pommery existe, de verdade, em carne e osso? Eis a pergunta insidiosa,
> que, se eu ñao tomo o cuidado de contestar peremptoriamente, era capaz de
> induzir a posteridade em erro crasso e fundamental. Mme. Pommery arriscava-
> se a decrescer às proporções de um mero símbolo, e a minha história ver-
> dadeira ao simples título de romance; e talvez menos. . . . Seja, pois, Mme.
> Pommery um símbolo, se o quiserem; que o não posso vedar. Mas, por amor
> da verdade, eterna e intangível, fica estabelecido este ponto:—que Mme. Pom-
> mery vive e respira, tão real e efetivamente como eu, que escrevo, e o leitor,
> que me lê, apenas com muito mais apetite e fôlego. (49)

❧

Does Madame Pommery exist, in flesh and blood? Behold the insidious question that, if I don't take care to answer preemptively, would be capable of turning posterity into a crass and fundamental error. Madame Pommery would
risk being reduced to a mere symbol, and my true story to a simple fiction; and

possibly less. . . . Madame Pommery is a symbol, if you wish; I can't hide that. But, for the love of truth, eternal and intangible, let this point be heard:—that Madame Pommery lives and breathes, as alive and real as I, who writes, and the reader, who reads me, but with a great deal more appetite and stamina.

Although he insists on the protagonist's historicity, the narrator cannot deny the rhetorical value of Madame Pommery. His exaggerated defense of the "eternal and intangible" truth exposes a tension in the text between reality and fiction, whether in reference to the literary genre or to the protagonist herself. He exploits this tension in order to create a new authority that challenges pre-modernist discourse and anticipates the literary heterogeneity of the modernists.[21] Yet what meaning can one extract from the fact that Madame Pommery is Jewish? Does "Jewishness" merely represent one more characteristic on a list of marginal qualities, or does it function as a discursive force that interrupts a pre-modernist homogeneity?

Far from being a one-dimensional caricature of marginality, Madame Pommery incorporates elements of contradiction and ambivalence. The daughter of Ivã Pomerikowsky, a Polish Jew, and Consuelo Sánchez, a Spanish nun who fled the convent to be with her Jewish lover, Ida Pomerikowsky embodies an ironic hybridity.[22] The narrator explains that Consuelo ended up leaving Ivã and their three-year-old daughter in order to run away with a new lover, a bullfighter from Barcelona, and that for this reason, Ida inherited few characteristics from the former nun. From her father, on the other hand, she inherited a crooked nose and a taste for finance, both stereotypically Jewish traits. Her financial talent helps her as a prostitute: she demonstrates the ability to "negotiate kisses."[23] While wandering through European cities as an itinerant prostitute, she changes her last name to Pommery, the reason for which is unknown, according to the narrator, though he suggests that the French brand of champagne has something to do with it: "Era natural que o adotasse, consideradas as vantagens da brevidade e da alusão" (it was natural that she would adopt it, considering the advantages of brevity and of allusion) (54). Her nontraditional genealogy, together with her peregrinations and her self-invention as a Frenchified lady, constitute Madame Pommery as a malleable, translatable figure. By codifying her in this way, Tácito privileges the act of assimilation, which is realized in the text on the level of form as well as content.

At the age of thirty-five, after a period in Marseilles, Madame Pommery travels to Brazil on the *Bonne Chance* with the desire to "do America."[24] After a difficult start in São Paulo, the wandering Jew-turned-prostitute opens a bordello (in the guise of a boarding house) called the Paradis Retrouvé, establishing herself as a property owner and, in this way, entering the São Paulo bourgeoisie.[25] The existence of the bordello differentiates this text from the chronicles cited by Ramos, in which one witnesses a public promiscuity, a promiscuity of the streets. Here, in contrast, one finds a site that is private, closed, controlled. The bordello thus represents a privileged space: Madame Pommery specializes in "high prostitution" and attracts an upper-class clientele. Among the residents of the Paradis Retrouvé are Leda Roskoff, a blonde Slav, the Italian Coralina, and Isolda Bogary, a Frenchwoman whose name combines with the protagonist's to remind the reader of Madame Bovary.[26] The international character of the bordello—headed by Pommery, a Frenchified Spanish-Polish Jew—juxtaposes the idea of cultural hybridity with promiscuity. Both concepts represent a transgression of limits, whether national, religious, familial, or sexual. Although these cultural references indicate contradictory messages within turn-of-the-century South American culture— "Jewishness" tends to represent the undesirable, while Frenchness implies the possibility of cultural superiority—they both serve the function of interrupting aesthetic and ideological homogeneity. Madame Pommery signals the possibility of bettering oneself in São Paulo and, at the same time, suggests a modernizing potential of the city itself; thus, the ambivalent attitude toward prostitution, money, and foreignness, acquires an affirmative tone in this text. In the same way that Madame Pommery appropriates a French name in order to climb the *paulistana* social hierarchy, the text seems to suggest that São Paulo possesses a similar ability to reinvent itself as modern.[27] The manipulation of "Jewishness" serves as a model for modernization in São Paulo and, by extension, in Brazil. Yet what kind of perverse modernity does the text postulate?

In addition to offering sexual pleasure, the marginal space of the bordello is populated with alcohol, especially Pommery champagne. The narrator relates to the reader the notion, popular in psychiatric thought at the time, that alcohol is the force that allows prostitution to exist. The protagonist's name, a synecdoche for the evils of society, doubly signifies these vices; further, it points to the causal relationship between the two phenomena. The narrator continues his argument by pointing out that poets, too, support this theory.

Os poetas . . . têm dito mais ou menos a mesma coisa . . . mas com muito mais graça e mais verdade. Donde concluo que a poesia sabe mais, ou melhor, que a ciência; mas não era aí que eu pretendia chegar. O que eu queria era mostrarme admirado da intuição de Mme. Pommery, que, neste assunto de álcool e de alcouces, sabia tanto como os sábios *e* os poetas. (101, emphasis added)

❦

The poets . . . have said more or less the same thing . . . but with much more grace and truth. Thus I conclude that poetry knows more, or better, than science; but that's not where I was heading. What I wanted was to demonstrate my admiration for the intuition of Mme. Pommery, who, on matters of drinking and drunks, knew as much as the scientists *and* the poets.

Of course, by pretending to state his intentions, the narrator is actually revealing a different motive: that of placing poetic discourse on par with scientific discourse, and ultimately of privileging the former. By linking alcohol with prostitution, the text simultaneously problematizes scientific authority and postulates a new category of knowledge, possessed by the heroine.

The deconstruction of scientific discourse is developed further through the character of Doctor Mangancha. The doctor, a bourgeois client of the bordello, represents the paulistana elite and scientific authority, though it is through his character that both are parodied. On the one hand, he is a famous surgeon; on the other, he is writing a book entitled "Of Alcoholism. Adaptation and Selection in the Human Species," a ridiculous manuscript which appropriates Darwinist discourse in order to postulate alcohol as an agent in the perfection of the human race. Doctor Mangancha, inebriated from having drunk two bottles of Pommery champagne, defends the civilizing effects of alcohol, citing Noah as the first alcoholic.[28] He compares alcohol with the sun, which has the ability to sustain life, though he also suspects that it has a degenerative effect on Europeans.

É certo que um sueco, um escocês, um alemão, definham nesses climas tórridos. É certo que, se trouxerem família, a prole irá degenerando de geração em geração. . . . Entretanto, depois de uma longa série de descendências, surge um tipo novo, fixo, resistente à combustão da soalheira, cheio de vigor e dotado de qualidades admiráveis, desconhecidas dos seus antepassados. (107)

❦

It's true that a Swede, a Scot, a German withers in this torrid climate. It's true that if they bring their families, their offspring degenerates generation after generation. . . . However, after a long series of descendants, a new type emerges, resistant to the burning sun, full of vigor and endowed with admirable qualities, unknown in his ancestors.

In this excerpt, the narrator inverts the pseudoscientific theory that asserts that African and indigenous "races" must mix with European blood in order to dilute the degenerative effect of living in the tropics. According to Mangancha, the European race becomes strengthened through contact with a tropical influence. This inversion suggests a new reading of the book's dedication, which is to the Eugenic Society, the early-twentieth-century Brazilian organization whose mission was the "moral and physical strengthening of the Brazilian people" (165n1). The author's ironic allusion to the society simultaneously appropriates the authority of eugenic discourse and questions its methods in order to propose an alternative Darwinism.[29]

Doctor Mangancha's thesis also appropriates the notion of the pathological genius, so in vogue among Symbolists, Parnasianists, and Spanish-American modernists.[30] He admits to the existence of decadence due to alcoholism, but insists that alcoholic geniuses compensate for the degenerates: "Goethe, por exemplo, bebia de cair, e até morrer, aos oitenta e três anos, não perdeu o costume de tomar pileques, por higiene. Beethoven era um maníaco, filho de um bêbedo; e bastam estes dois, porque so um Larousse pode conter os que não cito.... Viva o álcool, senhores, o benfeitor da humanidade!" (Goethe, for example, drank until he stumbled, and until his death, at eighty three years, he never lost his habit of having a drink for his health. Beethoven was a maniac, son of a drunk; and these two should suffice, because only a Larousse could contain all those I haven't cited. . . . Long live alcohol, gentlemen, the benefactor of humanity!) (113). In this quote one sees the humoristic reclamation of the category of the drunk in order to advocate a perverse modernization. Alcohol—represented by Madame Pommery, synecdoche of champagne—here becomes the protagonist of modern paulistana society. Although Mangancha's theories are not meant to be taken seriously—it is possible that the text parodies the doctor himself more than it does the positivist theories that he attempts to dismantle—there is no doubt that the theories of eugenics so popular in Brazilian culture are called into question. But it is only in the bordello, the space constructed by Madame Pommery, that such irreverence can occur; the fatal combination of "Jewishness" and prostitution creates the necessary conditions for an alternative discourse.

As Ludmer argues, the idea of the nation in early-twentieth-century Latin American culture was reinforced by the notion of the sexualization of money by the "Jew." In Tácito's text the "Jew" exercises this destructive power from the bordello, and this power is recodified as positive. Questioning the limits of genre, sexuality, and nation, Tácito appropriates positivist discourse in order to privilege the marginal; in this way, "Jewishness," prostitution, alcohol, and dangerous urban heterogeneity become the heroes of progress. This decentering move privileges poetic discourse, in addition to positing São Paulo as a protagonist of modernity. While the appropriation of scientific discourse situates Madame Pommery in an intertextual relationship with other works from the pre-avant-garde generation in Spanish-American letters (such as Darío's Los raros and Silva's De sobremesa), it also anticipates the linguistic and cultural heterogeneity and satire of the Brazilian modernistas. In this way the text performs assimilation and offers itself as a cosmopolitan model of the transition to modernity.

The next "case" involves a fraudulent text, a literary simulation: Versos de una . . . (1926)—a poetry collection penned by César Tiempo under the pseudonym Clara Beter, an imaginary Jewish prostitute who, like Tiempo, emigrated from the Ukraine to Argentina at the beginning of the twentieth century. Of note here is not merely the existence of a fictitious poet, but more precisely the way in which Tiempo realizes a series of inventions that involve and, in some cases, seduce his (mostly male) readers. In Versos de una . . . one encounters an example of text as event, that is, a notion of textuality that complicates ideas of both genre and gender (género textual, género sexual), as well as the relationship between literature and politics so fiercely debated in Tiempo's generation. Like Tácito's Madame Pommery, Versos de una . . . can be understood as a promiscuous text in its subversion of the boundaries between text and event, truth and fiction, literature and politics.

Clara Beter's collection of poetry was published by Editorial Claridad, whose journal of the same name served as the voice of the literary group Boedo. In the prologue to the collection Elías Castelnuovo, the unofficial leader of Boedo, presents the book as an expression of the ideological position of the group, which sought to create a social literature linked to the world of labor (Irizarry). Criticizing the more avant-garde rival group Florida (also called Martin Fierro after the periodical of the same name), Castelnuovo affirms the political nature of Boedo's literary work, emphasizing the importance of establishing a connection with the social reality of the city: "Para estudiar el puerto, pongamos por caso, es menester vivir en el puerto, trabajar en el puerto, palpitar con la gente del puerto. . . . El novelista que no vive con sus personajes no puede infundirles vida a sus muñecos" (To study the port, for example, it is necessary to live in the port, work in the port, share the beat with its people. . . . A novelist that does not live with his characters cannot infuse life into his dolls) (Beter 1998, 31). Clara Beter lyrically recounts the experience of being a prostitute, embodying in this way Castelnuovo's ideal of social literature: "Clara Beter es la voz angustiosa de los lupanares. Ella reivindica con sus versos la infamia de todas las mujeres infames" (Clara Beter is the anguished voice of the brothels. Through her verses, she vindicates the infamy of all infamous women) (33). The division between Boedo and Florida—a problematic opposition, particularly considering that writers like Roberto Arlt participated in the meetings of both groups—appears even more precarious when it becomes clear that Beter does not exist.[31] Moreover, this fiction exposes the dependence of the "revolutionary" poets on the transparency of language, the possibility of faithfully representing an identifiable reality.

The false dichotomy between Boedo and Florida cannot be disentangled from the imagined identities that sustain it. In this curious case one sees a series of invented names: César Tiempo is the pseudonym of Israel Zeitlin, while Castelnuovo signs the book's prologue with the name Ronald Chaves.[32] Moreover, Clara Beter's overdetermined identity offers clues to the attentive reader: if Clara serves as a thinly veiled reference to *Claridad*, Beter, which means "bitter," replicates the pseudonym of the socialist writer Gorky ("bitter," in Russian), one of the most significant intellectual models for the Boedo writers. Tatiana Pavlova, to whom Beter dedicates one of her poems, did exist, but—ironically—Beter's readers believed her to be an invention. This repeated disguising of the subjects involved not only implies another layer of meaning that must be considered when one analyzes the poetry but also calls into question the very conditions of possibility of representation (both aesthetic and political) strived for in the work of the Boedo writers.

Clara is not only the "author" and lyrical subject but also the object of enunciation in her verses. The first poem, "Quicio," introduces the lyrical "I" to the reader.

> Me entrego a todos, mas no soy de nadie;
> para ganarme el pan vendo mi cuerpo
> ¿qué he de vender para guardar intactos
> mi corazón, mis penas y mis sueños? (37)
>
> ❧
>
> I surrender to all, but belong to no one;
> to earn my bread I sell my body.
> What must I sell to preserve intact
> my heart, my sorrows and dreams?

In contrast to the elegant, cosmopolitan Madame Pommery, this prostitute is constructed as repugnant, miserable. The need to sell her body—the defining characteristic of the prostitute—brings the world of labor and the question of property and commodification to the immediate attention of the reader. But the female body is not the only item for sale: the dynamic of the *entrega* (surrender)—a body that is given over to the other—can also be understood to describe the poetic text as commodity, as an object that exists for the consumption of the masculine reader. The paradoxical condition of belonging to "everyone" and "no one," in this sense, functions as a metapoetic reference: on the one hand, the poem is in the world to be interpreted and appropriated by the reader; on the other hand, there is an element of the text that eludes the greedy public, an aspect that exceeds the limits of representation.

The relationship between the figure of Clara and her readers is crucial, given the collective hysteria inspired by her alleged existence. In a 1974 essay Tiempo recalls that a group of writers traveled from Buenos Aires to Rosario (where a fake address had been invented for Clara) in order to search for the prostitute-cum-poet.

> En el domicilio rosarino les informaron que allí no se alojaba ninguna tal. Una excursión más prolongada y detenida por los barrios bajos les permitió sorprender a una de las pupilas—francesa por más señas—escribiendo un epitafio rimado para un hijo que acababa de perder.—¡Vos sos Clara Beter!— saltó Abel Rodríguez tomándola por los hombros e intentando besarla a los gritos de ¡Hermana! ¡Hermana! ¡Venimos a salvarte! (20)

❧

> At the Rosario address they were told that no one by that name lived there. A longer, more thorough excursion through the poorer neighborhoods led them to one of the pupils—by all indications French—who was writing an epitaph in verse for a son she had just lost. "You are Clara Beter!" exclaimed Abel Rodríguez while he took her by the shoulders and attempted to kiss her. All the while they shouted, "Sister! Sister! We have come to save you!"

This anecdote, beyond providing entertainment, reveals the perverse link between the imaginary prostitute and her male readership, as well as the ethical complexity of this relationship, which culminates in an unfortunate assault on an innocent woman.

But the obsession with locating the "true" Clara Beter has its roots in the very lines of poetry attributed to the apocryphal prostitute. The insistence on the need to "guardar intactos / . . . mi corazón, mis penas y mis sueños" (preserve intact / . . . my heart, my sorrows and dreams) suggests the existence of an "authentic" essence that requires (and perhaps invites) protection. "Quicio" is not the only poem to evoke the notion of "purity" that hides behind the prostitute's mask: "Rosa de Jericó," too, alludes to the possibility of a "serene" interior that lurks beneath a painful surface.

> A veces me pregunto ¿cómo es que siendo tan
> mala para conmigo la vida, yo soy buena,
> ¿cómo conservo el alma tan suave y tan serena
> si el dolor es mi amante y la angustia mi pan? (63)

ℬ

> At times I wonder how it is that
> as harsh as life is to me, I remain good.
> How do I preserve a soul so tender and serene,
> if pain is my lover and anguish my bread?

Once again, one sees the attempt to idealize Clara's character, which has been corrupted by the harsh conditions of her life.

In the poem "Ayer y hoy," finally, it is the idea of the past that is essentialized with the same objective of painting the lyrical "I" as victim of her circumstances. Here, identity is structured around a central loss.

> Allá en los claros días de mi infancia lejana,
> en el muelle sosiego de la vida aldeana
> mi alegría era mía y era mío mi nombre (42)

ℬ

> There, in the clear days of my distant childhood,
> by the soothing dock of village life,
> my joy was mine, as was mine my name

An oppositional relationship is established between "here" (Argentina) and "there" (Ukrania), city and village, "mine" and "not-mine," confirming the dynamic developed in the previous poems. What follows is curious, given the circumstances of its publication.

> Hogaño en el estrépito de la ciudad hirviente,
> mi oscura vida añora la claridad ausente,
> debo entregar mi dicha y enmascarar mi nombre (42)

✽

Now, amid the din of the boiling city,
my darkened life yearns for that absent light,
I must surrender my happiness and mask my name

Yet another opposition is added to those mentioned above: the contrast between the "darkness" of Clara's life as a prostitute and the "clarity" of an innocent past. This distinction seems ironic if one takes into account that Editorial *Claridad* published these verses under the name *Clara*, as if through publication—the making "public" of an invented interior—the dark conditions of Clara's present life could be redeemed or cleansed. Moreover, the need to "mask" her name is crucial, in that it invites the question, conceal *what* identity under *whose* name? Is it the prostitute who must pose as the (innocent) other, or is it the (innocent) other who must disguise himself as a prostitute, and to what rhetorical end? Finally, how does the invented prostitute's "Jewishness" participate in this identitary hall of mirrors?

In *Madame Pommery* one sees that "Jewishness" functions as a characteristic central to the postulation of a translatable, assimilable figure. The Jewish prostitute, for Tácito, is a subject that can be invented and that can reinvent herself, in addition to participating symbolically in the logic of the transaction. The narrator of *Madame Pommery* explains that from her Jewish father Ida had inherited her knack for finances, an ability to "negotiate kisses." In Beter's poem "Atavismo" the lyrical subject, too, expresses gratitude for her Jewish heritage.

> Yo debo dar las gracias a mi raza judía
> que me ha hecho ahorrativa,
> mostrándome lejanos horizontes
> y anudando la prosa a la poesía.

✽

> —El presente es la prosa
> y el sueño de mañana, poesía—.

✽

> Hoy debemos sufrir—para nosotras
> esa es la ley suprema de la vida—,
> pero el futuro puede ser en nuestras
> manos, dócil arcilla. (83)

ॐ

I must give thanks to my Jewish race,
which has made me thrifty,
showing me faraway horizons,
adding prose to poetry.

ॐ

—The present is prose
and the dream of tomorrow, poetry—.

ॐ

Today we must suffer—for us
this is the supreme law of life—,
but the future can be, in our
hands, a malleable piece of clay.

By employing the hackneyed image of the parsimonious "Jew" and bringing it to the realm of prostitution, both texts seem to suggest that the "Jewess" makes a good prostitute because of her financial acumen. The "Jewish transaction" thus operates on both economic and rhetorical levels: at the same time that the figure of the Jewish prostitute negotiates with her clients, another type of negotiation is realized—this time discursive—with the cultural and political values and anxieties of this generation.

Moreover, "Jewishness" seems to be the only element that links the past to the present (and future) for the lyrical subject. If "Ayer y hoy" (in addition to other poems in the collection) establishes a dichotomous relationship between past and present, "Atavismo" suggests the possibility of continuity through an essentialized notion of race. Atavism—which refers to the unexpected reappearance of genetic traits and is linked, in the positivist philosophy of Cesare Lombroso, to criminality—erases the border between past and present, identity and mask. The prostitute's Jewish heritage determines her present state of misery (Jews have always suffered, the poem implies), but it also gives her the qualities necessary to endure it. Finally, her "Jewishness" is one of several personal traits that links the figure of Beter to her "creator," further complicating the question of an "authentic" subjectivity. The masking of César Tiempo, in this sense, is an autoreferential pose.

This ambivalence regarding the poetic subject causes one to rethink the transparency of language on which the ideological position articulated by Castelnuovo is based. *Versos de una . . .* is not only a fake, but also (or more specifically) a transvestite text, or the textuality of a transvestite subject: a male poet in drag. Yet one cannot conclude that César Tiempo is the "true" identity of Clara Beter; on the contrary, the drag queen (to draw on the gender theory of Judith Butler) destabilizes normative ideas about gender not simply by embodying a transgressive form of femininity, but rather by performing femininity and thus exposing *all* gender as performance. The inherent ambiguity involved in the act of masking one's name problematizes not only the authenticity of Beter but also the identity of Tiempo as the "true" poet, as well as the transparency of language-as-identifier in general. It is not that there is a "real" identity beneath a "false" mask; through a textual simulation, a new subjectivity is fashioned that does not pertain to either figure. This concept is useful if one understands, along with Ludmer, that simulation does not hide an empirical reality, but subverts the very division between "fiction" and "reality": "There is no real and true being against which to exhibit or simulate; there is no truth underneath the fiction at the very heart of the subject; one is what one represents" (2004, 205). The deconstruction of identity causes one to reassess the modes of representation theorized (and used) by the Boedo writers. What begins as a "literary joke" (Irizarry 1979) ends as a mockery of the literary practices of the moment: instead of "having fun" (in the transitive sense), this text "makes fun" (of the other). It thus becomes vital to reassess the conditions of possibility for a revolutionary literature, one that would radicalize the idea of the referentiality of language.

In *Madame Pommery* and *Versos de una . . .* one witnesses the elaboration and reinterpretation of several concepts central to the positivist ideology of the fin-de-siècle: the "Jew," the prostitute, and the simulator, objects of scientific analysis at the end of the nineteenth century and the beginning of the twentieth, come to occupy new discursive spaces in the 1920s. Both Tácito and Tiempo appropriate these figures or postures in order to articulate original subject positions. If for Tácito the figure of the "Jewish prostitute" suggests a potential for cosmopolitanism, for Tiempo it embodies the world of labor and marginality revindicated by the committed writers of his generation—yet both are symptomatic of a peripheral modernity. The simulator, too, becomes a protagonist of intellectual and cultural production: instead of signaling pathology, this figure offers the possibility of occupying "other" liminal social positions. Finally, it is the "Jew" as wandering signifier, open to interpretation by both writer and reader, who, assessed from a critical perspective, provokes a reevaluation of traditional forms of representation, demanding in this way a new mode of conceiving a politics of literature.

While Madame Pommery and Clara Beter are invented by their male authors as figures through which a heterogeneous modernity can be promoted
or questioned, in Borges's "Emma Zunz" one sees a distinct mode of promiscuous subject formation. In order to construct an alibi for the murder of
her father's nemesis, the eponymous heroine of "Emma Zunz" (re)invents
her "self" as both prostitute and rape victim and, in doing so, exposes the
nature of identity in general as fictional or performative. The Argentine literary and cultural critic Beatriz Sarlo has characterized the actions of the protagonist as both "reading" and "performance": "Emma está lista para que su
interpretación de los hechos se transforme en acción. Va a convertir su lectura de los hechos en una *performance*" (Emma is ready for her interpretation
of the events to become actions. She will transform her reading of the events
into a *performance*) (1999, 234). I build on Sarlo's argument by dwelling on
the connection between prostitution and "Jewishness," which, like so many
elements of Borges's fiction, is fraught with contradictions and inversions
of meaning. Just as the "Jew" is both capitalist (Loewenthal has a "passion"
for money) and victim of capitalism (Emanuel Zunz), murderer (Emma) and
justly murdered (Loewenthal), the character of Emma both is and is not a
prostitute. Rather, she *plays the part* of the prostitute as part of her plan to
avenge her father's death, then recodes her feigned prostitution as a rape in
order to construe her murder of Loewenthal as self-defense.

Emma's plan to eliminate Loewenthal is described as theater; it is a performance that she has rehearsed numerous times in her mind, repeating the
lines until she is sure that she can execute it flawlessly. As a work of art, it is
subject to interpretation and re-readings; as a created object, it exposes the
constructed nature of reality (Scarry 1985); as a performance, it is an event
that entails an element of surprise (Nancy 1998). Emma calls Loewenthal to
set up a meeting under the pretext of discussing a labor dispute. Before the
meeting, she goes down to the docks in the guise of a prostitute in order to
cruise the bars and find a "client" that will mark her body as sexually "im-
pure," which she will later use as her defense for murdering Loewenthal:
the confession she prepares for the police is "Abusó de mí, lo maté" (He
raped me . . . I killed him [Borges 2004b, 49]) (Borges 1999b, 66). The rape of
Emma by Loewenthal is thus an event that never actually occurs, but rather
fits neatly into her carefully constructed narrative. Each step of Emma's plan
bears multiple levels of interpretation: the writing of the plan, the performing of the part, and the meaning she ascribes to her actions interact to form

a complicated hermeneutic web to be disentangled—or further layered—by the reader.

Moreover, Emma's body functions as a blank slate onto which meaning can be inscribed. Hers is a Jewish body that, similar to those within the diagnostic scene, is not represented as "healthy" or "desirable." Even Emma regards her own body with disgust: "El temor se perdío en la tristeza de su cuerpo, en el asco. El asco y la tristeza la encadenaban" (Foreboding melted into the sadness of her body, into the revulsion. Sadness and revulsion lay upon Emma like chains [47]) (62). Inseparable from her body is her sexuality, which is also portrayed as abnormal, or possibly nonexistent: "Los hombres le inspiraban, aún, un temor casi patológico" (Men still inspired in her an almost pathological fear [45]) (60). Indeed, Emma regards the sexual act in which she must engage as worse than the murder itself: "Pensó que la etapa final [el asesinato] sería menos horrible que la primera [el acto sexual] y que le depararía, sin duda, el sabor de la victoria y de la justicia" (She reflected that the final step [the murder] would be less horrible than the first [the sexual act], and would give her, she had no doubt of it, the taste of victory, and of justice [46]) (61). In a sense, Emma prefers that the sexual act be worse than the violence, and for that reason, she chooses a man repugnant to her, rather than one for whom she might experience desire. It is as if the horror of the sexual act were to justify murder—somehow absolving her—whereas the possibility of enjoyment would destroy the realization of justice.

Immediately after Emma's encounter with the sailor, he departs, leaving money for Emma, whom he believes to be a prostitute. Emma destroys the money he has given her, even though she considers it a sin: "Romper dinero es una impiedad, como tirar el pan" (Tearing up money is an act of impiety, like throwing away bread [47]) (62). This act, on one level, is meant to hide the evidence of one sexual crime (the "real" one) in order to be able to claim to be the victim of a second, invented one. At the same time, her destruction of currency rewrites the event not as a transaction—not as prostitution—but rather as a situation constructed and controlled by Emma, one that fits into the performance she has rehearsed. In a sense, the story resists assigning economic value to human action: Emma does not sell her body for money, but rather for revenge. She meets with her boss not to negotiate salary demands, but to punish him for stealing money and framing her father. Thus, the implementation of justice trumps financial relations: divine justice transcends economics.

Emma's subversion of the economic transaction parallels her deconstruction of identity. Her sexual act is twice removed from the possibility of truth. It is neither prostitution nor rape; it is a dual simulacrum. Emma's double pose not only represents the flexibility of the "Jew," or her ability to mutate and masquerade as other, but also grants her a certain degree of agency. Within a context of fiction, Emma can create her own narrative. Further, she reinvents herself as a previously nonexistent person, a detail that is relayed as a premonition early in the story, as soon as she receives the letter that announces her father's death: "Furtivamente lo guardó en el cajón, como si de algún modo ya conociera los hechos ulteriores. Ya había empezado a vislumbrarlos, tal vez; *ya era la que sería*" (Furtively, she put it away for safekeeping in a drawer, as though she somehow knew what was coming. She may already have begun to see the things that would happen next; *she was already the person she was to become* [44]) (59, emphasis added). Despite this fatalistic tone, Emma's story (as well as her identity) is not as predestined as it might seem. The fact that she is unable to complete the pronunciation of the lines she has practiced repeatedly—"He vengado a mi padre y no me podrán castigar" (I have avenged my father, and I shall not be punished [49]) (66)—exposes a flaw in her creative act: the performance cannot mimic the rehearsal. At the same time, this flaw is what defines the act as an open text, subject to rewriting. The performance inevitably entails a reworking of the "essential" text, which of course was always already rewritten.[33]

Just as the category "truth" is a veiled and manipulable concept—the narrator claims that this is a true story, except for a few proper names, places, and circumstances—so is the category "Jew." The scene of prostitution in Borges represents a space within which hierarchies are simultaneously ordered and deconstructed, and truths are invented and manipulated. The hermeneutic malleability with which Borges writes the prostitution scene echoes the flexibility of Emma's "Jewishness." In this sense, Ludmer's argument that Emma may not be Jewish is worth considering; Emma's ethnoreligious identity, like her status as prostitute, remains subject to interpretation. The meeting of the categories "Jew" and "prostitute" in Borges's story produces a space within which identity can be written, performed, and read: a locus of enunciation and a place of invention, in which the malleability of the signifier is pushed to its limits.

Of course, the "Jew" is not the only figure employed in Borges's *ficciones* to decenter meaning and identity: the "female" and the "gaucho," to give only two examples, also serve as subjects of interpretation.[34] The figure of the "woman" in Borges (Emma, of course, is not only "Jewish" but also "female") is employed in distinct and contradictory ways. While Emma may be one of the sole examples of female agency in Borges's work, the figures of Juliana Burgos (in "La intrusa"), Azevedo Bandeira's lover (in "El muerto"), and Beatriz Viterbo (in "El Aleph") serve as intermediary figures for a privileged relationship or epiphany.[35] Readers of "La intrusa" ("The Intruder") have understood the figure of the "woman" as a stand-in or a place-holder for the larger question of homosocial relations: while Daniel Balderston writes that the figure of Juliana "is the token that allows the functioning of homosexual desire" (1995, 35), Herbert Brant echoes that the presence of the communal woman interrupts and, perhaps counterintuitively, makes possible the relationship between the Nilsen brothers who "use" her, share her, and ultimately expel her from the space of the homosocial (1999, 42).[36] In "El Aleph" ("The Aleph") one sees a wholly different dynamic: it is the (absent) figure of Beatriz Viterbo that brings the narrator to Carlos Argentino Daneri, who in turn leads him to the Aleph, hidden in the basement of his home. In both cases, however, the "woman" serves as a bridge to a privileged space: that of the homosocial in the former, and that of the cipher that contains nothing less than the secret of the universe in the latter.

The figure of the "gaucho" in such stories as "El fin" ("The End") or "El Sur" ("The South") enacts, in a way not unrelated to that of the "Jew," the deconstruction of a particular form of identity: that of the gaucho itself. But if the simultaneous thematization and exposure of the idea of "Jewishness" in "Emma Zunz" paves the way for a broader reflection on the constructed nature of meaning, the writing (and reading) of the gaucho plays a central role in the "killing off" (to echo the Latin American literary critic Patrick Dove) of a local, particular literary tradition, the gauchesque genre.[37] The narrator of "El Sur" undoes lo criollo not only by postulating a hybrid, cosmopolitan identity through the figure of the protagonist Juan Dahlman, but also, specifically, by identifying Dahlmann's "Germanic blood" as that which makes him or allows him to be authentically criollo, that which makes possible the election of a specifically Argentine (read: gauchesque) destiny: "Juan Dahlmann (tal vez a impulso de la sangre germánica) eligió el de ese antepasado romántico, o de muerte romántica" (Juan Dahlmann [perhaps impelled by his Germanic blood] chose that of his romantic ancestor, or that of a romantic death [1998c, 174]) (1986d, 86). Through this inversion of identity, Borges denaturalizes the link between "gaucho" and "Argentineness," exposing the constructed nature of this overdetermined figure.

It is not that Borges's reworking of the figure of the gaucho does not have implications for questions of reading and writing, meaning and identity "in general"—Dove maintains that the ambiguous conclusion to "El Sur" announces a literary problem, "how to give shape to or symbolize an encounter with that which eludes or falls out of symbolization" (2004, 87)—but rather that it is always and necessarily articulated in response to a particular tradition: the Argentine tradition of the gauchesque genre. If the figure of the "Jew" functions as a particular way of engaging the universal, the voyage to "universality" through the figure of the gaucho must involve an additional stop: the questioning of the tradition of the figure itself. In Borges's lecture "El escritor argentino y la tradición" the "Jew" offers a (particular) model to approach the universal. Borges's assertion that "nuestro patrimonio es el universo" (our patrimony is the universe) announces and enacts an original cosmopolitanism, as the Latin American literary critic Mariano Siskind has argued, in which the universal is articulated *necessarily* through the local, or the marginal.[38] The figure of the "Jew" serves as a model for such alternative cosmopolitanism: by populating the margins of the Occidental literary tradition, the "Jew" contributes uniquely, and better, to this tradition than someone who cannot view it from the outside. The intellectual production of the Argentine, by extension, not only belongs to the West but is more Western than the Western itself. Likewise, the strange history of "Emma Zunz" must be situated among Jews in order to arrive, indirectly, as a marginally universal, consciously constructed "truth."

In Rodolfo Enrique Fogwill's *Vivir afuera* (as in "Emma Zunz"), prostitution and "Jewishness" are not linked explicitly, but rather casually occupy the same terrain. *Vivir afuera* portrays a subaltern space in which all aspects of marginality coexist in a nonhierarchical relationship, thereby erasing any sort of difference. Promiscuity therefore does not represent a characteristic that describes the "Jew," nor is "Jewishness" a trait that alludes to prostitutes. Rather, both "Jews" and prostitutes are utilized rhetorically to populate and thus make a broader point about peripheral space and subjectivity in postmodern Buenos Aires.

Mariana, one of the six main characters of *Vivir afuera*, is a prostitute from the outskirts of Buenos Aires. Her geographical and socioeconomic marginality, along with her status as prostitute, characterize her as displaced from every sort of "center," a concept that does not seem to exist in Fogwill's novel. Each of the characters resides on the outside, but as the novel's back cover asks paratextually, "Outside of where?" Even Mariana's prostitution does not fall into traditional categories: her relationship with the character Wolff could be characterized as a sort of postmodern prostitution, a relationship that while involving both sex and money, has not been arranged by a formal contract in which the client pays for services rendered.

The two first encounter each other in a bar during early morning hours, both having just returned to Buenos Aires from the provinces, and they immediately notice one another. Although it is Wolff who approaches Mariana, they become acquainted based on mutual attraction. In fact, desire seems to be the only common denominator between these two characters, who differ in terms of class, education, age, and even accent. The socioeconomic, generational, and linguistic chasm that divides the pair, however, does not prevent them from going back to Wolff's apartment to take drugs and have sex. Wolff is aware of the fact that Mariana is a prostitute, even though she has decided not to charge him for their sexual encounter: "—Ni hablar de guita . . .—rió ella—. ¡Hoy todo corre por cuenta de la casa!" (Don't even talk about money . . .—she laughed—. Today, everything is on the house!) (Fogwill 1998, 118). They spend the entire morning talking; neither time nor sex is an issue, despite the fact that Mariana secretly hopes that Wolff will indeed give her some money: "*Seguro que por no cobrarle nada y por gozar el día menos pensado te tira un mil, o más. Los tipos son así*" (Surely for not charging him anything and for enjoying the day, he'll slip you a thousand, or more, when you least expect it. Guys are like that) (120). In fact, it is Wolff who appears more obsessed with money; he has just received a large check for a freelance writing job and cannot stop talking about his newfound wealth. Mariana—the less fortunate of the two—repeatedly points out that Wolff is fixated on money; Wolff's identity, it seems, depends on his poverty.

Their relationship becomes abruptly intimate when Wolff tells Mariana that he will accompany her to her doctor's appointment, at which time she will receive the results of her HIV test. On their outing, Wolff gives Mariana money so that she can pay her cab fare and buy a gift for her doctor, Saúl. That their relationship moves into the realm of the financial does not necessarily imply monetary compensation for their sexual encounter. Rather, sex and money simply coexist within the realm of the interpersonal, just as prostitute and "Jew" are juxtaposed within the margins of society. When Wolff offers Mariana money, having cashed his check, it is meant as a quasi-independent act, related to their affair only indirectly. Despite the lack of causality, however, money and sex are indeed linked to one another in a post-modern transaction. The exchange remains disconnected from any notion of reciprocity, its significance as fragmented as the lives of the characters.

The encounter between "Jew" and prostitute comes in the form of the doctor-patient relationship. Saúl, a hematologist, is repeatedly marked as Jewish in the novel, particularly in contrast to his upper-class, assimilated Jewish girlfriend, Diana Fridman. Indeed, it is the opposition between Diana and Saúl that delineates Saúl's exclusion from Argentine culture: while Saúl pronounces the "r" in Israel almost as a vowel (using a Hebrew accent), Diana pronounces it with a Spanish *erre*, "a la manera de los goi argentinos" (in the manner of Argentine goyim) (115). Saúl attempts to introduce Diana to the Jewish aspects of Borges—Argentina's national poet par excellence—when he recommends that she read "Emma Zunz" and "Deutsches Requiem" (175). Thus, to the extent that Saúl is "more Jewish" than Diana, he gravitates toward the margins of society, connecting more with his prostitute patient than with his own girlfriend.

Saúl and Mariana share a common obsession with AIDS. Saúl's fetish could be characterized as blood centered: "A él lo excitaba la sangre," the narrator comments as Saúl performs oral sex on a menstruating Diana, the ultimate transgression of the Jewish prohibition against physical contact during the two weeks surrounding menstruation. Mariana, for her part, remains paralyzed with fear that she will die of AIDS. Despite the fact that multiple HIV-tests come back negative, she continues to visit Saúl's office to repeat the exams. She arrives at her most recent appointment accompanied by Wolff, who has helped her select a gift for Saúl, a compact disc of traditional Jewish music, with which she is completely unfamiliar. Saúl is so moved by the gift—the CD contains his father's as well as his paternal grandfather's favorite song—that he develops a new affection for Mariana. Wolff narrates the quasi-love scene between Saúl and Mariana: "La miró a ella, miró los títulos de los temas y se inclinó sobre la mesa. La había tomado de los brazos. . . . Ahora yo tendría que desaparecer por la parte lateral del escenario y dejarlos a solas—se dijo Wolff, pensando—: Sería el final feliz de una película boba" (He looked at her, looked at the track titles and bent over the table. He had taken her by the arms. . . . Now I would have to disappear through the side of the stage and leave them alone—Wolff said to himself, thinking—: It would be the happy ending of a dumb movie) (245). In this scene, Mariana's feelings of transference toward her doctor are reciprocated, and they experience a moment that is more intimate—despite its kitschy sentimentality—than the mutual disgust and disrespect shared by Saúl and Diana. Here, the pathological space of the hospital creates the necessary conditions for prostitute and "Jew" to meet, in an over-romanticized manifestation of transference.

After a bomb threat has been called in to the hospital, Saúl, Cecilia (his Jewish colleague), Wolff, and Mariana leave for Wolff's apartment, where they spend the afternoon together. The experience reminds Wolff of the seventies: "Había un lugar, gente que se agrupaba creyendo que solamente los unía el azar . . . y se cumplían horas hasta que alguien, aburrido, proponía que fuesen a una casa, 'a mi casa'—decía—o 'a tu casa.' Y ahora esta mina . . . repite aquella escena" (There was a place, people that got together thinking that they were only united by chance . . . and hours would pass until someone, bored, would suggest that they go to a house, '"my house"—they would say—or "your house." And now this girl . . . repeats that scene) (271). The time warp in Wolff's mind superimposes a second level onto this arbitrary collection of people; this time, instead of a homogeneous group of outsiders, one sees a writer, a prostitute, and two Jews. Yet Wolff's association of this encounter with those of the seventies suggests that this collection of people is not as diverse as one might think. Despite cultural gaps and misreadings—Mariana doesn't comprehend why Wolff has so many books; Saúl doesn't understand why Wolff doesn't have a proper job; Mariana has never heard of Saúl's Jewish music; Saúl can't decide if Wolff is an anti-Semite—difference seems to be at least partially occluded in the novel.

Each character's particularities do not so much serve to distinguish one from the other, but instead function as qualifications to belong to the marginal space that Fogwill posits as the center of his fictional universe. The novel, which resembles more of a collage than a linear narrative, deconstructs the modern subject while never fully acknowledging any single alternative voice. The effect produced by this dynamic is that no one position is privileged, a result that although theoretically provocative remains ethically problematic. Fogwill's poetics recall Derrida's and Lyotard's use of "Jewishness" as a displaced category that possesses only rhetorical function, while completely suppressing the alterity of the "Jew." Fogwill's appropriation of the category "Jew"—as well as of the prostitute, the drug addict, and the patient—echoes the 1968 French protest slogan "Nous sommes tous des Juifs allemands" ("We are all German Jews"), Lyotard's reference to the category "jews," Derrida's postulation of a "Hebrew" philosophical genealogy as the Greek philosophical tradition's other. Ultimately, the characters of *Vivir afuera*—Jew, prostitute, writer—remain tools within a broader project to imagine subjectivity (perhaps for the author himself) in end-of-the-millennium Buenos Aires.

As evident in the promiscuous texts by Tácito, Beter, Borges, and Fogwill, the "looseness" of the Jewish, the female, and the prostitute's bodies in the Western cultural imaginary allows these figures to be utilized within literary discourse to differing, even contradictory, ends. Each of the works I analyze enacts promiscuity in a performative sense: that is, they realize on the level of form and content, discourse and theme, the very corruption of categories thought to be the work of the prostitute. The fact that Madame Pommery, an immigrant and prostitute, can rise within the social hierarchy of paulistana society suggests not only a flexibility within urban Brazilian culture but also a central role for Brazil within global modernity. Tiempo's Clara Beter and Borges's Emma Zunz both pose as prostitutes: while Tiempo invents Beter as a way to assume a "popular" locus of enunciation, parodying the terms of political literature, Emma feigns prostitution in order to write her own narrative, exposing the fragility of identity while insisting on the potential power of fiction. Fogwill's novel, finally, juxtaposes prostitute and "Jew" in order to create a broad category into which any "other" falls. In each of these examples, a textual transaction is realized, in which meaning is constructed through negotiations of identity and alterity, truth and fiction.

❧ ❧ ❧

After exploring these diverse scenes of transaction, it is important to consider what one is left with, the leftovers of these exchanges. Who are the casualties? Who are the survivors, those that outlive the totalizing processes imposed on them? What elements of the text serve its rhetorical ends, and what elements resist representation? If the different constructions of "Jewish transactions" imply the sexualization of money and the commodification of sex—in sum, a perversion of value—what kind of value/s are imagined in their place, or through the invention of their opposites?

The possibility of surplus, of that which transcends binary oppositions, is introduced by several of the texts I have treated in this chapter. In Noel Rosa's "Quem dá mais?" the auction serves as the site of the sale (or selling out) of Brazilian authenticity. The Jewish buyer creates surplus by purchasing a guitar, the symbol of Brazilian cultural patrimony, then reselling this object to a museum at double the price. By creating value, by extracting something superfluous from an inert object, the Jew's action at once represents the ultimate violation of Brazilianness, as well as the possibility of transcending the transaction. At the same time, the Jewish buyer creates a different kind of value by selling the artifact to a museum. Thus, the lyrics express a degree of undecidability with regard to the "Jew" and his financial activity, which simultaneously signal the creation and appropriation of value. The double function of the "Jew" moreover suggests a possible role for the sambista, a middleman in his own rite, and for the Brazilian in general, whose identity is repeatedly construed as hybrid or liminal.

Fogwill's *Vivir afuera*, too, suggests the possibility of that which escapes the financial transaction. Mariana's and Wolff's connection goes beyond the traditional relationship between prostitute and client; rather than trading money for sex, they trade both in an arbitrary, postmodern exchange that excludes contract and causality. The doctor-patient relationship between Saúl and Mariana is also completely reworked and displaced from its traditional function. Is it possible that the individual categories of "Jewishness" or "prostitution" or even "medicine" can be appropriated in the name of difference? Perhaps alterity can simultaneously be appropriated and granted agency. That is, while the notion of "Jewishness" remains a mere idea, a rhetorical tool, can it at the same time point to the possibility of something outside the totality of the modern subject?

Borges's "Emma Zunz" could be the most radical example of this dynamic, in that he includes a stereotypical Jewish character—Loewenthal—precisely in order to destroy such limiting categories. Loewenthal, who represents the hackneyed version of "Jewishness" witnessed in anti-Semitic discourse, must die, while the character of Emma, a dis-figured "Jew," serves as the protagonist of a story about the invention of identity and the fiction of truth. Even the construction of Emma as "Jew" (and prostitute) thematizes "Jewishness" (and prostitution) as a malleable signifier in order to make signifiers malleable. In other words, both traditional and rearticulated versions of "Jewishness" become the casualties of Borges's hermeneutic transactions *at the same time that he creates a space within the text that resists representation.*

There is an unresolved ambiguity present in the analysis of these narratives of transaction. Although I have explored the uses of "Jewishness" within broader projects of individual and collective subject formation, it remains unclear whether what I have denominated the "remainder" refers to waste, something squandered or discarded, or to surplus, an element that outlives the exchange. Does the remainder refer to the casualties or to the survivors of textual appropriations of "Jewishness"? Perhaps both concepts are two sides of the same coin, so that even that which is "thrown away" can signal the limit of the subject, the nation, or the text. By highlighting that which does not fit into the same, is it possible to imagine the other as that which resists representation?

✂ THREE

Textual Conversions

Jews had been able to escape from Judaism into
conversion; from Jewishness there was no escape.
—Hannah Arendt, *The Origins of Totalitarianism*

I f the scene of the diagnosis and the scene of the
transaction entail performative acts by which
"Jewishness" is constructed, negotiated, and pro-
cessed, leaving behind varying degrees of residual otherness, or remainders of Jewish alterity, the scene of
conversion offers perhaps the most radical example
of the appropriation of Jewish difference. The rhetoric of Jewish conversion—while concerned with the total absorption of the "Jew" into the imperialism of the
same—is simultaneously preoccupied with that which
is excluded from the process of assimilation, that element of Jewish alterity which resists the totalizing
forces of appropriation. As in the diagnosis, the scene
of conversion involves discursive operations through
which an individual or collective subject position is articulated vis-à-vis the other. At the same time, the act of
conversion, like that of the transaction, always implies

a remainder, a surplus, a "traumatic kernel" that refuses symbolization (Žižek 1989, 3). Discourse of conversion, finally, is inseparable from the extreme violence of the historical conversions of Jews, in particular during the Inquisition, the effects of which were felt on both sides of the Luso-Hispanic Atlantic.

While the history of Jewish conversion entails a series of diasporic circuits, forced exiles, and transatlantic expeditions during early modernity, it also involves numerous contemporary textual voyages in which this history represents a destination, an object of analysis, a hermeneutic leap in order to disguise or decipher the present. By exploring what I term *textual conversions*—discursive acts in which difference is assimilated into the totalizing project of the text—I intend to demonstrate that the figure of the converso serves as a body upon which the broader values and preoccupations of the writer and his culture can be inscribed. In modern literary representations of the converso another type of appropriation is realized, this time on the level of discourse. What does it mean to convert the other, if not to assimilate her to the religious, political, or aesthetic project of the self? What are the ethical implications of these historical and discursive appropriations?

Jewish conversion is a theme that, by definition, forms part of a transatlantic, transhistorical, and transcultural dynamic. The conversions that took place during the Inquisition—whether forced or voluntary—resulted in a subculture of New Christians, whose descendants populated the recently unified Spain and Portugal, as well as their fledgling colonies across the Atlantic.[1] As a result of the 1492 and 1497 expulsions of Jews from Spain and Portugal, which officially excluded them from the first voyages of conquest to the Americas as well, the Jewish presence on both sides of the Luso-Hispanic Atlantic from the sixteenth century through the eighteenth can be characterized as clandestine, invisible, subterranean. Because of the explicit exclusion but hidden inclusion of Jews through conversion, the converso comes to represent in Latin American literature an Other Within that serves as a reminder of the traumatic originary violence of the conquest. Given that the religious identity of the converso is always under suspicion—it is impossible to verify her true loyalties—the New Christian remains subject to interpretation, and this dynamic plays a critical role in the contemporary representations of this figure.

Of course, Spanish and Portuguese New Christians do not stand as the sole examples of Jewish converts; indeed, the very origins of Christianity could be understood as converso. The fact that the transition from what was initially a renegade Jewish sect to an autonomous religious community was realized through conversion—both of Jews and of Judaism itself—means that Christian identity is simultaneously dependent on and threatened by the idea of Jewish conversion.[2] In this sense, not only Judaism in general but Jewish conversion in particular stands as the condition of possibility of the emergence of Christianity, at the very same time that it marks its finitude, or impossibility. The double bind of conversion begins to explain why New Christians (as potential Judaizers) pose a far greater threat to the Inquisition in Spain and Portugal than do Jews themselves, and why, when Jews do appear as the target of politicoreligious aggression, it is because they are viewed as a bad influence on New Christians, not Old Christians.[3] (The Edict of Expulsion, while not explicitly distinguishing between New Christians and Old Christians, addresses the problem of Jewish proselytizing. Given the prohibition by Jewish law of such activity, it is more probable that New Christians who continued to secretly practice Judaism—crypto-Jews—relied on Jews for religious resources, both educational and material.)

What is interesting is the way in which figures of conversion—specifically, Jewish conversion—repeatedly emerge during moments of ideological and identitary instability, so that the Inquisition draws its strength from anxiety surrounding Christianity's origins, and modern Latin American narratives of race and nation return to the moment of the Inquisition and the scene of conversion in order to articulate the possibility of ethnic assimilation, national consolidation, and political transformation. When the boundaries between the same and the other become blurred, this ambiguity is displaced onto the Jewish convert.

The converso provokes a singular kind of anxiety due to the impossibility of fixing her identity. The German-Jewish philosopher Hannah Arendt argues that while religious conversion completely transforms Jew into Christian, cultural assimilation can never fully escape the modern, racialized concept of "Jewishness." Yet, as investigation of the history of conversion reveals, doubts regarding the status of the convert often linger. Although conversion promises total incorporation of the other into the universe of the self, there is always a potential resistance to this change. It is impossible to verify the loyalties, or the true identity of the converso: is she a faithful Christian? Does he secretly practice Judaism? Is it possible to identify elements of Jewish difference within the New Christian despite her religious transformation? The slippery nature of converso identity is disquieting, ultimately, because it calls into question the authenticity of the self. Zygmunt Bauman uses the term *proteophobia* to explain the unease toward "Jewishness" in the modern European imaginary: "The proper generic phenomenon of which the resentfulness of the Jews is a part is proteophobia, not heterophobia; the apprehension and vexation related not to something or someone disquieting through otherness and unfamiliarity, but to something or someone that does not fit the structure of the orderly world, does not fall easily into any of the established categories" (1998, 144). If "Jewishness" inspires anxiety in the modern European subject due to its resistance to classification, as Bauman suggests, the converso provokes a more extreme reaction by occupying an even less identifiable position.

A scene from Justo Sierra O'Reilly's *La hija del judío* (1848)—a novel that details the persecution of a New Christian by the Inquisition—highlights this anxiety toward the converso. After lecturing on the evils of Judaism, one of the characters, a Jesuit priest, asks, "Dime, pues, una cosa: un judío, por más virtuoso y recomendable que sea ¿deja de ser judío?" (Tell me then: does a Jew, despite how virtuous and commendable he may be, cease to be Jewish?) (Sierra O'Reilly 1959, 210). His question is answered in the negative by Don Luis: "Ya sé que no" (I know he does not) (ibid.). Their dialogue, a series of questions and answers, of instabilities and reaffirmations, reveals what is at the heart of the persecution of the New Christian during the Inquisition, as well as of anxiety surrounding "Jewishness" within modernity: its lack of fixedness. Hence the desperate need to assert the stability of the category "Jew": if the "Jew" will always be a "Jew," then I will always be myself as well. If this affirmation were actually believed or fully internalized, there would be no need to repeatedly state it as fact. This unsettling attitude toward "Jewishness" is present in all of the narratives of conversion I discuss. Each text simultaneously reacts with suspicion against that which can transform from one entity into another, from "Jew" into Christian, and sighs with relief when confronted with the other who, as planned, is fully absorbed into the self. Given the malleability of the convert, and the multiple ways in which she can be appropriated, what are the ethical implications of the literary recodifications of this figure?

In order to consider the problem of ethics and representation, I return to the work of Emmanuel Levinas, who, in his discussion of subjectivity, redirects Western philosophy's focus on the idea of Being to the relationship between same and Other. Rather than privileging the autonomous subject at the expense of the Other, Levinas discusses the call to responsibility that comes from the face of the Other as that which defines the subject. Through a response to the Other's call—by becoming *respons-ible*—the self is consti-tuted as a subject. It is therefore through the ethical encounter that one can begin to talk about subjectivity: "Responsibility [is] the essential, primary and fundamental structure of subjectivity" (Levinas 1982, 95). As a result of the "face to face" encounter—although Levinas does not talk about cause and effect in a temporal sense—the self assumes the status of subject by re-sponding to the demand of the Other.

Counterintuitively, perhaps, the encounter between self and Other is not characterized by reciprocity, but is rather best described as an asymmetrical relationship, in which the subject finds himself subordinated to the demand of the Other: "The intersubjective relation is a non-symmetrical relation. In this sense, I am responsible for the Other without waiting for reciprocity, were I to die for it. Reciprocity is his affair" (ibid., 98). Nor can one find evi-dence of union or identification between self and Other, but rather a *disfamil-iarization*, absolute exteriority. The Other, with her presence, interrupts the assimilating tendency of the self. Indeed, representing the other—that is, re-ducing the other to the terms of the self—implies the abolition of alterity, a complete totalization of the Other, incorporating any element of difference into the imperialism of the same. With its call to responsibility, the face of the Other suspends the assimilating tendency of the same.

In this sense, the issue of conversion forms part of a broader preoccupa-tion with the ethical treatment of the Other; after all, what does it mean to convert the Other, if not to assimilate him to the religion and culture of the self? Converting the Other implies an annihilation of difference, a rejection of any element of otherness that might threaten the identity of the self; con-version signifies the reduction of the Other to the same (Levinas 1993, 91).

What happens, then, when the converso—a figure whose difference is, by definition, already violated—is subjected to another sort of appropriation, that of the letter? In analyzing literary representations of the converso, can one think about the possibility of discursive violence, a textual conversion in which difference is annihilated through writing? Levinas finds no space within literature for the face of the Other; representing the Other necessarily involves the reduction of the face to a set of characteristics: eyes, nose, ears, mouth. Literary discourse, for Levinas, pertains to the category of rhetori-cal language, which by definition thematizes the Other, in contrast to ethical language, that pre-original language in which the self receives the demand of the Other. It is here, in the opposition between rhetorical and ethical lan-guage, where my analysis detours from Levinasian philosophy. In my reading of literary representations of Jewish conversion, I attempt to problematize this radical division, suggesting a possible interaction between rhetoric and ethics. Is there an element of difference within the text that survives the totalizing process of representation, an aspect of alterity that resists thematization? Must the representation of the Other automatically constitute a violation, as Levinas suggests? Is there a difference between the rhetorical use of the convert within a politics of resistance as opposed to a politics of assimilation? Is it possible to be politically correct and ethically irresponsible?

To address these questions, I first focus on a series of fictional works that, curiously, all portray Christian daughters of Jewish fathers. Jorge Isaacs's *María* (Colombia, 1867), Joaquim Maria Machado de Assis's "A cristã nova" (Brazil, 1875), and Alfredo Dias Gomes's *O Santo Inquérito* (Brazil, 1966) imagine a female Christian subject whose (explicitly or implicitly Jewish) mother is deceased or simply absent from the text. Of these three works—a novel, poem, and play—two are situated within the historical context of the Inquisition, the exception being Jorge Isaacs's *María*. I aim to unpack this nontraditional literary genealogy—why not a father-son or even a mother-daughter pair?—and propose that the female body is a productive site of conversion or malleability. I then investigate two texts in which a more figurative form of conversion takes place. Heitor Carlos Cony's *Pessach: A travessia* (Brazil, 1967) and Mario Vargas Llosa's *El hablador* (Peru, 1987) both utilize "Jewishness" to suggest a potential for other types of conversion: political transformation, ethnic assimilation, and national consolidation. While these works do not turn to the violent history of the New Christian and the Inquisition, they highlight the radical malleability of the converso by pushing the symbolic potential of Jewish conversion to its limits.

These works do not reflect the sole instances of Jewish conversion in modern literature; nor is this phenomenon restricted to Latin American literature. Rather, the representation of conversos and conversion belongs to a broader, transatlantic tradition that includes the nineteenth-century Spanish writer Benito Pérez Galdós's *Gloria* as well as his *Torquemada* novels, George Eliot's *Daniel Deronda*, James Joyce's *Ulysses*, the Portuguese playwright Bernardo Santareno's *O Judeu*, Antonio Gala's theatrical work *Las cítaras colgadas de los árboles* (performed and published in Francoist Spain), and the Majorcan writer Carme Riera's novel *En el último azul*, to name only a few examples. I explore this phenomenon by asking the following questions: how can we explain the uncanny presence of the converso within modern Latin American literature? What symbolic value does this figure possess, and how does it differ from that of the "Jew"? By utilizing the converso, a historical figure, to articulate contemporary issues, does another sort of conversion take place? What are the ethical implications of these aesthetic appropriations?

THE JEW'S DAUGHTERS: THE GENEALOGY OF ASSIMILATION

Published in 1848–49 in El Fénix, after Justo Sierra O'Reilly's return to Mexico from a diplomatic post in Washington, La hija del judío (The Jew's daughter) recounts the story of María, the adopted daughter of don Alonso de la Cerda (Castro Leal 1959, xix). This innocent young Christian girl is persecuted by the Inquisition when it is learned that she is actually the daughter of the despised Jew Felipe Alvarez de Monstreal. While she is not condemned to death—as are many "daughters" of the Santo Oficio—she is exiled from Mexico, her conversion and adoption by a Christian family deemed a failure.

Sierra O'Reilly's María is not the only example of an imaginary "hija del judío," but rather is accompanied by a number of other fictional Christian daughters of Jewish fathers within the Latin American literary tradition: Isaacs's María (María), Machado de Assis's Ângela ("A cristã nova"), and Dias Gomes's Branca (O Santo Inquérito), all of whose names are overdetermined—one is tempted to say hackneyed—symbols of purity and innocence. This alternative genealogy of the Jewish father and Christian daughter is not an exclusively Latin American occurrence, but rather parallels a similar phenomenon across the Atlantic.

In his book Shakespeare and the Jews the early-modern-literature scholar James Shapiro details the Elizabethan preoccupation with and fictionalization of Jewish conversion, arguing that in the early modern English imaginary, Jewish women are converted and married off to Christian men, while "male Jewish converts are invariably old and impotent, condemned to remain unwed and at the periphery of the Christian community" (1996, 132). While Shakespeare's Merchant of Venice is far from the only example of this dynamic, it is certainly the most widely known. Jessica's betrayal of her father, Shylock, by converting to Christianity in order to marry Lorenzo serves multiple functions: it foreshadows Shylock's forced conversion at the hands of the court; it marks the beginning of the Jew's downfall; it establishes Jessica as a counterexample to Portia, whose loyalty to her own father places her at the center of the play's moral universe; and it reveals the impossibility of completely converting the Jew (Jessica's sadness at sweet music reveals that the melancholy cultivated in the "hellish" house of her Jewish father has not disappeared; her tragic "Jewess-ness" remains).

The presence of the Christian daughter and Jewish father pair returns in nineteenth-century English literature. In *Figures of Conversion* the literary critic Michael Ragussis analyzes a number of Victorian historical romances in which the problem of difference and assimilation is dramatized through a converted daughter set in the context of the Spanish Inquisition: "Focused on a daughter's duty to her father and her fatherland, and the threat of her conversion, these romances define the role of women in the construction of the modern nation-state. When writers of historical romance situated the converted daughter at the founding moment of Christian Spain, she became a sign of the ideology that required Jews to convert before they could become full-fledged (English) citizens" (1995, 128). How can one understand the use of the converted daughter to articulate broader preoccupations with difference and assimilation within nineteenth- and twentieth-century Latin American culture (particularly since the question of Jewish conversion to Christianity was not the pressing issue in Latin America that it was in Victorian England)? What malleable potential does the female body offer in this curious textual phenomenon? How is masculinity represented within this father-daughter pairing, and what function does it serve within broader attempts to codify conversion?

Jorge Isaacs's *María* (1867) is a fascinating example of discourse on conversion in nineteenth-century Latin American literature, due at least in part to the history of the Isaacs family. The author's father, George Henry Isaacs, was an English Jew who had converted to Christianity in order to marry Manuela Ferrer Scarpetta, the Catholic daughter of a Catalan official (Mejía 1978, 210). The religious history of his father, as well as Jorge Isaacs's own geographical trajectory (he was an Englishman who emigrated to Colombia via Jamaica) is repeated in *María* through the figure of Efraín's father. Efraín, the narrator and protagonist of Isaacs's novel, recounts the controversial romance between his Jewish father and a Christian woman: "La madre de la joven que mi padre amaba exigió por condición para dársela por esposa que renunciase él a la religión judaica. Mi padre se hizo cristiano a los veinte años de edad" (The mother of the young woman my father loved demanded, as a condition to give her daughter's hand in marriage, that he renounce the Jewish religion. My father became a Christian at the age of twenty) (1978, 11). In this passage, Isaacs establishes autobiographical links between Efraín's father and his own. Through Efraín, Isaacs articulates his own ideological and spiritual oscillations—not only what Doris Sommer characterizes as an "undecidability" between Catholicism and Freemasonry, between "nostalgic conservatism and New World liberalism" (1991, 179–80), but also what one might call a *converso trauma*, the fictional reworking of a heterogeneous religious past.

Of course, Efraín's father is not the only converso in Isaacs's novel: María, Efraín's cousin and love interest, has also converted to Christianity in order to join her family in Colombia. Her conversion, however, is not voluntary like her uncle's, but decided by her father, Solomón, and uncle when she is three years old. Efraín recounts his father's reunion with Solomón in Jamaica, after the latter has just lost his wife, Sara, to a mysterious disease—the same illness, of course, that will prohibit the consummation of Efraín and María's romance. Solomón is despondent and able to find solace only in his cousin's new religion, which he decides to accept as his own. Efraín's father convinces Solomón to baptize his daughter, Ester, so that she may be brought to live with their family in Colombia, given Solomón's inability to care for her.[4] Solomón agrees to the conversion, conceding that Christianity can promise more to his daughter than Judaism.

> Las cristianas son dulces y buenas, y tu esposa debe de ser una santa madre. Si el cristianismo da en las desgracias supremas el alivio que tú me has dado, tal vez yo haría desdichada a mi hija dejándola judía. No lo digas a nuestros parientes, pero cuando llegues a la primera costa donde se halle un sacerdote católico, hazla bautizar y que le cambien el nombre de Ester en el de María. (12)

> ❧

> Christian women are sweet and good, and your wife must be a saintly mother. If Christianity provides, during profound misfortunes, the kind of comfort you have offered me, perhaps I would bring unhappiness to my daughter by allowing her to remain Jewish. Do not tell our relatives, but when you reach the first coast that has a Catholic priest, have her baptized, and change her name from Ester to María.

Cognizant as he is of the transgression he is committing against their Jewish family, Solomón nonetheless recognizes the redemptive value of Christianity, embodied in the figure of the *cristiana*. By depicting the female Christian as "sweet," "good," and "saintly," he assures himself that his cousin's wife will make a good mother for his daughter. At the same time, he designates a future identity for Ester: by changing her name to María, she will be transformed from Hebrew queen into the saint that her female co-religionists personify.

María's undiagnosable disease stands for that aspect of "Jewishness" that cannot be eradicated through conversion, as well as the idea of racial alterity that will not be successfully integrated into the nation and, therefore, must die (as Sommer argues in *Foundational Fictions*). In this sense *María* is at once a story about illness and about conversion; more precisely, it is a narrative about disease as the impossibility of conversion. Sylvia Molloy and Doris Sommer both indicate the ways in which racial ambivalence is played out through the figure of María, who is simultaneously represented as exotic Jewess and pure Christian. María, whose Jewish disease is neither diagnosable nor treatable, is ultimately inassimilable to the family (and, on an allegorical level, to the nation). In contrast, Efraín, who is marked as Jewish by his biblical name, successfully assimilates into a Christian subject, though it could be argued that this is a conscious project on the part of the family, which sends him to London to be educated as a doctor. His socialization as a scientific authority, the embodiment of medicine, parallels his completion of the process begun by his father, who, like María, has also only "partially" converted from Judaism, as evidenced by his failing health.

But if the impossible romance between Efraín and María dramatizes contrasting narratives of conversion, why is it that the male protagonist represents a successful assimilation, while the female remains marked as other and is eventually killed off? This is particularly interesting given that the male half of the converso pair bears a Hebrew name, while seemingly leaving behind this aspect of his identity. María's figure deviates in this sense from Machado de Assis's and Dias Gomes's *filhas de judeus* (daughters of Jews) in that she is the daughter of a Jewish mother, and therefore ultimately inconvertible. While the other genealogical pairings elect to make the father Jewish, breaking the traditional matrilineal link to Jewish heritage, Isaacs posits the father-son lineage (Efraín and his father) as potentially transformative, leaving religious continuity to the mother-daughter (María and Sara).[5] Although Solomón plays a role in his daughter's conversion, his ultimate abandonment of María invests the mother with a stronger genealogical presence, albeit through her undiagnosable disease. The significant members of the older generation, in *María*, are those whose inconvertible "Jewishness" prevents both romantic consummation and national consolidation, those that refer to the multiple conversions in Isaacs's own history.

If the literary codification of conversion in *María* is more autobiographical than historical, Machado de Assis's poem "A cristã nova" (1875) and Alfredo Dias Gomes's play *O Santo Inquérito* (1966) are two examples of literary creations that return to the historical scene of the Inquisition in colonial Brazil in order to address issues of racial and ideological difference in the nineteenth century and the twentieth. Both Machado de Assis's and Dias Gomes's works have as their heroine the daughter of a *cristãos novo*, whose religious past represents an element of conflict for each of their respective societies. The bodies of Ângela and Branca, as conversas and as women, mark sites of racial and ideological contestation. Both figures cross boundaries that are at once religious and sexual: their romances with *cristãos velhos*—another element shared by European narratives of converted daughters—are just one example of this dynamic. By considering the textual conversions of Ângela and Branca, I hope to initiate a discussion about the rhetorical flexibility of the *cristã nova*—the female Jewish convert—signaling a link between historical and discursive violence.

Machado de Assis's long poem "A cristã nova" (The New Christian) lyrically relates the story of a father's and daughter's attempted integration into early-eighteenth-century Brazilian culture.[6] As both immigrants (from Palestine to Brazil) and converts (from Judaism to Christianity), this family of two experiences a dual displacement that constitutes their lyrical identities. While the poem is structured around a series of losses—the geographical and the religious being only two examples—a lyrical mourning is undertaken, launching the family into a new, redemptive state that ultimately proves untenable. Through the figure of the converted daughter, "A cristã nova" imagines a problematic transculturated national subject, displaced from the racially complex moment of the poem's publication onto an early-eighteenth-century context.

"A cristã nova" first appeared in 1875 in *Americanas*, Machado de Assis's third collection of poetry. The portrayal of religious conversion in this poem can be interpreted as an allegory for race in late-nineteenth-century Brazil; in reading it, one should thus bear in mind the positivist notion of *branqueamento*, or racial whitening, in vogue at the time (Skidmore 1993, 64–69). Racially speaking, 1875 was a critical time in Brazilian social history. While slavery was not officially abolished until the following decade, the Lei do Ventre Livre granted freedom to the children of slaves in 1871, creating a population of free people of color.[7] Thus, the moment in which Machado wrote "A cristã nova" was a time of flux, a time of shifting boundaries, evolving identities, transitions: it was a time for conversion. Considered by many to be Brazil's foremost novelist and poet, Machado de Assis himself was a descendant of freed slaves. As a writer of mixed racial descent, Machado operated in a space of crossover, liminality, assimilation, on the threshold between self and other, "black" and "white." Given these realities—both national and individual— the alternating tension between and fluidity of the categories "Christian" and "Jew" are worth exploring; they serve as lenses through which debates surrounding positivism and national identity can be articulated.

Machado de Assis figuratively approaches these identitary issues in "A cristã nova" by positing a series of overdetermined oppositions: night and dawn, darkness and light, age and youth, sea and land, old and new, "Jew" and "Christian," Palestine and Brazil. The first scene of the poem is set in Guanabara Bay, the shoreline of the then fledgling Rio de Janeiro, emphasizing the notion of a borderland, a liminal space. In this textual opening the shore marks a site of arrivals and departures, of local and global, of native and foreign; Guanabara also epitomizes—to an almost stereotypical degree—Brazil.[8] One is thus situated in an identifiable location, *a site where place can identify itself as place*. The seashore allows one to see where Brazil begins and ends, and therefore exactly what it is, for that is one of the objectives of this book. Entitled *Americanas*, the text reflects a desire to poetically thematize the female inhabitants of the New World, as well as to define the New World itself.

As the poem begins, instead of being introduced to the *americana* who will later emerge as the text's lyrical heroine, one first meets her father, an aging man with a long, white beard. It is nighttime, and he is gazing at the sea, reminiscing about his native land, Palestine. He remembers a Palestine associated with his ancestors, with sadness, with strife, with death—"Toda essa vida que morreu" (That entire life that died) (Machado de Assis 1971–74, 1.3.22)—and the opening scene quickly evolves into one of mourning, grief, and loss.[9] This picture of nostalgia and sadness, of night and death, must be established in order to contrast the world of his New Christian daughter, Ângela, to whom the reader is introduced in the fourth section.

In her first appearance Ângela is sitting at the feet of her Jewish father. While there is a certain hierarchy implicit in her pose and, consequently, a note of deference and respect toward the old world of her father, his tradition threatens to be supplanted by the new world of his American, Christian daughter. Ângela is described as a beautiful virgin with black eyes and dark skin, the stereotypical Orientalist image of the Jewess characteristic of

Romantic literature (she is accompanied intertextually by Isaacs's María and by the nineteenth-century Brazilian poet Castro Alves's muse in "Hebraia," among myriad other literary Jewesses). At the same time, her exotic beauty is linked to the freshness of her adopted (*New* Christian and *New* World) identity. The eponymous cristã nova is likened to a "flor que Israel brotou do antigo tronco, / corada ao sol da juvenil América" (flower that Israel germinated from an ancient trunk, / tanned by the sun of a youthful America) (1.4.15–16). This is the first mention of "América" in the poem, and she is modified by the adjective "youthful," in contrast to the decrepit universe of the father. The opposing worlds of father and daughter are further highlighted through their divergent gazes.

> Mudos viam correr aquelas horas
> da noite, os dois: ele voltando o rosto
> ao passado, ela os olhos ao futuro. (1.5.1–3)

❦

> Mute they saw those night hours
> passing, both of them: he turning his face
> to the past, her eyes to the future.

In this stanza the dichotomies set in place from the opening stanza become personified through the figures of the Jewishly identified father (despite his apparent conversion) and his Christian daughter.[10] Their religious discord is articulated verbally through an interruption; as the father characterizes Moses as the savior of Israel, his converted daughter reacts emotionally to his ostensible betrayal of their "new" savior, Christ.

> " . . . o nome
> do que há salvo Israel, Moisés . . ."
> "—Não! Cristo,
> filho de Deus! Só ele há salvo os homens!" (1.7.38–41)

❦

> " . . . the name
> of the one that saved Israel, Moses . . ."
> "—No! Christ,
> son of God! Only he has saved mankind!"

The break in the father's discourse due to Ângela's proclamation of her faith signals their dissonant spiritual allegiances: while the father remains loyal to the idea of Moses as the liberator of the Jewish people, his daughter naïvely interjects the exceptionality of Christ as the sole savior of men.[11]

Despite the agitation of this scene, the intimacy shared by father and daughter guarantees that the opposition between the Old World and the New, Judaism and Christianity, is not necessarily antagonistic. Rather, the aging Jew and his daughter feel mutual affection for one another, just as the father experiences nostalgia for his parents and his ancestral land. Such shared adoration, however, does not imply complete identification. The father dreams of the daughter's choice of a man of "nossa raça" (our race), placing the pair in a shared category of racial identification. The daughter, on the other hand, refers to the divide (both geographical and conceptual) between her land and the world outside Brazil.

> Formosa, oh! quão formosa a terra minha!
> . . . além desses compridos serros,
> além daquele mar, à orla de outros,
> outras como esta vivem? (1.6.11–14)
>
> ❧
>
> Beautiful, oh! How beautiful my land is!
> . . . beyond these extensive mountains,
> beyond that sea, at the edge of others,
> do others like this one exist?

The fact that Ângela articulates Brazil as her own when she refers to "terra minha" is significant. She further confirms her geographical loyalties when she wonders aloud about the existence of other lands across the sea. The ocean, again, becomes the boundary between self and other, a threshold that her father has crossed only partially.

Part 2 of "A cristã nova" is replete with images of dawn, renovation, and light, in sharp contrast to the darkness, night, and death of part 1: "Era naquela doce e amável hora / em que vem branqueando a alva celeste" (It was that sweet and lovely hour / when celestial dawn is turning white) (2.1.1–2). Dawn is linked to the process of branqueamento, the racial implications of which would not have been lost on Machado's public, the intelligentsia of the nineteenth century well versed in (if not proponents of) positivism and social Darwinism. The "whitening" of the dawn that one witnesses here is more than simply the overdetermined romantic characterization of nature; it also connotes cultural and racial transformation. The use of words such as "renovação" (renovation), "juventude" (youth), "sol" (sun), and "luz" (light) suggests that the family's emigration to Brazil, as well as their religious conversion, offers the possibility of redemption for the family, however tenuous.

The potential integration of the daughter into an American cultural and political context is further strengthened by her relationship with a cristão velho (Old Christian), Nuno, who—in addition to contrasting with the racial and religious marginality of his betrothed—proves to be a military hero. His part in the victory over foreign invaders (an allusion to the 1710 attack by the French on Rio de Janeiro) metonymically links him with the emergence of the protonational (or, indirectly, of the national, from the perspective of the lyrical subject narrating from the end of the nineteenth century, as well as of Machado de Assis and his contemporary readers). Moreover, Ângela's father's reluctant acceptance of her relationship with Nuno (he "hands over" his daughter to her new guardian in anticipation of his own death) seems to point in the direction of a successful conversion or assimilation. The transformation of Ângela's blood is affirmed by Nuno himself.

> . . . "Puro sangue é ele,
> se lhe corre nas veias. Tão mimosa,
> cândida criatura, alma tão casta,
> inda nascida entre os incréus da Arábia,
> Deus a votara à conversão e à vida
> dos eleitos do céu. Águas sagradas
> que a lavaram no berço, já nas veias
> o sangue velho e impuro lhe trocaram
> pelo sangue de Cristo . . ." (2.6.27–35)

> ✲

> "Pure blood is it,
> that runs in her veins. Such a delicate,
> candid creature is she, such a pure soul,
> despite being born amongst the skeptics of Arabia,
> God granted her conversion and the life
> of the chosen in heaven. Sacred waters
> in which she was bathed in the crib, already in her veins
> the old, impure blood was replaced
> by Christ's blood . . ."

The promise of purity, insured by the substitution of Ângela's formerly im-pure blood by Christ's, ostensibly confirms the possibility of total conver-sion, albeit at the price of her past and of her father, whose life is threatened by the Santo Ofício. Machado's use of blood as the marker of Ângela's alter-ity (as well as of its potential erasure) simultaneously points in two episte-mological directions: first, to the Inquisition's conception of *pureza de sangue* (purity of blood) as a religiously delineated notion of sameness and differ-ence; second, to a nineteenth-century, (pseudo)scientifically defined concept of race.

While Ângela's future bloodline seems promising, her father describes his own fate as sealed by the arrival of the Santo Ofício.

> " . . . O cárcere me aguarda,
> e a fogueira talvez; cumpri-la, é tempo,
> a vontade de Deus. . . ." (2.15.5–7)

ᘒ

> " . . . Prison awaits me,
> and death by fire perhaps; it is time to abide
> God's will. . . ."

That he attributes his destiny to the will of God signals a certain resignation, a surrender of agency to the transcendent force of God or tragic fate. The loss that has been building throughout the poem now seems immanent—"'Vamos: é já tempo!'" ("Let's go: the time has come!") (2.16.2)—and the fa-ther, contradicting his previous desire for his daughter to live—"'Vive / ao menos tu'" ("Live / at least you") (2.15.23–24)—surprisingly requests that she die along with him: "'Convosco descerei à campa fria, / juntos a mergul-har na eternidade'" ("With you I shall descend to the cold tomb / and together dive into eternity") (2.16.13–14). It is here that the poem takes a double turn: Ângela accepts, her filial loyalty and faith in Christ ultimately overpowering her desire to live, and having witnessed the power of his daughter's faith in the face of death, her father renounces Judaism in favor of Christianity: "'Ó Nazareno, ó filho do mistério, / se é tua lei a única da vida / escreve-me no peito'" ("Oh Jesus, oh son of the mystery, / if your law is the only one in life / inscribe it upon my chest") (2.19.12–14).

This unexpected dual shift in the poem—Ângela's renunciation of her "American" future and her father's subsequent abandonment of his obses-

sively mourned religious past—simultaneously signals the erasure of difference as well as its impossibility. While the father's conversion seems to reject the idea of the survival of religious (or racial) difference, the departure
of father and daughter to "Old Europe" to face the Inquisitorial authorities suggests the unfeasibility of assimilation. It is as if the nostalgic tone
present from the beginning of the poem were to prepare or preserve the conditions of possibility of "return" (the father's sadness signifying his and Ângela's nonbelonging in the New World). Yet their voyage is not constructed
as circular; father and daughter do not return to Palestine, but are once again
displaced, ostensibly to Portugal and to death. In this sense their repeated
departures, accompanied by two seemingly genuine professions of faith in
Christ, establish an aporia of identity that, when read from the perspective of
nineteenth-century Brazilian culture, acquires additional significance. Given
the ideological context of branqueamento, as well as Machado's own racial
ambivalence, the poem appears to point to "whitening" as desirable while
ultimately discrediting it as a viable option. However, although the double
bind of religious or racial difference is left unresolved, the concept of nation
seems to remain intact.

A century later, the idea of conversion still proves to be a productive rhetorical site on which to project questions of difference and nation. Although
"A cristã nova" and O Santo Inquérito (1966) both return to the historical scene
of the Inquisition in order to articulate modern racial and ideological preoccupations, there has never been historical documentation that would prove
the existence of Machado's Ângela. In contrast, O Santo Inquérito, penned by
the leftist playwright and television writer Alfredo de Freitas Dias Gomes
and performed during the early years of the Brazilian dictatorship of the
1960s, is based on the life of Branca Dias, a New Christian who lived in
northeastern Brazil and suffered the persecution of the Inquisition. Accounts
of her life, death, and religious practices vary and contradict one another:
while some historians situate her in Pernambuco in the sixteenth century,
others maintain that she lived in Paraíba during the eighteenth century. Several versions of her story describe an auto-da-fé in Portugal in which Branca
burned at the stake; still others claim that she died peacefully at home, despite having clandestinely run a synagogue on her plantation. Whatever the
"true" story of Branca Dias may have been, it is the divergent interpretations of
her life and the process of textual conversion that takes place in Dias Gomes's
rewriting of this highly mythologized figure that are of interest here.

O Santo Inquérito tells the story of the arrest, interrogation, and eventual murder of Branca and her fiancé, Augusto, by the Santo Ofício in Paraíba. In Dias Gomes's text she is not portrayed as a crypto-Jew who clandestinely organizes religious services in her home, but rather as a pious Christian who is wrongly accused of Judaizing by the authorities.[12] Though it is learned throughout the play that she does indeed descend from a line of crypto-Jews, it also becomes clear that Branca is unaware that her family has secretly observed Jewish rituals in their home. Branca's claim that she is an "authentic" Christian to the authorities is confirmed by the text itself, which shows her reciting Hail Mary's even when she is alone. Moreover, she appears bewildered by the entire Inquisitorial process.

> BRANCA: . . . O que não entendo é por que estou aqui. Não fui convertida, nasci cristã e como cristã tenho vivido até hoje. Cristãos de nascimento são também meu pai e meu noivo, que também estão presos, afastados de mim. Na verdade, senhores, não entendo coisa alguma. (Dias Gomes 1962, 102)

> ℬ

> BRANCA: . . . What I don't understand is why I'm here. I wasn't converted, I was born Christian and as a Christian I've lived until today. My father and fiancé, also Christians by birth, are also being held prisoners, isolated from me. To tell you the truth, sirs, I don't understand a thing.

While Branca is depicted as innocent of practicing Judaism, however, "Jewishness" itself is never ultimately absolved of its own crime of alterity. Rather, Dias Gomes's work exhibits an ambivalent attitude toward the "Jew," which simultaneously symbolizes the victim of an oppressive regime and signifies that undesirable aspect of difference that remains excluded from the collective subjectivity of the Left.

"Jewishness" enters *O Santo Inquérito* through the figure of Simão, Branca's father. He is marked as other by his name, which is Hebrew in origin, as well as by his possession of the family secret that Jewish rituals have been practiced in the family home. Simão also stands for the opposite of the heroic subject: unlike Branca and Augusto, who refuse to comply with the Inquisitorial process, he breaks at the first hint of torture, confessing all of the family sins and even inventing false information in order to placate the Inquisition officials.

> SIMÃO: Desde o primeiro momento compreendi que devia aceitar tudo, confessar tudo, declarer-me arrependido de tudo. Vamos nós discutir com

êles, lutar contra êles? Tolice. Têm a fôrça, a lei, Deus e a milícia—tudo do lado deles. Que podemos nós fazer? (136)

❧

SIMÃO: From the beginning I understood that I should accept everything, confess everything, repent for everything. Are we going to disagree with them, fight against them? Nonsense. They have the force, the law, God and the militia—all on their side. What can we do?

Simão—whose fatalistic attitude is reminiscent of Ângela's father's resignation—thus signifies the weak subject who does not stand for any ideals; rather, he is a Judas-like figure who betrays the pure, Christian martyr. "Jewishness" is associated with this weakness in character that Branca leaves behind; her conversion and subsequent martyrdom signal her realization as a revolutionary subject.

The dichotomy established between Branca and Simão signifies a distinction between alternate modes of political citizenship. When read as an allegory of the dictatorship, the play establishes a hierarchy of value between the actions of father and daughter: while the Christian daughter remains faithful to the transcendent values of loyalty, truth, and love, Simão betrays his family as well as his faith. Although it is Branca who is punished within the fictional horizon of the play—Simão is set free while his daughter burns at the stake—it is the more Jewishly portrayed Simão who is judged by the text itself. The father's conversion is incomplete, while Branca has successfully assimilated into a principled, pious young woman.

Branca's conversion is fully realized, in a figurative sense at least, by her death, at which time her status is confirmed as a politically committed martyr. That Branca's identity can be manipulated and reinterpreted by the Santo Ofício, by Dias Gomes's text, and by Brazilian popular culture in general reveals the malleability of the New Christian. Because the religious allegiances of the convert can never fully be ascertained—there will always be an element of her identity that defies interpretation—Branca functions as a *convertible signifier*, a rhetorical figure that can be translated and misread according to the ideological and aesthetic needs of the text.[13] Although Dias Gomes's rewriting of Branca as Christian creates a necessary space of resistance against the dictatorship, in textually converting her he simultaneously silences another voice: that of the historical Branca, that aspect of Jewish alterity that resists the violently totalizing process of conversion. Exploring the representation of Branca Dias in O Santo Inquérito thus helps one to understand two distinct but related processes: the construction of a site of opposition to the dictatorship, and the rhetorical use of the converso. The fact that Dias Gomes's reading of Branca suppresses difference, rather than celebrating it, suggests that it is only through a homogenization of alterity, through the absorption of the other into the totality of the self, that a collective identity can be constructed.

In each of these three scenes of conversion, a curiously gendered pattern emerges, which begs several questions: what is it about the female body that makes it an easily convertible signifier? Why do these Christian daughters consistently descend from Jewishly portrayed fathers? Finally, why must all three daughters die, while the figurative converts (both male) of Cony and Vargas Llosa survive? The idealization with which the textual conversions of María, Ângela, and Branca are realized suggests that their status as Christian *daughters* is not incidental. Isaacs, Machado de Assis, and Dias Gomes all resort to the romanticization of femininity in order to articulate the spiritual purity of these three hijas del judío. Moreover, the fathers in each text are depicted as weak: María's father can't seem to manage without his wife; Ângela's father sits on the beach all day crying and ultimately places his life in God's hands; and Branca's father surrenders to the Inquisitorial authorities before they have even begun to torture him. It could thus be argued that their daughter's conversion has not only to do with a vision of femininity as malleable but also with the lack of strength exhibited by the Jewish fathers. That is, the Christian daughters and their Jewish fathers *both* occupy the space of femininity. Such a dynamic is not unique to these texts, but rather common in the broader Western imaginary. Sander Gilman's work on representations of "Jewishness" and masculinity reveal that male Jews are imagined in much the same way that femininity (Jewish or non-Jewish) is constructed in the culture at large, so that at the end of the nineteenth century, for example, the Jewish male was associated with the hysteria normally attributed to the female reproductive system (1991, 56). For their part, Jewish women tend to be represented as exotic beauties, in contrast to their repugnant male counterparts (Garb 1995, 26).

That the juxtaposition of discourse surrounding "Jewishness," femininity, and masculinity should enter the scene of conversion is not surprising. If literary appropriations of the converso emphasize the bleeding of religious, sexual, racial, and ideological categories, grounding this rhetoric in the highly charged, fertile space of gender and sexuality proves to be particularly productive. As if to form a triangle of sexual and religious crossover and mixing, each of the three hijas has a Christian love interest: the fully converted

Efraín, the war hero Nuno, and the martyr Augusto. Of course, none of these relationships is ever consummated (unlike in the cases of their English counterparts, described by Shapiro and Ragussis), so that while each text proposes the possibility of romantic harmony, the death of each heroine prohibits the fulfillment of the desire for the other, sustaining instead this desire in its purist (unrealized and unrealizable) state.

FIGURATIVE CONVERSIONS

While literary reconfigurations of the converted Jewess prove fruitful in the articulation of cultural, religious, and political transformations, as well as in their implications for individual and collective (national, racial, or other) subjectivities, neither the hija del judío in particular nor the New Christian in general represents the only figure through which Jewish difference can be interpreted and performed as flexible or "convertible." In Heitor Carlos Cony's *Pessach: A travessia* (1967) and Mario Vargas Llosa's *El hablador* (1987), two twentieth-century works within which "Jewishness" is juxtaposed with diverse notions of transformations, assimilations, or crossings, the "Jew" appears in figurative scenes of conversion that, although not always grounded in historical instances of Jewish conversion to Christianity, radicalize the rhetorical potential of Jewish malleability. The wandering signifier is pushed to its limit, converting the "Jew" into *guerrilheiro* and *machiguenga*, as part of broader projects to suppress, absorb, or subvert the divide between same and other.[14] While Cony's *Pessach* employs the biblical story of Exodus, in which the Jews are freed from slavery in Egypt, to refer to the ideological liberation of the protagonist within the context of the Brazilian dictatorship, Vargas Llosa's *El hablador* depicts the cultural conversion of a Jewish limeño (inhabitant of Lima) into a Machiguenga storyteller as a way to imagine the possibility of national consolidation in Peru.

Pessach: A travessia (Passover: The Crossing) recounts the story of Paulo Simões, an assimilated Jewish *carioca* (inhabitant of Rio de Janeiro) who becomes a militant revolutionary immediately following the military takeover in 1964. The novel commences on the fortieth birthday of the protagonist-narrator, a politically disengaged existentialist writer who can commit neither to a cause nor to a relationship. Several characteristics connect the protagonist to the author: both are writers with a string of ex-wives and ex-lovers (Cony has been married six times); both were born in the 1920s and became politically committed in the 1960s (Cony was arrested on numerous occasions during the military dictatorship of the 1960s and 1970s); and both have last names that appear to be "Brazilianized" versions of Jewish surnames (Simon, in the case of the protagonist, and Cohen, in the case of the author, though the Jewish origin of the latter has never been affirmed). Just as the protagonist of *Pessach* successfully leaves his "Jewishness" behind, so, too, does he transform himself into a committed guerrilheiro. *Pessach* ("passing over," in Hebrew) doubly signifies Paulo's cultural assimilation into Brazilian society and his political transformation into an engaged subject.

The protagonist's fortieth birthday causes him to reflect on his identity as he recalls repeated instances from his past in which he has denied his "Jewishness." He characterizes himself as individualistic and alienated, describing his experience as a cynical loner in the Brazilian military twenty years earlier: "A Pátria é uma droga" (The Fatherland is a drug) (Cony 1967, 5). He depicts the solitude of the years of his military service, during which time he encounters a Jew named Isaac.

> Havia outro rapaz que também não fôra assimilado pelos grupos. . . . Um dia, me interpelou:
> —Você é judeu?
> —Quem? Eu?
> —Sim. Você.
> —Judeu uma ova!
> —Vi o seu nome complete, na secretaria. Você se assina Paulo Simões, mas há um nome que você omite: Gorberg. E seu nome não e Simões, é Simon.
> —E daí? É possível que tenha sangue judeu, diluído por aí, há muita gente assim, mas não sou um judeu.
> Isaac ficou ofendido com a violência daquela frase, *mas não sou um judeu.* . . . No fundo, temia que êle espalhasse o nome que eu aprendera, com meu pai, a omitir. (7)

ℬ

> There was another guy who hadn't been assimilated into the groups either. . . . One day, he addressed me:
> "Are you Jewish?"
> "Who? Me?"
> "Yes. You."
> "Jewish my foot!"
> "I saw your full name, in the office. You call yourself Paulo Simões, but

there's a name that you omit: Gorberg. And your name isn't Simões, it's Simon."

"And? It's possible that I have some diluted Jewish blood, there are many people who do, but I'm not a Jew."

Issac was offended by the violence of that statement, *but I'm not a Jew.* . . . The truth is, I was afraid he'd tell everyone about the name that, like my father, I'd learned to omit.

The interaction between the two outsiders, in which Paulo is identified as Jewish by a fellow coreligionist, anticipates the interpellation that occurs later in the novel, when Paulo is called to duty by members of a guerrilha group. In both cases an external voice demands responsibility of Paulo, whether for the sake of ethnic identification or ideological commitment.

The encounter with Isaac also highlights the secret that Paulo has always carried with him. He admits to having a phobia, caused by a traumatic experience with a childhood bully, that he would discover hidden traces of circumcision on his penis: "Quando, num dia da infância, o garôto me chamou de judeu, corri para casa e fui me espiar. Sempre tive pavor de descobrir, um dia, o talha da circuncisão que nunca me fôra revelada" (When, one day as in my childhood, a boy called me Jew, I ran home to inspect myself. I always lived in fear of discovering, one day, the mark of circumcision that had never been revealed to me) (13). His apprehension has not only to do with the threat of his "secret" identity being exposed to others (that Isaac will reveal his "true" family name to everyone); it has equally to do with the potential discovery of a hidden mark of otherness that has been concealed from him. In his traumatic memory the accusation of being a Jew creates in Paulo the sense that there is an aspect of difference in him that escapes him, that he cannot contain. The notion that this characteristic is repressed to such a degree that Paulo cannot access it, but that it could return unexpectedly one day, generates a fear of a surprise visit: "Tenho mêdo que alguém me surpreenda, nu assim, sem as máscaras que me protegem" (I am afraid that someone will surprise me, naked, without the masks that protect me) (13).

Yet it is Paulo who surprises his parents—who don't remember that it is his birthday—with a weekday visit. Paulo's father, who is in the throes of a panic attack, explains that Paulo has caught them off guard, that they haven't had time to prepare for his arrival.

—Foi bom que você aparecesse hoje, assim de repente, sem esperarmos. Geralmente, nos domingos, eu e sua mãe nos preparamos para a visita, queremos que você encontre aqui a imagem que sempre lhe vendemos do nosso lar. Mas hoje, de supetão, eu não estou preparado para continuar mantendo essa imagem.Você vai me ver nu, com meus pânicos, meus suores frios. Está no meu sangue, filho, no nosso sangue. (78)

✎

"It was good that you showed up today, all of a sudden, without us expecting you. Generally, on Sundays, your mother and I prepare for your visit, we want you to find the image that we've always projected of our home. But today, unannounced, I'm not prepared to continue maintaining the illusion. You're going to see me naked, with my panics, my cold sweats. It's in my blood, son, in our blood."

That it is Paulo who surprises his father "naked"—precisely the fear he himself had articulated earlier—is not a coincidence, for the nakedness both men strive to conceal is their circumcised penis, whether figurative or literal, real or imagined. Paulo's surprising of his father is reciprocated when his father "comes out" to him as a Jew with paranoid fears of anti-Semitic violence, identifying the origin of his panic as "in his blood." To make matters worse, his father also confesses that he continues to observe religious rituals in secret. While Paulo had admitted to himself (and, reluctantly, to others) that his father had Jewish ancestors, he had convinced himself that this Jewish blood had been overridden by his desire to assimilate: "–Não sou judeu. . . . Meu pai é bastante diluído e totalmente assimilado. Eu nem tenho que preocupar-me com isso" ("I'm not Jewish. . . . My father is very diluted and completely assimilated. I don't have to worry about that") (33). It therefore comes as a shock to Paulo when his father reveals that he never stopped observing Yom Kippur, the Jewish Day of Atonement. His father, a modern-day crypto-Jew, continues his confession by revealing his suspicion that the Jews will be persecuted by the Brazilian military government: "–Aprenda isso, meu filho, que está em meu sangue, e, até certo ponto, em seu sangue também: quem paga por tudo, no fim das contas, somos nós, os judeus" ("Understand this, my son: it's in my blood and, to a certain degree, in your blood as well: in the end it is we, the Jews, who pay for everything") (78).[15] The father's echoing of "my blood . . . our blood" in "my blood . . . your blood" performatively relays an identity of persecution to his son. Tracing this history of oppression back to "os egípcios," he situates the locus of Jewish suffering in the moment immediately preceding the Exodus.

The father's revelation does not lead Paulo to a reclamation of his Jewish heritage, but rather represents one in a series of events that disrupt Paulo's complacency, that inspire in him an awareness of oppression. This genealogy of slavery is articulated through the motif of pessach, which reappears in the novel as the allegory whereby the ideological liberation of the protagonist is codified. Paulo himself is aware of the multiple implications of the parable, if not its political ramifications, then at least its literary potential. He explains that for years he's considered writing the story of a man who betrays his religion, which he would situate symbolically in the context of the Exodus.

> A noite em que todo um povo resolve abandonar o cativeiro dourado das margens do Nilo e partir para o deserto, para as pedras e as montanhas do deserto. Esta noite, que decidiu a história de um povo—e foi, até certo ponto, a noite mais importante do mundo—seria diluída em acontecimento menor, individual: um homem escolheria a árdua caminhada pelo deserto, em busca de uma terra que jamais alcançaria. Seria essa a sua passagem, a sua travessia: conquistar a liberdade—ou a paz—e o importante não era a conquista em si, mas a travessia, a busca. (79–80)

❧

> The night in which an entire people resolved to abandon the golden captivity at the shores of the Nile and depart for the desert, for the stones and the mountains of the desert. That night, which decided the history of a people—and which was, to a certain degree, the most important night in the world—would be diluted into a minor, individual event: a man would choose the arduous walk through the desert, in search of a land that he would never reach. This would be his passage, his crossing: conquering liberty—or peace—and the key would not be the conquest in itself, but rather the crossing, the search.

This passage, which of course refers to the novel *Pessach* itself, designates one possible avenue of interpretation to the reader: that of the individualization of the Exodus myth. It is as if Paulo the crypto-Jew has shifted into Paulo the narrator, indicating the allegory he will develop throughout the rest of the novel as Paulo the crypto-Jew begins his process of ideological liberation from slavery.

His Exodus, the seeds of which are planted in the first part of the novel (entitled "Pessach: A passagem por cima"), is realized on the level of action in the second part ("A travessia"), in which Paulo is recruited by an old friend, Sílvio, and his comrade, Vera, to become a member of a guerrilha group fighting the Brazilian military. Paulo's politicization does not occur on a conscious level. His participation in the leftist group is not the result of a personal decision; nor, however, does he resist his incorporation into the movement. He neither agrees nor refuses to join; instead, at the end of the first part of the novel, Vera is simply waiting for him in his car. The second part begins with him driving at breakneck speed through the streets of Rio, "abandonando a cidade" (abandoning the city) (123). His first words in this scene signal his near-passivity: "O acelerador lá em baixo, sinto o pé dormente de tanto comprimi-lo contra o chão do carro" (The gas pedal all the way down, I feel my foot asleep from pushing so hard against the car floor) (123). Paulo's numb foot metonymically signals the paradox of his political commitment: he is simultaneously active and passive, awake and asleep, driving and being driven. The unaccounted-for space between the two halves of the novel, the silent lack around which his transformation takes place, posits his political engagement as more absence than presence. He is summoned to responsibility, but he (and the reader) becomes aware of his response only after he is already responding: in a sense, this moment of interpellation is the realization of Paulo's encounter with Isaac twenty years earlier.

Despite having accompanied Vera out of the city to reunite with the other members of the resistance, Paulo never actually decides to join them. Nor does he choose to abandon them, instead justifying to himself that the country may provide him with the space he needs in order to write. It is not until the last scene of the novel, after having lived with the guerrilheiros for months, that Paulo finally assumes agency. Under attack by the Brazilian military, Paulo arms himself and sets out with Macedo, the group's leader, and Vera to cross the border. Curiously, it is Macedo who likens their situation to that of the Hebrew slaves in Egypt.

> Para minha surprêsa, Macedo me lembra a passagem do Mar Vermelho. Deixo-o falar. Encontrei-o certa tarde, lá na Fazenda, examinando meu esbôço de romance. Ele pensara no assunto, meditara no problema de Moisés, a libertação de um povo, e fala, fala como certa febre, tenho a impressão de que delira. . . . –Carne queimada—acrescenta êle. Nenhum homem mutilado como eu pode ser um Moisés. Que cada um seja o seu próprio Moisés, atravesse o rio. (288)

❧

> To my surprise, Macedo reminds me of the crossing of the Red Sea. I let him talk. I found him one afternoon, there at the ranch, examining the draft of my novel. He must have thought about the matter, meditated on Moses's prob-

lem, the liberation of a people, and now he speaks, he speaks feverishly, I have the impression that he's delirious. . . ."Burnt flesh," he adds. "No man as mutilated as I am can be a Moses. Everyone must be his own Moses, and cross the river."

Paulo finds himself unable to shoot the enemy during the battle (whether due to lack of courage or to ineptitude), and once Macedo and Vera have been killed, he finds himself alone. Facing the border, the solitary figure who was celebrating his fortieth birthday at the beginning of the novel finally assumes agency: "Desenterro a metralhadora—e avanço" (I dig up the machine gun—and I go forward) (301). These closing words of the novel mark his successful conversion into a committed revolutionary, yet they do so without discarding the individualist tone that his character has cultivated throughout the text. In this sense, it is not sufficient to say that the Jewish pessach allegorically represents Paulo's political conversion, but rather that both transformations—the religious as well as the ideological—work together to constitute the protagonist as an existential hero.

If Cony's novel, not unlike Dias Gomes's play, utilizes the notion of Jewish conversion in order to postulate an ideological alternative to totalitarianism, the Peruvian writer, intellectual, and would-be politician Mario Vargas Llosa's El hablador (The Storyteller) appropriates the Jewish convert as a way to imagine the absorption of the indigenous other into the nation. Within a vastly distinct cultural and geopolitical context, Vargas Llosa's novel recounts the transformation of a half-Jewish Peruvian ethnographer into an indigenous storyteller. El hablador is a narrative of metamorphosis—conscious of its ties to the German-Jewish writer Franz Kafka's tale of an equally uncanny conversion from man into insect—which reflects on the problem of social marginality and ethnic exclusion within the context of a late-twentieth-century, modernizing Peru. By oscillating between two narrative subjects—the first a semiautobiographical limeño writer living in Italy and the second a Machiguenga storyteller—the novel considers the process of becoming other, as well as the inverse possibility of the other becoming the same. This transformative potential is articulated through the character of Saúl Zuratas, the Jewish middleman who serves as a bridge between the urban, cosmopolitan space occupied by the first narrator and the highly exoticized, "prehistorical" universe of the Machiguenga.

El hablador opens in Florence, Italy, with the limeño, the first of two alternating narrators, explaining his expatriate status: "Vine a Firenze para olvidarme por un tiempo del Perú y de los peruanos y he aquí que el malhadado país me salió al encuentro esta mañana de la manera más inesperada" (I came to Firenze to forget Peru and Peruvians for a while, and suddenly my unfortunate country forced itself on me this morning in the most unexpected way [Vargas Llosa 1989, 3]) (Vargas Llosa 1987, 7). This preliminary statement situates the locus of enunciation simultaneously inside and outside the nation: while the limeño does not explain why he might need to flee the national scene, it becomes immediately evident that this is an unrealizable project. In the very same breath, the limeño announces the possibility and impossibility of escaping Peru. Passing a photography exhibition on the Peruvian Amazon, he finds himself interpellated by the scenes depicted in several of the images: "Fueron tres o cuatro fotografías que me devolvieron, de golpe, el sabor de la selva peruana. . . . Naturalmente, entré" (It was three or four photographs that suddenly brought back to me the flavor of the Peruvian jungle. . . . Naturally, I went in [3]) (7).[16] Here, the expat's encounter with lo peruano ("Peruvianness") is constructed as something unavoidable, in an essentialist sense; he is "naturally" drawn to the photos of the landscape of his native land. When he enters to take a closer look, he is surprised to realize that the subject of one of the photographs is a Machiguenga storyteller. His visual recognition of the hablador, whose storytelling will make up the content of the second narrator of the novel, reminds him of an old friend from his university days in San Marcos, Saúl Zuratas, a half-Jewish limeño who had transformed into a member of the Machiguenga tribe in the Peruvian Amazon.

This introduction situates the limeño protagonist—who, as Doris Sommer argues (1996, 92), shares more than a few characteristics with Vargas Llosa—as the primary and privileged narrator of the novel. Beginning in the third chapter, he will be accompanied by an additional narrative subject, the secondary and arguably subordinate voice of the eponymous hablador, the traditional Machiguenga storyteller. The relationship between the two narrative voices—far from exhibiting a dialogic dynamic in the Bakhtinian sense—is both hierarchical and complementary; the second narrator does not disrupt, but rather affirms the authority of the first. While the indigenous storyteller lends a degree of credibility to Vargas Llosa's effort to represent the nation, it is the elite intellectual who retains the ultimate right to write Peru. The relationship between narrators is constituted as uneven during the opening scene in the Italian gallery, in which the storyteller appears as the object of the cosmopolitan artist's gaze (that of the Peruvian writer as well as of the Italian photographer whose work is being exhibited). This subject-object positioning is not incidental: one learns, through the course of the novel, that the narrator has tried in vain for decades to write about the storytellers: "¿Por qué había sido incapaz, en el curso de todos aquellos años, de escribir mi relato sobre los habladores?" (Why in the course of all those years, had I been unable to write my story about storytellers? [157]) (152). It is implied that this text is the realization of this project. El hablador therefore represents an attempt to write the story of Saúl Zuratas's conversion into a Machiguenga storyteller, as well as the desire to penetrate the most intimate core of Peru's Other Within—"Sentir y vivir lo más íntimo de esa cultura" (to feel and live in the very heart of that culture [244]) (234)—that element of alterity that refuses incorporation into the criolla nation.

Immediately following the final sentence of the first chapter, which identifies the figure in the photograph as an hablador, the second chapter opens with a description of Saúl Zuratas, who is linked with the storyteller through juxtaposition. The narrator introduces Saúl by referring to the large birthmark on his face, the physical manifestation of his position as an outsider: "Saúl Zuratas tenía un lunar morado oscuro, vino vinagre, que le cubría todo el lado derecho de la cara y unos pelos rojos y despeinados como las cerdas de un escobillón. El lunar no respetaba la oreja ni los labios ni la nariz a los que también erupcionaba de una tumefacción venosa. Era el muchacho más feo del mundo" (Saúl Zuratas had a dark birthmark, the color of wine dregs, that covered the entire right side of his face, and unruly red hair as stiff as the bristles of a scrub brush. The birthmark spared neither his ears nor his lips nor his nose, also puffy and misshapen from swollen veins. He was the ugliest lad in the world [8]) (11). His aberrant Jewish body, like that of Futoransky's Laura Kaplansky, Glantz's Nora García, or Borges's Emma Zunz, signals his status as misfit. The nickname used by Saúl's friends and enemies alike, Mascarita, signals a complete identification between the mark and the man.

The son of an immigrant Jewish father and a provincial, uneducated criolla mother, Saúl is doubly marginalized from the bourgeois limeña society in which he finds himself. That he is the product of a mixed marriage is not incidental, given the emphasis placed on national integration in the novel. The heterogeneous nature of Saúl's family already begins to address the problem of ethnic difference, though it appears that in this criolla experiment, the product has come out defective. Saúl's pet, a parrot named Gregorio Samsa, metonymically links him with Kafka's protagonist, the prototypical "minority" figure (following Deleuze's and Guattari's classification of Kafka's work as minor literature). The parrot reappears later in the novel, within the hablador's narration, his repetitive speech a symbol of the storyteller's cyclical recounting of myths. The talking bird mirrors Saúl's identity in a second way as well: once Saúl has converted into a Machiguenga, he baptizes the parrot with his former nickname, Mascarita. Thus, man and parrot continuously mimic one another; in taking on Saúl's literal and figurative names, the animal performs the same function as his owner: that of serving as a mirror for the identity of the other.

During his years at the University at San Marcos, Saúl pursues ethnography as a career and begins to work with the Machiguenga tribe of the Peruvian Amazon. While the narrator reads this choice as a result of the mark on his face—"¿Estaba ahí la clave de la conversión de Mascarita?" (Was this the key to Mascarita's conversion? [27–28]) (29)—Saúl's father interprets his connection with the Machiguengas as an identification between the Jewish and indigenous experiences of persecution (29–30). In both versions, the birthmark, the "Jew," and the Machiguenga reside in the space of alterity, in contrast to the subject position of the narrator.

The limeño narrator recalls the arguments that develop between the two classmates about the fate of the traditional cultures of the Peruvian Amazon as Saúl becomes more involved with the Machiguenga tribe.

A veces, para ver hasta dónde podía llevarlo <<el tema>>, yo lo provocaba. ¿Qué proponía, a fin de cuentas? ¿Que, para no alterar los modos de vida y las creencias de unas tribus que vivían, muchas de ellas, en la Edad de Piedra, se abstuviera el resto del Perú de explotar la Amazonía? ¿Deberían dieciséis millones de peruanos renunciar a los recursos naturales de tres cuartas partes de su territorio para que los sesenta u ochenta mil indígenas amazónicos siguieran flechándose tranquilamente entre ellos, reduciendo cabezas y adorando al boa constrictor? ¿Debíamos ignorar las posibilidades agrícolas, ganaderas y comerciales de la región para que los etnólogos del mundo se deleitaran estudiando en vivo el potlach, las relaciones de parentesco, los ritos de la pubertad, del matrimonio, de la muerte, que aquellas curiosidades humanas venían practicando, casi sin evolución, desde hacía cientos de años? No, Mascarita, el país tenía que desarrollarse. ¿No había dicho Marx que el progreso vendría chorreando sangre? Por triste que fuera, había que aceptarlo. No teníamos alternativa. Si el precio del desarrollo y la industrialización, para los dieciséis millones de peruanos, era que esos pocos millones de calatos tuvieran que cortarse el pelo, lavarse los tatuajes y volverse mestizos—o, para usar la más odiada palabra del etnólogo: aculturarse—, pues, qué remedio. (23–24)

✾

Occasionally, to see how far his obsession might lead him, I would provoke him. What did he suggest, when all was said and done? That, in order not to change the way of life and the beliefs of a handful of tribes still living, many of them, in the Stone Age, the rest of Peru abstain from developing the Amazon region? Should sixteen million Peruvians renounce the natural resources of three-quarters of their national territory so that seventy or eighty thousand Indians could quietly go on shooting at each other with bows and arrows, shrinking heads and worshiping boa constrictors? Should we forgo the agricultural, cattle-raising, and commercial potential of the region so that the world's ethnologists could enjoy studying at first hand kinship ties, potlatches, the rites of puberty, marriage, and death that these human oddities had been practicing, virtually unchanged, for hundreds of years? No, Mascarita, the country had to move forward. Hadn't Marx said that progress would come dripping blood? Sad though it was, it had to be accepted. We had no alternative. If the price to be paid for development and industrialization for the sixteen million Peruvians meant that those few thousand naked Indians would have to cut their hair, wash off their tattoos, and become mestizos— or, to use the ethnologists' most detested word, become acculturated—well, there was no way around it. (21–22),

Despite the narrator's disclaimer that these comments are meant as a provocation, they nevertheless serve a function within the scope of the novel. Even if the dialectic between the limeño narrator and Saúl is purely rhetorical, the views expressed in this citation justify, to a certain extent, the move to annihilate ethnic alterity in the name of progress. Further, they presuppose that the primary motivation of protecting a traditional culture would be to serve the interest of the intellectual, in particular the ethnographer. At the same time—and perhaps paradoxically—this passage protects an essentialized vision of the communities it describes. It is therefore an argument for an inevitable "progress" that depends on a fixed notion of Amazonian tribes, in which the reduced or nonexistent contact with the outside world is equated with a prehistorical or ahistorical status. In this version of (non)history, the Indians shoot one another with bow and arrow, shrink each others' heads, and worship a boa constrictor. Put in these terms, it certainly seems foolish to restrict Peruvians' use of "their" natural resources for the sake of anthropology and a snake-based idolatry.

Yet the narrator that utters these clichés is at the same time fascinated by the very cultures he minimizes. When he has the opportunity to visit the Amazon himself, years after his discussion with Saúl, he finds himself seduced by the idea of a primordial paradise that, rather than being excluded from his notion of Peru, also makes up a part of the nation.

> La fuerza y la soledad de la Naturaleza . . . sugerían un mundo recién creado. . . . Cuando llegábamos a las tribus, en cambio, tocábamos la prehistoria. Allí estaba la existencia elemental y primeriza de los distantes ancestros. . . . También eso era el Perú y sólo entonces tomaba yo cabal conciencia de ello: un mundo todavía sin domar, la Edad de Piedra, las culturas mágico-religiosas, la poligamia, la reducción de cabezas. (71)

❧

> The strength and solitude of Nature . . . brought to mind a newly created world. . . . When we reached the tribes, by contrast, there before us was prehistory. . . . This, too, was Peru, and only then did I become fully aware of it: a world still untamed, the Stone Age, magico-religious cultures, polygamy, head-shrinking. (72–73)

If one thinks about Vargas Llosa's own aesthetic and political history, the existence of the magical-religious realm within Peru serves several functions: it is useful for a boom writer, as well as for a would-be politician (he would run for president only three years after the publication of El hablador). For the limeño narrator, also a writer like Vargas Llosa, the Machiguenga tribe offers something unique in the form of the storyteller. When Saúl asks him about his obsession with the habladores, the limeño narrator replies, "Son una prueba palpable de que contar historias puede ser algo más que una mera diversión" (They're a tangible proof that storytelling can be something more than mere entertainment [94]) (92). That is, the central role of the storyteller within the traditional Machiguenga culture promises a nobler role for the writer as well, rather than simply being relegated to the realm of entertainment.[17]

Yet this tribe and its storyteller remain unavailable to the limeño narrator. In order to penetrate the culture of the Machiguengas, as well as the traditional practices of its storyteller, he requires a translator, a middleman. It is here that he turns to Saúl, who, as an ethnographer and outsider, promises entry into an otherwise inaccessible space. The limeño narrator immediately writes a letter to his Jewish friend: "Le contaba que había decidido escribir un relato sobre los habladores machiguengas. ¿Me ayudaría?" (I told him I'd decided to write something about Machiguenga storytellers. Would he help me? [104]) (102). By this time, however, Saúl has disappeared and cannot be located by the narrator or anyone from the university. Though a rumor suggests that he made *aliyah* and moved to Israel, the death of Saúl's parents make the verification of this information impossible. Thus, Saúl, too, becomes inaccessible, absorbed into the space of the other that precludes comprehension.

The last chapter returns to Florence and to the moment with which the novel opens. After having left and returned to the exhibit on numerous occasions, as well as having reflected on Saúl's story, the limeño narrator has decided that the hablador pictured in the photograph is his Jewish friend, that he has transformed from a limeño ethnographer to Machiguenga storyteller. The first reference to this metamorphosis is announced by the narrator-hablador, who has been recounting stories about the tribe's mythological origin and subsequent displacement, as well as his own personal history. In a slightly obscure passage, the referent of which one understands only once the true identity of the hablador has been revealed, he describes his own transformation: "Me había convertido en insecto, pues" (I'd changed into an insect, that's what [203]) (196–97). This statement, in which Kafka's novel is alluded to for a third time, sets the stage for the limeño narrator to claim that the hablador is actually Saúl. In an attempt to explain or interpret his friend's complete absorption by the exotic world of the Machiguengas, he turns to the trope of conversion: "Mascarita entró en contacto con un mundo que lo intrigó y lo sedujo. Lo que debió ser, al principio, un movimiento de curiosidad intelectual y simpatía por los hábitos de vida y la condición machiguenga, fue . . . tornándose en una conversión, en el sentido cultural y también religioso del término" (Mascarita came into contact with a world that intrigued and attracted him. What must in the beginning have been a feeling of intellectual curiosity and sympathy for the customs and conditions of life of the Machiguengas became . . . a conversion, in both the cultural and the religious meaning of the word [241]) (231).

But what function does this conversion serve? To begin with, it provides an entry through which the limeño narrator can imagine—via Mascarita—the site of alterity that has escaped him for the past decades, this intimate space which simultaneously eludes and is critical to both the nation and to the artist who would write this nation. Describing Saúl as a converso, the limeño narrator expresses disbelief that such a transformation could take place: "Convertirse en un hablador era añadir lo imposible a lo que era sólo inverosímil. . . . Porque hablar como habla un hablador es haber llegado a sentir y vivir lo más íntimo de esa cultura. . . . Es ser, de la manera más esencial que cabe, un machiguenga raigal" (Becoming a storyteller was adding what appeared impossible to what was merely improbable. . . . Talking the way a storyteller talks means being able to feel and live in the very heart of that culture. . . . It means being, in the most profound way possible, a rooted Machiguenga [244]) (233–34). At the same time, Saúl—whose name refers intertextually to the first Jewish convert in Western literature, the biblical Saul/Paul—embodies the realization of the limeño narrator's longing to enter the realm of the other. Saúl's conversion carries this fantasy to its limit: beyond merely entering the Machiguenga community, he literally becomes the other.

The discourse on conversion has political implications as well, particularly in light of the heated debate between the limeño narrator and Saúl regarding the future of the Amazonian tribes. By narrating the full transformation of Jew into hablador, the novel seems to imply that the reverse could also happen: if the "modern," cosmopolitan subject can become the "pre-historical" Indian other, so, too, can the Machiguenga tribes assimilate into criollo Peru. But by enacting this acculturation merely symbolically, or, rather, by displacing it onto Mascarita, the novel can suggest the possibility of the assimilation of Amazonian tribes without sacrificing the essentialist, exotic vision of these communities that has been constructed. Thus, Vargas Llosa's text would like to have it both ways (and successfully carries this out on a rhetorical level): the other simultaneously becomes absorbed into the imperialism of the same while simultaneously remaining wholly other. Yet this is not the radical exteriority referred to by Levinas; rather, the novel's Machiguenga other remains thematized, in the realm of the said, rather than of the saying. In this sense, the Machiguenga narrator—which is, of course, an appropriation of the indigenous voice by the cosmopolitan intellectual—functions in the service of the first. No disruption, no trauma takes place here. Instead, the Machiguenga storyteller fits neatly into the aesthetic and ideological project of the writer and the nation, both of which attempt to represent—textually or politically—Peru's ethnic minorities. The Jewish convert, once again, remains limited to a purely rhetorical role, a tool through which Peru's "real" other can be approached.

As one can see from Cony's and Vargas Llosa's novels, the Jewish other can be appropriated to fit the needs of a politics of resistance as well as a politics of assimilation. Although the figurative conversion is less explicitly linked to the violent history of Jewish conversion, it nevertheless draws on this history in order to theorize distinct modalities of political, cultural, and ethnic transformation. In both texts alterity is incorporated into the nation, albeit within two very different ideological projects: while *Pessach* employs the trope of the Jewish exodus from Egypt as a way to imagine the transformative potential of political engagement, *El hablador* displaces the problem of ethnic marginality onto the Jewish other, implying the potential absorption of the indigenous other into the nation.

⅏ ⅏ ⅏

Is there a distinction between the appropriation of the converted Jew within a project of resistance as opposed to a project of assimilation? While one's instinct may be to condemn the right-wing politics of Vargas Llosa, who utilizes the Jewish other in order to propose what amounts to the annihilation of a whole culture, is this entirely different from the rhetorical use of the converso to articulate an opposition to the Brazilian dictatorship, as in Dias Gomes and Cony? Is it possible to justify the act of appropriating the other for the sake of creating a space for difference? Is the fictional murder of the female convert of Isaacs, Machado de Assis, and Dias Gomes distinct from the figurative annihilation of Jewish difference in Cony and Vargas Llosa? When the Jewish convert is thematized, turned into a purely rhetorical figure, a convertible signifier, does this discursive act preclude ethics?

After having analyzed the textual linking of "Jewishness" and conversion, one is left with more questions than answers. One has seen several interrelated paradoxes in the textual conversions of María, Ângela, Branca, Paulo, and Saúl: the impossible but necessary conversion of the other for national consolidation, the suppression of difference for the sake of political resistance, the rhetorical use of the Jewish convert as part of a discursive opposition to totalitarianism. Is it that one is left facing an aporia, an impasse, from which there is no exit? Or is it precisely through the aporia that it becomes feasible to expose the inherent paradox between rhetoric and ethics, creating in this way the possibility of their coexistence? Perhaps one can view the task of the literary critic as that which can open a space for the other, even if it is only through signaling that which remains excluded from the text. To do so, one must explore in greater depth the limits of literary discourse, the conditions of simultaneous possibility and impossibility of a rhetorical ethics, a space within which absence just might be signaled through presence.

The Limits of Representation

T he scene of conversion provides a useful context from which to reflect on those of the diagnosis and of the transaction because, in a sense, each scene of "Jewishness" I have investigated could be characterized as a textual conversion: each work appropriates the Jewish other, molding and transforming "Jewishness" for use within a specific geopolitical and aesthetic framework, absorbing Jewish difference into the same. Yet there seem to be slivers of difference, remainders to these totalizing processes. The very acts of diagnosis, transaction, and conversion are fueled by anxiety toward that which doesn't fit, whether one is talking about undiagnosable diseases, remainders of symbolic transactions, or elements of alterity which refuse conversion. But are these figurative misfits obliterated beyond the point of recognition? Is one dealing with survivors or casualties? Can the face of the Other be present within literary discourse? How does exteriority—the unsayable—relate to the interior of the text? When considering the place of exteriority within the literary text, can one begin to outline the contours of a relationship between ethics, politics, and aesthetics?

Jorge Luis Borges's "Deutsches Requiem" (1946), Ricardo Piglia's *Respiración artificial* (1980), and Sergio Chejfec's *Los planetas* (1999) are three Argentine works in which the idea of "Jewishness" is employed as part of "postmodern" aesthetic projects that challenge and expose the limits of representation. The reading of these narratives provides an opportunity to retreat from the previous three textual scenes in order to meditate on the uses of "Jewishness" within texts that expose their own limitations as representational apparatuses. Each of the three works was written during or in response to totalitarianism—Borges's in the wake of the Holocaust and in the context of Peronist nationalism, Piglia's under the repressive dictatorships of the 1970s, and Chejfec's reflecting back on that period decades later—and ostensibly seeks to totalize (difference, truth, memory, meaning) as little as possible. Yet each work relies on some notion of "Jewishness"—Jewish identity, Jewish history, or Jewish space—precisely in order to reveal the bounds of the narrative or textual subject. If one is to take seriously the challenge of ethics and writing, it is vital to consider this apparent paradox within the act of narrating that acknowledges the hither side of representation. Moreover, the fact that the three works in question were all written in response to fascism—whether in the context of the Holocaust or the Dirty War—suggests that what I call "ethical signifying" has implicit and explicit political consequences. Is it possible, in these three texts that are haunted by the violence of fascism and disappearances, to think about an *oblique politics of representation*, that is, of a politics approached by way of the ethical within the aesthetic?

The debatable ideological position of Borges or, even more difficult to decipher, of Borges's work has been taken up by Annick Louis. She describes the tendency of Borges's readers to see him either as a reactionary, in light of his relationship to the dictatorships of the 1970s, or as a militant antifascist due to his critical stance vis-à-vis Nazism, both of which she views as opposite sides of the same coin: "Que el rechazo del sujeto Borges por el nazismo nos tranquilice tanto como nos molestaba su temporaria adhesión a las dictaduras militares latinoamericanas no implica que sus referencias al nazismo constituyan una mera expresión de esta toma de posición" (That the rejection of Nazism by Borges's subject soothes us as much as it bothered us that he temporarily adhered to Latin American military dictatorships does not imply that his references to Nazism constitute a mere expression of this position) (1997, 118). In other words, in order to critically engage the political nature of Borges's work, one needs to take a step back from the question of theme and instead focus one's attention on the use of rhetoric, that is, the way in which Borges does not express a political position, but rather performs one.[1] If one cannot properly classify Borges's work as *literatura comprometida* (committed literature), what are the political implications of a story such as "Deutsches Requiem," the protagonist of which is a Nazi commandant and convicted murderer?

Edna Aizenberg suggests that one understand "Deutsches Requiem" as both postmodern and post-Auschwitz, that is, as a work that engages with the violence of fascism by dismantling the violence of signification: "Borges questions the limits of representation as a way of finding a new discourse commensurate with a new genocidal reality, not as a means of liberation from any relation to reality" (1997, 149). Her argument takes that of Louis a step further by suggesting that Borges creates a work in dialogue with a politically charged reality through aesthetic language, through a complicated relationship with the order of representation. In my reading of "Deutsches Requiem" I investigate the interplay between aesthetics, ethics, and politics by reading the short story as a text that traverses the limits of literary discourse.

Borges's story, originally published in *Sur* in 1946 and included in the 1949 collection *El Aleph*, takes as its historical context the period immediately following the Holocaust. Written just after the commencement of the Nuremberg Trials, "Deutsches Requiem" is an appropriate, if haunting, way to address the question of survival, of remains, given its subject matter. The story is narrated from the perspective of Otto Dietrich zur Linde, the assistant director of the fictional Tarnowitz concentration camp, and seems, at first glance, to validate the ideology or at the very least to empathize with the experiences of this murderous figure (which may quite possibly account for the scarcity of criticism published on the story until very recently).[2] The decision to narrate in the first person seems odd at best, and the reception of this story has been ambivalent, perhaps in reaction to this ethically questionable move. Yet Borges creates the possibility of an "other side" of Nazi rhetoric and subjectivity, beginning with the inclusion of a secondary figure, the Jewish poet and camp inmate David Jerusalem. In his attempt to approximate both Nazi protagonist and his Jewish victim Borges pushes the limits of representation to its extreme. By exploring the various narrative strategies used in this work, I address the aporetic relationship between rhetoric and ethics, between what Emmanuel Levinas calls le dire (the saying) and le dit (the said), and ask what the political implications of such a poetics might be.

"Deutsches Requiem" opens with the protagonist about to face his death. As Otto Dietrich zur Linde prepares for his execution, he recalls the heroic deaths of his ancestors.

> Uno de mis antepasados, Christoph zur Linde, murió en la carga de caballería que decidió la Victoria de Zorndorf. Mi bisabuelo materno, Ulrich Forkel, fue asesinado en la foresta de Marchenoir por francotiradores franceses, en los últimos días de 1870; el capitán Dietrich zur Linde, mi padre, se distinguió en el sitio de Namur, en 1914, y, dos años después, en la travesía del Danubio. En cuanto a mí, seré fusilado por torturador y asesino. (Borges 1999a, 83)

> ❦

> One of my forebears, Christoph zur Linde, died in the cavalry charge that decided the victory of Zorndorf. During the last days of 1870, my maternal great-grandfather, Ulrich Forkel, was killed in the Marchenoir forest by French sharpshooters; Captain Dietrich zur Linde, my father, distinguished himself in 1914 at the siege of Namur, and again two years later in the crossing of the Danube. As for myself, I am to be shot as a torturer and a murderer. (Borges 2004a, 62)

This final soliloquy introduces the short story and, in doing so, frames the life of its protagonist. Otto's death, the end of his "self," serves as an opportunity to construct the limits of this self, to delineate the boundaries of his identity. By referring to the heroic deaths of his forefathers, the Nazi is able to highlight the bravery of his party, nation, and family, imagining in this way his own heroism. His self-proclaimed objective is that the reader should understand the history of Germany, and the future history of the world in light of the Nazi defeat. As a martyr, his defeat reveals, by contrast, an epic Nazi past. The narrator's monologue, to which the reader serves as interlocutor, functions as an unapologetic tribute to Germany's Third Reich; yet, as with every attempt to construct a national or subjective identity, some element must remain in the margins. In a rhetorical move typical of Borges, the reader learns of the Nazi's "other" through a footnote to the narrative, penned by an apocryphal editor who explains that: "Es significativa la omisión del antepasado más ilustre del narrador, el teólogo y hebraísta Johannes Forkel" (It is significant that zur Linde has omitted his most illustrious forebear, the theologian and Hebraist Johannes Forkel [62n1]) (83n1). This paratextual discourse, the narrator's exclusion that is included by a fictional editor, reveals a "Hebraic" element of the protagonist's lineage—if not by blood, by intellectual curiosity, which of course is probably more significant from Borges's point of view. The omission of this relative—the most distinguished member of the family—is announced in the footnote as an early voice of dissonance in the text. The presence of "Jewishness" serves to interrupt what began as a cohesive narrative about the autonomous self and the possibility of referentiality.

After this textual opening, the narrator continues by recounting his own life, as well as the process by which he became a member of the Nazi Party. Perhaps surprisingly, Otto's past is filled not with military exploits, but rather with an aesthetic and philosophical trajectory that leads to his adoption of Nazism as an ideology. A passion for music, metaphysics, and poetry—specifically the works of William Shakespeare, "otro nombre germánico" (another colossal Germanic name [63]) (84)—leads to the study of Nietzsche and Spengler and, two years later, to his inscription in the party.[3] That he has left behind his love of theology echoes the ostracization of the Hebraist ancestor relegated to a footnote in his family history. Though Otto lacked a "vocación de violencia" (calling for violence [64]) (85), he awaited the war that would confirm the faith of his comrades. His career as a soldier was interrupted—by fate, as he describes it—when he was injured in an unheroic battle, an event so small the press didn't even pick it up. On a street behind the synagogue—an overdetermined site of conflict—our protagonist was shot twice in the leg, which it later became necessary to amputate. In another parodical footnote, it is mentioned that the consequences of this wound were quite grave.[4] On a figurative level, of course, the injury and subsequent amputation leave the protagonist a partial man. This pseudocastration evokes an anti-Semitic paranoia, a kind of sexualized blood-libel. When analyzing the symbolic power of this injury, it is interesting to think about the sensation of feeling many amputees describe having in the missing body part, a "phantom limb." While our narrator does not refer to his missing leg, however, there is another absence that haunts him: that detested, abject (read: Jewish) aspect of his identity. Once again, "Jewishness" appears as the hidden trait that Otto fails to suppress completely; after all, it is no coincidence that he was shot behind a synagogue.

The other consequence of his injury is that in 1941 he is named assistant director of the Tarnowitz concentration camp, in which he meets his nemesis, David Jerusalem. Here, the "Jewishness" that until this moment only appears in footnotes and foot injuries finally assumes a whole body. An inmate of the concentration camp, David Jerusalem, as his name gives away, could not be more Jewish: "Hombre de memorables ojos, de piel cetrina, de barba casi negra, David Jerusalem era el prototipo del judío sefardí, si bien pertenecía a los depravados y aborrecidos Ashkenazim" (A man of memorable eyes, sallow skin, and a beard that was almost black, David Jerusalem was the prototypical Sephardic Jew, although he belonged to the depraved and hated Ashkenazim [66]) (89). David Jerusalem's facial attributes are depicted, while eclipsing his "face" in the Levinasian sense. His eyes, skin, and beard appear as fetishized, fragmented characteristics that conceal his face, that human element of the Other that demands responsibility in the subject. As Levinas explains, "You turn yourself toward the Other as toward an object when you see a nose, eyes, a forehead, a chin, and you can describe them. The best way of encountering the Other is not even to notice the color of his eyes! When one observes the color of the eyes one is not in social relationship with the Other" (1982, 85). The thematization of the face—the replacement of the naked face with objectified characteristics—is, of course, what allows the relationship between self and Other to be violent. And what more appropriate context for such thematization than the concentration camp? It is no coincidence that Levinas's *Otherwise than Being* is dedicated "to the memory of those who were closest among the six million assassinated by the National Socialists, and of the millions on millions of all confessions and all nations, victims of the same hatred of the other man, the same anti-semitism." The Holocaust and its victims frame Levinas's philosophy on the ethical relationship between the same and Other.

In Borges's story, however, literature commits its usual sin, in Levinas's view, of violating the Other, of fitting the Other into the totality of the self. Indeed, each aspect of "Jewishness" in "Deutsches Requiem" remains relegated to the hidden corners of the hero's body and soul. David Jerusalem, after all, is a poet, representing the protagonist's forgotten passion for poetry and theology, and reminding one of the famous relative omitted by Otto in his narrative genealogy. The Jewish poet disturbs the narrator, resisting his attempts to suppress or eliminate those undesirable aspects of himself. As the Nazi describes, Jerusalem "no era un hombre, ni siquiera un judío; se había transformado en el símbolo de una detestada zona de mi alma" (was not a man, not even a Jew; he had become a symbol of a detested region of my soul [66–67]) (89–90). Jerusalem is the Nazi's Other, violated in the fullest sense, both discursively and physically. Indeed, Otto admits having driven Jerusalem to suicide in 1943.

Yet Otto confides in the reader that Jerusalem is not just a detested Jewish other that he would like to annihilate; his feelings of disgust are accompanied by an attraction, even admiration for the poet. To begin with, Otto's loathing of Jerusalem is complicated by a respect for his poetry: "Aún puedo repetir muchos hexámetros de aquel hondo poema que se titula *Tse Yang, pintor de tigres*. . . . Tampoco olvidaré el soliloquio *Rosencrantz habla con el Ángel*" (I can still recite many hexameters from that profound poem titled "Tse Yang, Painter of Tigers." . . . Nor shall I ever forget the soliloquy "Rosenkrantz Talks with the Angel [66]) (89). Furthermore, the Nazi confesses that the poet nearly drives him to experience the most loathsome of all human emotions: mercy. The danger of feeling compassion toward his victim goes beyond being a mere ideological conflict; it threatens his very autonomy as a subject: "Fui severo con él; no permití que me ablandaran ni la compasión ni su gloria. Yo había comprendido hace muchos años que no hay cosa en el mundo que no sea germen de un Infierno posible; un rostro, una palabra, una brújula, un avioso de cigarillos, podrían enloquecer a una persona, si ésta no lograra olvidarlos" (I was severe with him; I let neither compassion nor his fame make me soft. I had realized many years before I met David Jerusalem that everything in the world can be the seed of a possible hell; a face, a word, a compass, an advertisement for cigarettes—anything can drive a person insane if that person cannot manage to put it out of his mind [66]) (89).

The perils of mercy described by the narrator are reminiscent of Levinas's vision of the ethical relationship between same and Other. It is remarkable that Borges should name the face as that which can potentially drive the self to madness; after all, what is more powerfully present than the face of the Other? What resists the totality of the self with such defiance, if not the face? As Levinas so poetically remarks, "Absolutely present, in his face, the Other—without any metaphor—faces me" (quoted in Derrida 1978, 100). This presence is unmediated by rhetoric, as Derrida confirms in "Violence and Metaphysics," his seminal essay on the philosophy of Levinas: "The face is not a metaphor, not a figure" (1978, 101). And yet, paradoxically, the face is only able to command the self through speech, through the "Thou shalt not kill." It is thus not a coincidence that another element on the narrator's list of forces powerful enough to inspire insanity should be the word. The critical conjugation of face and word is that which threatens to destroy the ego, for it is opposite the speaking face that the self becomes a slave to the Other's demands. Without the marriage of face and language, violence reigns, as Derrida remarks: "Violence, then, would be the solitude of a mute glance, of a face without speech" (ibid., 99).

The question then becomes whether the spoken word, the speaking face, the "Thou shalt not kill" can enter a written text. Is there room, within literary discourse, for the face of the Other? Does David Jerusalem speak in "Deutsches Requiem"? On a literal level, no. The character never utters a word within the parameters of the story. The fact that he dies—commits suicide—as a result of the Nazi's lack of mercy complies only too fluidly with Levinas's view of ontological violence: the totality of Otto's self does not allow for the survival of the Other. What's more, one never learns of Jerusalem's suffering, of his experiences in the concentration camp, of that which drives him to suicide. Without question, his is a muted voice. But is the speech of a fictional character the only avenue toward responsibility for the Other? Can the face speak in another way, and if so, can this occur within the confines of a literary text? Levinas believes that this is not possible; he distinguishes between rhetorical language, which violates the Other, and ethical language, which allows the subject to respond to the Other. But if one follows Jill Robbins's suggestion that these dualistic categories "interpenetrate and contaminate" one another, it is possible to detect poetic discourse within Levinas's own description of the ethical encounter: after all, the Other's demand, the "Thou shalt not kill," is not a literal commandment expressed in words, but is itself a metaphor.

Does the text move beyond the literal speech—or lack thereof—of David Jerusalem? Is it possible to contend that David Jerusalem speaks? Or, more specifically, that David Jerusalem's face speaks? Is it present? Perhaps, if one thinks about presence as absence, following Derrida: "For the Other not to be overlooked, He must present himself as absence" (1978, 103). The absence of Jerusalem—as well as other forms of "Jewishness"—exhibits a palpable presence in Borges's text, from the footnote about Otto's Hebraist relative to the ellipsis omitting the crimes committed against his Jewish victim(s): "Determiné aplicar ese principio al régimen disciplinario de nuestra casa y . . ." (I decided to apply this principle to the disciplinary regimen of our house, and . . . [66]) (89). Yet another footnote follows this ellipsis, explaining to the reader that "ha sido inevitable, aquí, omitir unas líneas" (here, the excision of a number of lines has been unavoidable [66n1]) (89n1). Borges's use of textual silences—footnotes, ellipses, even humor itself—serves to highlight that which is glaringly lacking in the text: the ethical treatment of exteriority, the obedience of the commandment. He thus broadens the possibility of literary discourse and allows a miniscule bubble to float within the body of the text, in which the face speaks, albeit quietly. By drawing attention to the lack of ethics present in the relationship between oppressor and oppressed, there is a near inaudible suggestion of responsibility, of what responsibility could look like, how it would sound, how it would read.

And yet I must contradict this argument and question its optimism, so that it does not itself become a totalizing idea. I must allow the obliteration of otherness and the quiet possibility of responsibility to coexist, in unhappy contradiction. Is it possible that, while the violence of the text divulges the secret of the vulnerable Other, the most oppressive aspects of the texts appear in such humanistic lines as the following: "Yo agonicé con [Jerusalem], yo morí con él, yo de algún modo me he perdido con él" (I suffered with him, I died with him, I somehow have been lost with him), followed by "Mientras tanto, giraban sobre nosotros los grandes días y las grandes noches de una Guerra feliz" (Meanwhile, the grand days and grand nights of a thrilling war washed over us [67]) (90)? What does this ostensibly collective suffering and joy signify? Who is this "nosotros" and what difference does it suppress? Is it not in these phrases, pregnant with camaraderie and identification with the Other, that this Other is murdered, absorbed into the totality of the self?

Rather than attempting to resolve the intrinsic contradictions of "Deutsches Requiem," I conclude by turning to the last lines of the story: "Miro mi cara en el espejo para saber quién soy, para saber cómo me portaré dentro de unas horas, cuando me enfrente con el fin. Mi carne puede tener miedo; yo, no" (I look at my face in the mirror in order to know who I am, in order to know how I shall comport myself within a few hours, when I face the end. My flesh may feel fear; I myself do not [68]) (91). In this final moment, which mirrors the opening scene, Otto Dietrich zur Linde faces his death, the absolutely Other. In this moment he is forced to confront the various others that have populated his life, but he ends up encountering his own face. This perfect circle, much like Ulysses's return, excludes the possibility of difference; Otto ultimately chooses not to accept responsibility for his actions toward the Other.[5] However, he is not the only relevant subject of the text: in "Deutsches Requiem," self and Other are continuously shifting between Otto and Jerusalem, on the one hand, and the reader and text on the other. Although Otto does not respond to the vulnerability of his victim's naked face, the reader is made aware of hints of suffering through silences, footnotes, and ellipses. And while Jerusalem does not literally speak, does not articulate his torment, there is some element of the text, a tiny splinter, that perturbs the reader, that allows one to go beyond one's own experience, to go beyond the limits of one's own subjectivity, as well as the subjectivity of the protagonist, to the realm of the Other.

Perhaps what one has witnessed in this reading, the characteristic that would distinguish it from myriad other texts, is the acknowledgement *within the text itself* of the hither side of representation, the exception to being. By closing the signifying circle of the protagonist while simultaneously signaling the existence of something else, an *otherwise than being*, Borges indicates both the limitations as well as the potential of literary discourse. So, the answer to the question of whether the face of the Other might enter the text would—at least in this case—seem to be in the negative. At the same time, by announcing this failure, Borges opens up a certain ethical space within the confines of the text. The Other can thus be present through the acknowledgment of the impossibility of this presence. This recognition of an impossible presence is not exactly an absence, however, but more specifically, a *signal of* absence, one that is ultimately only made "real" through the act of interpretation. More than an ethics of writing, then, it seems appropriate here to talk about an ethics of reading. If the readerly subject is interrupted, traumatized by the violence of a open text, by the ambiguity of a murderer-hero (whose other side is revealed indirectly), it seems that one could begin to conceive of an ethics, or even a politics, of reception: an ethics understood as exposure to the absent face of the Other, a politics approached obliquely, a politics understood as that (always unknown, unconfirmed) event which might occur "following" this exposure.

The notion of the absent face, that element of exteriority that interrupts the totalizing self, that complicates the written text's aim to comprehend, acquires heightened significance within the context of the Southern Cone dictatorships of the 1970s. The phenomenon of the disappeared—violent acts of kidnapping and murder by the military—is a particularly poignant example in that the "truth" of the other's violation remains secret, yet simultaneously demands justice. Writing on the disappeared during and after Argentina's Dirty War, Ricardo Piglia, in *Respiración artificial*, and Sergio Chejfec, in *Los planetas*, both attempt to imagine that which escapes representation: literally, what exceeds one's scope of knowledge or comprehension. As in Borges, the idea of "Jewishness" becomes a useful tool in articulating that which defies representation within the broader geopolitical context of fascist violence. While Piglia, too, figuratively returns to the scene of "Auschwitz" to discuss the notion of unspeakability, Chejfec thematizes the idea of "Jewishness" in Argentina as part of a larger meditation on sameness and difference, identity and representability.

Respiración artificial (1980) has hardly suffered from the lack of critical attention that Borges's "Deutsches Requiem" did. While Borges's public perhaps did not know what to do with a story that, at least on the surface, had a Nazi as its protagonist and (anti)hero, the subtlety of the fiction writer and critic Ricardo Piglia's allegorical writing of the disappeared (which is never named directly) has, deservedly, attracted a great deal of interest. In one of the more well-known analyses of the novel Idelber Avelar characterizes Respiración artificial as a texto sin afuera: a text without an outside (1995, 416). Why, then, would a completely enclosed text be of concern to a discussion of the treatment of exteriority in literary discourse? If, as Avelar claims, Piglia writes a self-contained narrative, what space is created for the absent other (the disappeared, the past, the present) which undoubtedly haunts his work? What role does "Jewishness" play in the impossible but necessary enunciation of truth: the truth of history, the truth of the disappeared, the truth of the other?

Piglia's detective novel begins with the question, "Hay una historia?" calling into question the very basis of the narrative which is about to unfold.[6] The hi/story in question concerns the protagonist's correspondence with and subsequent search for his missing uncle (who, in turn, has a textual relationship with another absent figure, the nineteenth-century political figure Enrique Ossorio). The nephew-uncle relationship between Emilio Renzi and Marcelo Maggi—a reworking of the more traditional father-son pairing—is constructed consciously, and does not escape narrative commentary: "Alguien, un crítico ruso, el crítico ruso Iuri Tinianov, afirma que la literatura evoluciona de tío a sobrino (y no de padres a hijos)" (Someone, a Russian critic, the Russian critic Yuri Tynianov, declares that literature evolves from uncle to nephew [and not from fathers to sons] [Piglia 1994, 17]) (Piglia 2000, 21). This decentering of the conventional literary genealogy establishes the novel as a sort of alternate universe. The question of what this narrative is an alternate to, that is, what exists on the hither side of this story, lies at the heart of the novel's preoccupation with writing and representation, allegory and truth.

While a facile interpretation of Respiración artificial might understand Renzi's search for Maggi as an allegory for the tens of thousands of disappeared during Argentina's Dirty War—indeed, that is the immediate historical and political context within which Piglia is writing, and the repressive military government in power would not allow a direct or literal treatment of this issue in literature—Avelar explains that allegory works on a far more complex level. Rather than reading the novel (x) as a direct, albeit figurative, representation of the "real" history occurring at the moment (y), Avelar turns to the philosophy of Walter Benjamin to understand the way in which allegory works, particularly in the context of totalitarianism. If, as Benjamin contends, destruction is idealized in the symbol, in allegory one is confronted with history as a face, or as a skull (Benjamin in Avelar 1999, 3). In allegory, furthermore, one stands before the remains of that which is absent: that which, by definition, exceeds one's cognitive, aesthetic grasp. Piglia employs the allegorical precisely in order to designate that which lies outside the order of representation: "Disertar infinita, neuróticamente, acerca de la imposibilidad de narrarnos; así como de la imposibilidad de no narrar esta imposibilidad" (He neurotically narrates the impossibility of narrating, as well as the impossibility of not narrating this impossibility) (Avelar 1995, 417). The anxiety of representation appears constantly in such references as Coleman Hawkins's expression "Escucho una música y no la puedo tocar" (I hear a tune and I cannot play it [Piglia 1994, 35]) (Piglia 2000, 39) or Luciano Ossorio's preoccupation with the loss of speech: "Tengo un solo temor. . . . Llegar a concebir [la verdad . . .] y no poder expresarla" (I have just one fear. . . . Finally grasping [meaning . . .] and being unable to express it [Piglia 1994, 45]) (Piglia 2000, 49). Yet these very references are unstable: they are mentioned indirectly through the narrator, who is not certain of their origins. Moreover, the novel's parallel histories (Ossorio and Maggi, the nineteenth century and the twentieth) do not complement one another, do not fill in the gap left by the other, but rather highlight this very gap. Allegory does not resolve the problem of absence, or exteriority; it underscores the problem and (awkwardly, uncomfortably) brings it to our attention.

The question remains, however, as to how such narration is possible: what is the role of figurative language in saying the unsayable? How is it possible to allude to that which cannot be articulated in literary discourse? In addition to other strategies employed in *Respiración artificial* and analyzed by Avelar, the notion of "Jewishness" becomes a useful tool in confronting the double bind of history and narrative.[7] Piglia does this in several ways: through the figure of Tardewski (who may or may not be Jewish), through the idea of *ungeziefer*, paradoxically used by both Kafka and Hitler, and by characterizing "Auschwitz" as the realm of the unspeakable.

Renzi becomes acquainted with Tardewski when he travels to Concordia in search of his missing uncle. Tardewski, a Polish immigrant to Argentina and a friend of Professor Maggi, had been entrusted by the professor with the notes for his unwritten novel before he disappeared. Tardewski is related to the central problem of the novel in several ways: he possesses Maggi's papers, ostensibly the "key" to unlocking the mystery of his absence; he represents the "other face" of Maggi, as his companion and intellectual interlocutor; and, finally, he stands for the Old World culture of Europe, as well as its demise. Through Tardewski, Renzi (and, the reader is led to believe, Maggi) learns of Argentina's other: the European cosmopolitan center against which and in dialogue with which Argentine culture has defined itself.

The relationship between Tardewski and Maggi (in addition to the coupling of Tardewski and Renzi) is one of a long list of intellectual pairs described in the novel. The professor, Renzi explains, was fascinated by the phenomenon of the European artist or thinker who emigrated to Argentina, came to "incarnate universal knowledge," and would form a "duet" with a local intellectual: "De Angelis-Echeverría en la época de Rosas. Paul Groussac-Miguel Cané en el 80. Soussens-Lugones en el novecientos. Hudson-Güiraldes en la década del 20. Gombrowicz-Borges en los años 40" (De Angelis–Echeverría in the Rosas period. Paul Groussac–Miguel Cané in the 1880s. Soussens–Lugones at the turn of the century. Hudson–Güiraldes in the twenties. Gombrowicz–Borges in the forties [116–17]) (120). This act of doubling—which creates, instead of a mirror effect, an excess of difference—is repeated in the dynamic between Tardewski and Maggi, described as "la unidad de los contrarios" (a unity of opposites [186]) (237). Tardewski, whose name is repeatedly misunderstood (Renzi comes looking for a "Tardowski," and the Polish immigrant's sole article is published using the same erroneous spelling), does not quite belong; he is the novel's foreign "misfit."[8] Yet at the same time that he stands as Argentina's other (as a European intellectual, and a failed one at that), he also occupies the position of the other in his native (Nazi-dominated) Poland. Reflecting back on the events that brought him to Concordia, he hypothesizes that he could have ended up in a concentration camp had he not fled to Argentina.

En su juventud, dijo, jamás se le hubiera ocurrido imaginar que iba a pasar cuarenta años en este rincón del mundo. A veces, dijo, se le daba por pensar qué hubiera sido de su vida de haberse quedado en Europa o de haber regresado al final de la guerra. Quizás hubiese muerto en un campo de concentración o quizás, dijo, de haber seguido en Londres sin la ocurrencia de irse a veranear a Varsovia justo en agosto de 1939 y en ese caso de haber sobrevivido los bombardeos, tal vez, en ese caso, dijo, hubiera terminado mi doctorado y hoy sería profesor de filosofía en alguna universidad inglesa o norteamericana (192–93).

❧

In his youth, he said, he had never imagined that he would spend forty years of his life in this corner of the world. At times, he said, he started thinking about what his life would have been like had he stayed in Europe or had he returned after the end of the war. Perhaps he would have died in a concentration camp, or perhaps, he said, he would have continued in London without having the idea of going to spend the summer in Warsaw in August 1939, no less, and had he survived the bombing raids, perhaps, in that case, he said, I might have finished my doctorate and now I would be a professor of philosophy at some British or North American university. (155)

The existence of other potential versions of his life attests to the possibility of *something else*, at once underscoring the finitude of his destiny and exposing its arbitrariness. It posits history—whether individual or collective—as possessing an "other" side, suggesting, once again, that the narrated story is not the "real" story and that the "real" story is always ultimately unattainable.[9] Moreover, Tardewski's "alternate destiny" as a Holocaust victim, while not confirming his Jewish identity, places him alongside the "Jew" within the broader category of the marginal, the undesirable, within the symbolic universe of the novel: "A medida que las tropas nazis iban arrasando la cultura europea, yo mismo iba siendo arrasado, como si fuera su representante" (As the war in Europe progressed, as the Nazi troops were flattening European culture, I felt myself being flattened, as if I were its representative [175]) (177). Through the utterance of this (alter)egology, Tardewski becomes a figure for the hither side of history and representation.

It is through Tardewski, as well, that one learns of yet another "odd couple," the uncanny (and borderline humorous, if it were not so disturbing) pairing of Adolf Hitler and Franz Kafka.[10] As a philosophy student in England, Tardewski accidentally stumbles on a strange discovery in the British Library, due to the mistaken classification of Hitler's *Mein Kampf* under the entry for the Greek sophist Hippias. Tardewski's reading of this version of Hitler's book, annotated by the German historian Joachim Kluge (who, Tardewski explains, is an exile and friend of Walter Benjamin), leads him to the bizarre connection between Nazism and Kafka's work, traceable to the co-incidental meeting of the two in a café during the "wandering years," the intellectual Bildungsroman, of the future leader of the Third Reich. Kluge suggests that Hitler spends this period in Prague, frequenting the Arcos Café, the meeting place of local artists and intellectuals, including Kafka. Kafka, for his part, refers to an Austrian named Adolf with whom he conversed at the café, according to Tardewski's methodical research. In their conversations Adolf narrates to Kafka "la utopía atroz de un mundo convertido en una inmensa colonia penitenciaria. . . . Y Kafka le cree. Piensa que es posible que los proyectos imposibles y atroces de ese hombrecito ridículo y famélico lleguen a cumplirse y que el mundo se transforme en eso que las palabras estaban construyendo" (the atrocious utopia of a world converted into an immense penal colony. . . . And Kafka believes him. He thinks it is possible that the impossible and atrocious projects of that ridiculous hungry little man may come to pass and that the world may be transformed into what the words were constructing [206–7]) (208). Decades after this unlikely conversation, Kafka goes on to fictionalize this hell, while Hitler goes on to realize it. The proof, says Tardewski, of this implausible coincidence lies in the German word *ungeziefer*: the term that Hitler uses to characterize his concentration-camp victims and that Kafka employs to describe what Gregor Samsa turns into, one morning in bed. Kafka's and Hitler's work meet in the space of the ungeziefer, and Tardewski narrates this frightening anomaly.[11]

The lexical intersection between artist and fascist has particular meaning for Tardewski's work, whose objective is to theorize the downfall of European culture during the first half of the twentieth century. It is also significant on the level of macronarration: the repudiated object is central to Piglia's rhetorical project in its articulation of that which is cast aside, the exterior which is always, of course, inside as well. But if the ungeziefer signifies vermin—the alienated modern other for the Jew writing in German in Prague, as well as the vile other that must be exterminated for Hitler—what about that element of alterity that escapes signification? The unspeakable, within the fictional universe of *Respiración artificial*, is not that element of society that is called ungeziefer, but the very scene within which the ungeziefer is imagined and murdered, the concentration camp.

> Sobre aquello de lo que no se puede hablar, lo mejor es callar, decía Wittgenstein. ¿Cómo hablar de lo indecible? Ésa es la pregunta que la obra de Kafka trata; una a otra vez, de contestar. O mejor, dijo, su obra es la única que de un

modo refinado y sutil se atreve a hablar de lo indecible, de eso que no se puede nombrar. ¿Qué diríamos hoy que es lo indecible? El mundo de Auschwitz. Ese mundo está más allá del lenguaje, es la frontera donde están las alambradas del lenguaje. Alambre de púas: el equilibrista camina, descalzo, solo allá arriba y trata de ver si es posible decir algo sobre lo que está del otro lado. (214)

❦

What we cannot speak about we must pass over in silence, Wittgenstein said. How to speak of the unspeakable? That is the question that Kafka's work tries over and over again to answer. Or better still, he said, his work is the only one that in a refined and subtle manner dares to speak of the unspeakable, of that which cannot be named. What would we say is the unspeakable today? The world of Auschwitz. That world is beyond language, it is a frontier filled with the barbed wire of language. Barbed wire: the tightrope walker walks, barefoot, alone up there, and tries to see if it is possible to say anything about what is on the other side. (212–13)

It is in this monologue by Tardewski, the uncertain symbol of a fallen civilization, that the primary concern of the novel is brought to light: how to acknowledge, using language, the world beyond language. Of course, in this tribute to Kafka ("truly great writers are those who constantly face the almost absolute impossibility of writing"), there is a double message: on one level, it is a modest recognition by the writer that his aspirations are unrealizable; at the same time, however, isn't it also an affirmation that by failing, Piglia succeeds in positing himself as a "truly great writer"?

Does Piglia follow Wittgenstein's dictum and pass over the unspeakable in silence? What words, what signifiers, are necessary to attempt to remain quiet? Like Borges, Piglia turns to the scene of "Jewishness" in order to acknowledge the unsayable. Specifically, the scene of "Auschwitz" becomes, in its horror, a convenient rhetorical tool. Returning to Avelar's reading of Piglian allegory, it is not as though "Auschwitz" (x) were a direct representation of the Dirty War (y), but rather that "Auschwitz" points to all that cannot be said about both x, y, and everything else. Yet a contradiction remains, and it is worth acknowledging: in order to cease to thematize, it is necessary to thematize. This is the double bind one sees in another form in Borges's writing, in which the construction of the "Jewish" figures Emma Zunz, Aaron Lowenthal, and David Jerusalem are central to the project of unsaying "Jewishness." Perhaps this is the aporia inherent in the relationship between ethical language and rhetorical language, Levinas's *saying* (*le dire*) and the said (le dit). Ultimately, all saying falls into the said, becomes a the-matization without which, paradoxically, the saying is impossible. In Tar-dewski's words, this is the barbed wire of language, the prison of discourse without which the nightmare remains unacknowledged. One is left facing the double bind of ethics but also the challenge of politics: how to move from exposure to representation, responsibility to justice.

Written nearly two decades after Respiración artificial, Los planetas (1999), by the fiction writer and essayist Sergio Chejfec, also confronts the difficul-ties inherent in the intent to approximate the unspeakable. Like Borges's and Piglia's texts, Los planetas confronts the dire political reality of the sec-ond half of the twentieth century without expressing an explicit ideological position, choosing instead to occupy the complicated terrain of literary rep-resentation. If Piglia turns to the nineteenth century in order to articulate the problem of totalitarianism and disappearance of the (then) present, Chej-fec's narrative takes place a few years after tens of thousands of Argentines were disappeared and thus brings the problem of memory into the dynamic of representation seen in Respiración artificial. The novel is narrated primarily from the perspective of S, a forty-year-old writer living in Buenos Aires, who recalls his childhood friend M, kidnapped and likely murdered during the early years of the Dirty War. Organized around a series of anecdotes and frag-mented recollections of M, the novel deals with questions of violence and history, memory and mourning. The central tension of the narrative has to do with the (over)identification of S with M (amounting, in its extreme form, to the near appropriation of M's identity by S), despite the fact that M's mem-ory, as well as S's writing, relies on the existence of difference in the face of the same. Like Borges and Piglia, Chejfec is concerned with the problem of exteriority and its relationship with the interior of the text. In order to ad-dress this philosophical and narrative quandary Chejfec draws on the image of the void, that emptiness around which all meaning is structured. He em-ploys the notion of "Jewishness" as an empty signifier that must be filled as a way to articulate the aporetic relationship between identity and difference, absence and presence.

Just as Respiración artificial is organized around a series of pairs, so, too, is Los planetas structured around a central relationship: the touching friend-ship between the narrator and his childhood companion (the two are alter-nately referred to as Miguel and Sergio, M and S, M and "the other," and M and "I"). If Piglia turns to the idea of the intellectual "duo" in order to reflect on the intersection between lo argentino and lo europeo, aesthetics and politics, history and representation, Chejfec delves into the memory of the boyhood twosome as a way to subvert the division between same and other. The relationship between identity and alterity becomes a crucial motif in this novel because it structures the conditions of possibility *and* impossibility of the representation of the other. By becoming the other (the narrator contends that M was the "real" writer), S acquires the authority necessary to relate the story of his friend's disappearance. Yet the extreme form of this identification—publishing a novel under the name of Miguel, an option proposed by a bureaucrat when Sergio tries to legally change his name to that of his disappeared companion—would eliminate the possibility of memory, because there would no longer be a Sergio to remember Miguel (nor would there be an external Miguel to be remembered).

The author's unapologetic autobiographical references (S is occasionally called Sergio, is from Buenos Aires, is a writer, nearing forty, Jewish, etc.) seem gratuitous, as if Chejfec were giving the reader a freebie, taking away at the same time her ability to interpret. Reading, one is always tempted to say, "I wonder if this is the author revealing his 'true' feelings, experience, history, and so on. Yes! S must 'really' be Sergio, and this story must 'really' be 'true'!" Yet by giving multiple and, ultimately, extremely quotidian clues, Chejfec simplifies the author-narrator connection, robbing the reader of the right to insist on any sort of fixed meaning in his writing. This link is further complicated by his explanation of the initial M: "M de Miguel, o de Mauricio; también podría decir M de Daniel, ya que, como sabemos, detrás de las letras puede haber cualquier nombre" (M for Miguel, or Mauricio; it could also be M for Daniel, since we know that behind letters there can be any name) (Chefjec 1999, 18). As Isabel Quintana (2004) points out, M also signifies death (*muerte*); it could also stand for martyr or mark. Indeed, S explains that M's disappearance was a defining force in the lives and identities of his surviving friends: "M era el *mártir*, pero no porque su sacrificio estuviera dirigido a nuestra salvación sino porque su desaparición era nuestra *marca*" (M was the *martyr*, but not because his sacrifice was directed toward our salvation, but because his disappearance was our *mark*) (22, emphasis added). The letters S and M, although easily interchangeable with Sergio and Miguel, ultimately prove to be arbitrary signs, linked but not married to their subjects.

The question of what name is behind the initial, as well as what identity is behind the name, is radicalized in the section "Primera historia de M" (First Hi/story of M), which recounts a practical joke that M and S play on their parents.[12] One day at school, they decide to return to the home of the other, assuming the name of and pretending to be the other. While they anticipate a good laugh, knowing that their parents will see through their efforts at deception, they are horrified when the parents respond unfazed. Of course, there is already something a bit eerie about their actions, which the narrator compares to the experience of attending one's own funeral, that is, seeing the world absent oneself. The joke becomes increasingly frightening, however, when their parents call them by the name of the other as if nothing were out of the ordinary. In addition to the unexpected behavior of the parents is the haunting feeling that the house of the other is really no different from their own: "Todo les resultó familiar y extraño a la vez" (Everything seemed familiar and strange at once) (48). If, as the narrator suggests, one normally associates terror with the unknown, what frightens here is the sense that the unknown appears embedded in the familiar (a reminder, perhaps, of what the world would be like if difference were to cease to exist altogether). This feeling of uneasiness increases as the night goes on, as each boy approaches what should be the most private point of the day—bedtime, sleep, solitude— but whose singularity is instead hijacked by the parents' refusal to acknowledge the difference between the two boys.

Of course, the disquiet portrayed is precisely what Freud aims to describe in his discussion of the uncanny: "For Freud, the uncanny derives its terror not from something external, alien, or unknown but—on the contrary—from something strangely familiar which defeats our efforts to separate ourselves from it" (Morris 1985, 307). The scene of the practical joke thus simultaneously explores two aspects of the uncanny: the dreadful, anxiety-producing power of elusive difference masquerading as the same, as well as the dystopic prospect of the complete elimination of difference (the ultimate aim of totalitarianism). What begins as boyhood play quickly spirals downward into the nightmarish possibilities of fascism, and it is from this potential void that the narrator must rescue M's memory.

The problem of identity and difference is elaborated further through the motif of "Jewishness," specifically, through the figures of the Orthodox Jews observed by M and "the other" while riding on a city bus. The two friends argue over the question of whether these ultrareligious men and boys represent the "authentic" face of Judaism: "M dijo, señalando con el dedo, que esos judíos eran verdaderos, auténticos. 'Ellos son genuinos,' murmuró. '¿Quiénes?,' preguntó el otro. 'Ellos, los ortodoxos, ¿No son más auténticos?,' respondió M" (M said, pointing with his finger, that those Jews were real, authentic. "They are genuine," he murmured. "Who?" asked the other.

"Them, the orthodox ones, aren't they more authentic?" M answered) (45–46). M's affirmation, followed by a question, revisits the tension between identity and alterity, and the complicated interdependence of the two categories. The insistence on the authenticity of the religious Jews, M clarifies, does not mean that they are *more* Jewish, but that their Jewish "nature" is expressed through more tangible qualities, in contrast to the secular, assimilated M and "the other": "Nuestra naturaleza está marcada por el abandono, la ausencia, los restos de una plenitud poco a poco más remota y algo exótica. . . . En cambio ellos con cada paso señalan una confirmación, reafirman una continuidad" (Our nature is marked by abandonment, absence, the remnants of a fullness slowly becoming more remote and somewhat exotic. . . . They, on the other hand, with every step marked a confirmation, reaffirmed a continuity) (46). Eliciting the notion of "abandonment" or "absence," this scene is vital to the broader preoccupation of the novel: how to identify that which escapes one's grasp, how to name that which eludes the domain of the (writing) subject.

The dynamic of the religious and secular Jews in Chejfec—the seeming opposition between plenitude and lack—is reminiscent of the phenomenon described by Slavoj Žižek in his analysis of modern European anti-Semitism, in The Sublime Object of Ideology. Žižek explains the modern incarnation of anti-Semitism—which, in contrast to its premodern, religious roots, reacts to a secular, pseudoscientific, racialized concept of "Jewishness"—by drawing on the example of the *Invasion of the Body Snatchers* (Siegal 1956). In this horror film what frightens is not that which is easily identifiable as "other" (*"pure difference perceived as Identity"* [Žižek 1989, 99]), but rather the other that approximates the same, once again, Freud's uncanny: "They look like human beings, they have all their properties, but in some sense this makes them all the more uncannily strange" (Žižek 1989, 89). This is the same dynamic at work in modern anti-Semitism: "Jews are 'like us'; it is difficult to recognize them, to determine at the level of positive reality that surplus, that evasive feature, which differentiates them from all other people" (Žižek 1989, 89). M and "the other" exemplify this secularized concept of "Jewishness" in their abandonment of tradition, or in the absence in them of any easily definable trait. Žižek describes this absence as "lack . . . perceived as a point of supreme plenitude" (1989, 99). This lack of positive essence is present in the Orthodox Jews as well; it is simply more apparent in the figure of the secular Jews. The Orthodox are thus a reminder of the lack of "identity" in the secular, who, in turn, embody and make evident the hidden lack in the Orthodox.

The narrator elaborates on the complicated overlapping of the identitary categories "Jewish" and "non-Jewish" in his description of the strange location of M's family home.

> Pese a estar en un barrio genéricamente judío, el sitio no corespondía a un area considerada como tal. Esta contigüidad, como es costumbre, ponía en evidencia el deslinde, al contrario de lo que pudiera suceder en otros casos, precisamente como el de mi familia, que no vivía en una zona considerada judía, circunstancia que sin embargo no llamaba la atención de nadie. (27)

⌘

> Despite being in a generically Jewish neighborhood, the house did not belong in an area considered to be so. This proximity, as commonly occurs, made boundaries more evident, contrary to what otherwise might be the case, such as that of my family, who did not live in a zone considered Jewish, a circumstance that did not, however, draw anyone's attention.

While M's house is oddly located, due to its simultaneous belonging and nonbelonging to an easily identifiable "Jewish" space, the narrator's family—also Jewish—lives in a non-Jewish neighborhood, which does not appear as bizarre since it does not juxtapose identity and alterity in the same unsettling way. The geographical is then reproduced in the architectural: the family home is structured such that M's room extends over the house of the next-door neighbor's, infusing his room with the smells of the other family, rather than his own (78). The uncomfortable overlap between the realm of the same and that of the other, "Jewishness" and "non-Jewishness," is vital to the broader problematic of the novel, which attempts to enter the realm of the other through language and memory, in the end intentionally failing.

The narrator's description, finally, of "Jewishness" as "un vacío o hueco que precisa ser llenado por atributos diferenciados" (an emptiness or void that must be filled by differentiated attributes) (28) conjures the image of the "void," which is central to the novel's preoccupation with the representation of disappearance and death. This concern is voiced early in the novel, during the first mention of M's kidnapping.

> Entre el secuestro y la noticia había un lapso de varios días, un lapso que ahora no me atrevo a calcular, en parte porque no estoy seguro de poder hacerlo: esos días no fueron días, era una interminable masa de tiempo, también insustancial y capaz de reproducirse sin término, que por esas crueles situaciones del destino, como a veces se dice, precisamente habría de encontrar en el

diario de esa tarde la promesa de terminar, si no de completarse por lo menos de cesar, adquirir alguna forma y de esta manera quedar a la espera de un después. (18)

⅋

Between the kidnapping and the news there was several days' lapse, a lapse that I do not dare calculate now, partly because I am not sure I can do it. Those days were not days, they were an unending mass of time, insubstantial and capable of reproducing itself endlessly; and because of destiny's cruel jokes, as it is sometimes said, I would find precisely in that afternoon's newspaper the possibility of finishing—if not reaching completion, then at least stopping, acquiring some shape, and in this way remain, awaiting an after.

The "lapse" between the event (M's kidnapping) and its codification (the news) underscores the void at the heart of the act of representation. Here, the notion of a "lapse" is mentioned in relation to time—"un lapso de varios días" (several days' lapse)—but it also describes a period during which the "proper" limits of time, whatever they might be, are exploded, in which events, reality, truth exceed the limits that traditionally bound them, or at least their conceptualization. It is in this sense that the narrator confesses that he wouldn't "dare" to calculate the amount of time that passed, as if to signal that the act of calculation (measurement, representation) would be a transgression, somehow, of the enormity of the event.

Rather than trying to close this gap, the novel instead opts to respect and meditate on it. The idea of the void appears and reappears throughout the novel: it is the void within M's mourning parents ("La ausencia del hijo producía un *vacío*" [The absence of the son created a *void*] [21]); the well uncovered by S's own traumatic memory of his friend ("El *pozo* abierto por el recuerdo de M sólo se cubrió poco a poco–los días, después las semanas y los años–con la desolación que deja la barbarie" [The *well* opened by the memory of M was covered only little by little—the days, then the weeks and years—by the despair left behind by barbarism] [19]); as well as the glaring absence of M's name on the list of the disappeared ("Se ignora el nombre de muchos secuestrados; sin embargo sólo su *ausencia* en las listas públicas nos habla a nosotros, que lo conocimos, de un *vacío* que pone en duda la misma existencia" [The names of many of the missing are unknown; however, it is only their *absence* from public lists that speaks to us, who knew him, of an emptiness that puts in doubt existence itself] [43]).[13] The excessive repetition of the idea of "emptiness" obsessively rehearses the act of representation while exposing its limits: the void cannot be approached, but the unapproachable void can be signaled again and again and again.

It is precisely this type of ethical signifying to which the leftist French philosopher Alain Badiou refers in his discussion of the event in *Ethics*. The situation, he argues, is structured around a void (*vide*), an absence, so that the event (the locus of ethical experience) would entail a "'naming' of this absence" (2002, 68). Badiou explains that "the event names the void inasmuch as it names the not-known of the situation" (ibid., 69). In order to illustrate this dynamic, he offers the example of Marx-as-event: "Marx is an event for political thought because he designates, under the name 'proletariat,' the central void of early bourgeois societies . . . absent from the political stage" (ibid.). If ethics, in this context, refers to fidelity to an event, might not ethical language be understood as that which is faithful to the sign of the void? Given that Badiou seems to be interested in the ethical only insofar as it can provide the conditions of possibility for revolution, how can one infer the political implications of a poetics which engages alterity by announcing its impossible presence? That is, how does the void of the ethical become infused with the content of the political?[14]

Finally, how does the signifier "Jew"—as a symbolic container that is always embedded in the historical and the ideological—enter into this negotiation between presence and absence? To dialogue with Žižek, in what way does the idea of "Jewishness" get invested with one's unconscious desire? Why is it that the "Jew" periodically "enters the framework of fantasy structuring our enjoyment" (Žižek 1989, 126)? It is because, Žižek will claim, this fantasy shields the subject from the void, from the nothingness that is the Real. We therefore have to distinguish between what Žižek calls the "objectification of [the] void" (ibid., 95) and Badiou's "'naming' of [the] absence," the former referring to a thematization of absence, the latter suggesting its unrepresentability. Through the construction of a symbolic order around the lack in the other, the subject (individual or collective, aesthetic or ideological) constitutes itself by protecting itself from this excessive lack, as well as its own immanent failure. This is the phenomenon one witnesses in the obsessive reiteration of the signifier "Jew" in the texts I have analyzed in this book, and thus it is not surprising that Žižek characterizes this transformation of the presymbolic Real into the symbolized reality as a "conversion" (ibid., 230). In these (one could argue, in all) textual conversions, the desire— as well as the suffering—of the other remains outside of the order of representation. One cannot know what the other wants, just as one is never able to comprehend the suffering of David Jerusalem in Borges, the whereabouts of Professor Maggi in Piglia, or the "truth" of M's kidnapping in Chejfec.

Yet there also always remains the option of signaling this impossible knowledge, and it is in this paradoxical space that I conclude. I began with an image of concentric circles, the smallest designating constructions of "Jewishness," the middle standing for inventions of "other others," and the largest indicating the problem of representation and alterity in general. Perhaps the core of this image does not consist of a point, but rather of an absent center, an empty space which eludes representation altogether, but which may in fact point in the direction of an as-yet-undefined politics. Paradoxically, one arrives at this nonplace through literary discourse, or through an announcement of the failure of literary discourse. If, as Annick Louis contends, Borges approaches the political not as content, but rather by exposing the "truth" of the Nazi (2000, 63), perhaps one can understand the road to politics, in Borges, Piglia, and Chefjec, as an oblique one: one that must pass through the scene of the ethical. The possibility of justice is infinitely postponed but also repeatedly demanded through the ethical interruption. Finally, it is enacted or performed within the realm of the literary: it is no coincidence that the unnarratable "others" that interrupt the totality of the self in Borges, Piglia, and Chejfec, are all writers.

⌀ NOTES

INTRODUCTION ⌀ "JEWISHNESS," ALTERITY, REPRESENTATION

1   I place the terms "Jew," "Jews," and "Jewishness" in quotation marks in order to denaturalize their meanings and challenge the essentialist assumptions that often accompany their use. While I occasionally refrain from using quotation marks—generally to refer to real people or historical communities—I do not mean to oppose "figurative Jews" and "real Jews." Quite the opposite, I intend to underscore the processes whereby even "real" Jews construct their own "Jewishness."

2   As of 1994, there were 208,000 Jews in Argentina (0.6 percent of the total population) and 100,000 in Brazil (0.06 percent). While Mexico's 40,800 make up 0.04 percent of the population, the Jews of Colombia and Peru account for a mere 0.01 percent of the total population in each country (5,000 and 2,900, respectively); these figures pale in comparison not only to those of Argentina and Brazil but especially to those of the United States, whose Jewish population is 5,675,000, or 2.16 percent of the total population (Elkin 193). The statistics for 1989

published by U. O. Schmelz and Sergio DellaPergola (1991) approximate those reported by Laiken Elkin.

3 I am thinking of "A cristã nova," *As minas de prata*, *De sobremesa*, *Macunaíma*, "Deutsches Requiem," "Emma Zunz," "El milagro secreto," *Los siete locos*, *El amor y otros demonios*, *El hablador*, *Respiración artificial*, and *Stella Manhattan*, to name only a few.

4 While Rubén Darío hails from Nicaragua, the *modernista* poet and essayist lived and published much of his work in Chile, Argentina, Costa Rica, and France.

5 The notion of the "wandering signifier" draws on the mythical figure of the wandering Jew, as well as on the idea of the signifier as a linguistic sign that is open to multiple interpretations, originating in the work of the Swiss linguist Ferdinand de Saussure and expanded on by structuralist and poststructuralist literary theorists throughout the twentieth century.

6 I tend to favor the use of the term "figurative Jew" (as well as "rhetorical," "symbolic," or "imaginary," though these terms should not be read in a Lacanian sense) to refer not (only) to the human being who calls himself a Jew (or is called a Jew) but also to the signifier "Jew," which exists as a result of our imaginings, creations, and anxieties. That is, while the "figurative Jew" is related to "real" Jews (a problematic relationship that I outline below), I would like to center my discussion on the creative process of imagining "Jewishness," whether by Jews or non-Jews.

7 Cheyette discusses this ideological ambivalence in his earlier work as well: "The indeterminacy of the semitic representations under consideration meant that 'the Jew' can be constructed to represent both sides of a political or social or ideological divide" (1993, 9).

8 For more on the origins of this myth, see George Kumler Anderson's *The Legend of the Wandering Jew* (1965), particularly chapter 2, "The Beginnings of the Legend."

9 Tamar Garb asserts that "ambivalence has been the salient attitude toward the Jew in Christian consciousness" (1995, 20), while Artur Sandauer describes allosemitism as "a radically ambivalent attitude" (quoted in Bauman 1998, 143). Bauman asserts that "the Jew is ambivalence incarnate" (1998, 146).

10 See, in particular, Castro's *España en su historia* (1984) and Menocal's *The Ornament of the World* (2002), as well as *The Spanish Inquisition* by Henry Kamen, who characterizes the intercultural relations of medieval Spain as an "uneasy coexistence" (1998, 1).

11 Sidelocks, skullcaps, and fringed ritual undergarments are just several examples of external, tangible marks of Jewish difference, particularly before the secularization of Jews during modernity.

12 Geoffrey Bennington, a scholar of continental philosophy and literary theory, questions Lyotard's appropriation of the term "the jews": "'The jews' are not the jews, though there seems to be an essential relationship between them and the [real] jews: but on the other hand it looks as though the sense Lyotard is able to

make of the real jews is provided by the possibility of their 'jewishness' not being confined to them, uniquely identified with them, as real jews, but something more like a structural feature that could be, and is, shared by others, notably writers and thinkers" (1998, 193).

13 See Silverman 1998, 201. Max Silverman also poses the question, "Where are real Jews here?" pointing to "the recruitment of 'the Jew' to serve the allegorical function of some universalism or other" even in contemporary theoretical debates (ibid., 198).

14 Daniel Boyarin's work on constructions of Jewish masculinity, for example, explores the replacement of the feminized "*Yeshiva-Bokhur* male ideal (the later mentsh)" with the "'New Jewish Man,' 'the muscle Jew,'" approaching both figures as cultural inventions (1998, 65). Boyarin's *Unheroic Conduct* (1997) expands on this thesis.

15 According to Orthodox and Conservative Jewish law, patrilineal descent does not constitute a valid means by which Jewish identity can be transmitted.

16 Žižek, referring to the Jew as an "ideological figure," details the way in which the Jew "is invested with our unconscious desire." Of course, one should ask, who is this first-person plural for whom Žižek speaks when he talks about "our" desire? We Europeans? We non-Jews?

17 I am in dialogue here with Elaine Scarry's concept "generous imaginings" (1999).

18 The historian Dennis Showalter and Zygmunt Bauman use different terms to allude to symbolic and real Jews. While Showalter distinguishes between the "Jew next door" and the "mythological Jew" (quoted in Bauman 1991, 187), Bauman talks about the abstract Jew and the empirical Jew or "the Jew as such" versus "the Jew next door" (1998, 148).

19 While the majority of the texts analyzed in this book are by non-Jews, I include the works of several Jewish writers: Luisa Futoransky, Margo Glantz, César Tiempo, Sergio Chejfec, as well as the more ambiguously identified Jorge Isaacs and Heitor Carlos Cony. While Julián Martel is perhaps the most explicitly anti-Semitic author treated here, and Jorge Luis Borges is generally considered to be philo-Semitic, the rest are far more difficult to define. I find this ambiguity to be a challenge, yet ultimately a potential source of subtlety and nuance in my readings.

20 All translations of essays, unless otherwise stated, are my own. When a published English translation of a text is used, it is indicated by an accompanying page number.

21 See DiAntonio and Glickman 1993; Goldberg 2000; Igel 1997; Liwerant, Gojman de Backal, and Soriano 1999; Senkman 2000; Bernardo Sorj 1997; Bila Sorj 1997; Sosnowski 2000; Stavans 2001.

22 "Jews have been numerically insignificant in all countries where they have dwelt... yet they have profoundly influenced arts and letters, science, the economy, the administration of justice, and foreign policy, to name only major areas" (Elkin 1998, xiv).

23 European ambivalence toward the "Jew" was in this way reproduced in Latin America, though within a radically different political and social climate.

24 I intentionally use the term *converso* to refer to the figure of the "Jewish convert" in general, in order to demonstrate the prevalence of this figure beyond the historical and religious context of the Inquisition.

25 It has been documented that after living as a practicing Catholic, Isaacs became a member of the Freemasons, a moral and metaphysical fraternal organization and secret society. See Witalec 1999 for more on this.

26 In her essay "Exclusões (e inclusões) na literatura latino-americana: Índios, negros e judeus" (1998), the Latin American comparatist Lúcia Helena Costigan argues that while the indigenous and "black" other play a crucial role in imagining national identity in Latin American literature, the Jew is largely absent or excluded from the national landscape. The Brazilian literature scholar Nelson Vieira (1995) also emphasizes the invisibility of the Jew in Brazilian literature. Research on constructions of race and ethnicity in Latin America, of course, is abundant (Dain Borges 1993; Castillo 1995; Grandis and Bernd 2000; Helg 1990; Lesser 1995, 1999, 2001; Skidmore 1990, 1993; Stepan 1991).

27 The anti-Jewish sentiment during the Vargas period has been detailed by scholars such as Robert Levine (1968) and Maria Luiza Tucci Carneiro (1988). In a 2002 article, however, Roney Cytrynowicz goes against this line of interpretation, arguing that despite the xenophobic rhetoric and official policy of the Vargas government (which, he claims, did not target Jews any more than other "foreign" groups), Jews succeeded in maneuvering around and within these restrictions in order to flourish institutionally. Thus, while one can draw parallels between the anti-Semitic rhetoric of nationalist governments on both sides of the Atlantic during the late 1930s and early 1940s, Cytrynowicz insists that the Vargas regime cannot be understood as a Latin American equivalent to Nazi Germany. In an earlier work on this period Jeffrey Lesser discusses the paradoxical increase in Jewish immigration to Brazil despite anti-immigration sentiment and policy (1995, 51–57).

28 I do not intend to essentialize or generalize European representations of Jewishness; one need only consult the excellent studies by Bryan Cheyette (1993) and Sander Gilman (1991) to see radically distinct approaches to the symbolic "Jew" in English and German cultures. Likewise, I hope to highlight the differences among national and individual projects in Latin American literature as they engage metaphors of "Jewishness" in order to articulate broader subject positions.

29 See Sarmiento 1977. Joshua Lund rightly warns against the pitfalls of such terminology in *The Impure Imagination*: "The danger is that the constant critique of racial democracy that hinges on calling it a 'myth' ends up participating, by surprise, in the very same 'exceptionalism' that secures Brazil's identification as a relatively harmonious space of race relations. It does so by turning racial democracy into the example against which that exceptionalism rests. . . . Racial democracy becomes a mistake ascribed to the past, from which we (Brazilians and/or students of Brazilian culture) learned, and which we now recognize as mere myth-

making, a project in which we no longer participate" (2006, 144). While I agree with Lund's argument, I retain the phrase for the purposes of my study only because I believe it to be valuable insofar as it reveals a crucial element of collective representations of race.

30 While the period of the Conquest contains some of the bloodiest massacres in colonial history, modern Latin American attempts to deal with the ethnic "other" do not frequently advocate extermination or expulsion, at least on the level of rhetoric. Thus, while massacres continue to occur, it is generally in spite of a discourse of inclusion.

31 While Cornejo Polar begins to develop his theory of heterogeneity in the 1970s (see, for example, his 1978 essay "El indigenismo y las literaturas heterogéneas: Su doble estatuto socio-cultural"), his book Escribir en el aire (Writing in the air) marks a key theoretical intervention in the fields of Latin American literary and cultural studies. Marilyn Miller points out that in his later work—in particular, the essay, "A Non-Dialectic Heterogeneity"—Cornejo Polar "called for a new emphasis on 'migrancy' as an alternative to mestizaje [because he] feared the term had exhausted almost all its explanatory capacity" (2004, 5). Mabel Moraña traces the development of this concept in her 1995 essay "Escribir en el aire: Heterogeneidad y estudios culturales."

32 For an astute critical engagement of theories of hybridity in García Canclini and others, see Kraniauskas 2004.

33 Julia Kristeva's notion of being "strangers to ourselves" approaches this concept from the perspective of psychoanalytic theory, asking whether one becomes a foreigner in another country "because one is already a foreigner from within" (1991, 14).

34 Bauman argues that the Jewish "stranger within" in Germany leads to an "Age of Gardening," in which the foreign other is weeded out of the national landscape (1998, 152).

35 Most English publications on (and translations of) the work of Emmanuel Levinas spell the term "Other" with an upper-case "O." However, the term "O/other" refers to four different Levinasian expressions: l'Autre, l'autre, Autrui, and autrui, which appear in his work without consistency (Critchley and Bernasconi, 2002, 16; Levinas 1996, xix). Levinasian scholars have made contradictory decisions on how to deal with this issue (Critchley 1992, 5, 50; Llewelyn 1995, xii; Levinson 2004, 104). I generally capitalize "Other" only in reference to Levinas's work.

36 For a brilliant discussion of the problem of ethical subjectivity in Kant and Levinas, see Gabriela Basterra's Seductions of Fate, especially part 5.

37 Subjectivity does not exist before the ethical relationship with the Other, but rather responsibility is already inherent in subjectivity: "Responsibility in fact is not a simple attribute of subjectivity, as if the latter already existed in itself, before the ethical relationship. Subjectivity is not for itself; it is, once again, initially for another" (Levinas 1982, 96).

38 Levinas explores the concept of the "imperialism of the same" in his essay "The Trace of the Other" (quoted in Robbins 1999, 4).

39 Levinas describes the saying as "pre-original language, the responsibility of one for the other, the substitution of one for the other, and the condition (or the un-condition) of being hostage" (1998, 6).

40 Diane Perpich explains that "In 'Reality and Its Shadow,' published in 1948, Levinas argues that art is essentially disengaged from moral and political concerns, adding that it is constituted by a dimension of evasion and irresponsibility as potentially wicked, egoist, and cowardly as 'feasting during a plague'" (2001).

41 "In Totality and Infinity (1961), the language of the polemic is more subdued, less rhetorical, though ironically rhetoric itself has become the central target" (Perpich 2001).

42 Robbins's text details the way in which Levinas performs a relationship with literature (1999, xxiii, 11).

43 See Robbins 1999, 13; Derrida 1978, 84.

44 "The way of thinking proposed here does not fail to recognize being or treat it, ridiculously and pretentiously, with disdain, as the fall from a higher order or disorder. On the contrary, it is on the basis of proximity that being takes on its just meaning. In the indirect ways of illeity, in the anarchical provocation which ordains me to the other, is imposed the way which leads to thematization, and to an act of consciousness" (Levinas 1998, 16).

45 One of the most powerful examples of that which does not, cannot, enter the text is physical pain, according to Scarry in The Body in Pain (1985).

46 This reflection brings to mind a similar question posed by Alain Badiou in Ethics: "There is always only one question in the ethic of truths: how will I, as some-one, continue to exceed my own being? How will I link the things I know, in a consistent fashion, via the effects of being seized by the not-known? . . . How will I continue to think?" (2002, 50).

ONE ❧ DIAGNOSING "JEWISHNESS"

1 "El objetivo de este libro es dar cuenta del pacto de sentido entre literatura, nacionalismo, y saber médico en que se fundan las ficciones exclusivas del naturalismo argentino y su visión corporalizada de la nación" (Nouzeilles 2000, 11–12, emphasis added).

2 I am, of course, referring to the political thinker Benedict Anderson's seminal work, Imagined Communities, though I am concerned not only with the construction of national identities but with continental, regional, ethnic, aesthetic, ideological, and individual subjectivities as well.

3 Musselwhite, to name one example, undertakes a psychoanalytical reading of the Ashanti interlude as the repressed 'other' side of the novel.

4 I borrow the term lacrimogenous from Sylvia Molloy (1984, 36).

5 Unless noted otherwise, all literary translations from Spanish to English are by Citlali Martínez. When a published English translation of a text is used, this is indicated by its accompanying page number.

6 Colombia was "practically the only Latin American country that did not achieve some kind of national consolidation in the nineteenth century" (Sommer 1991, 178).

7 Paradoxically, very few Jews lived in Buenos Aires at the time that Martel wrote *La bolsa* (Fishburn 1981).

8 "El corazón de las corrientes humanas que circulaban por las calles centrales como circula la sangre en las venas, era la Bolsa de Comercio" (At the heart of the human currents that circulated through the main streets, like blood circulates through the veins, was the Stock Exchange) (7).

9 For an original take on the issue of the parasitic, see Derrida's *Of Hospitality*, in which he elaborates on the relationship between parasite and host within the context of "hospitality" (2000, 59). In the propagandistic film *Der Ewige Jude* the "Jew" is described as a parasite on the host country, a metaphor which leads to the necessary extermination of the Jews.

10 It is relevant to note here that Dr. Glow is an attorney, not a medical doctor. Yet, I would still argue that his name nevertheless signifies health.

11 Beyond its very useful application to a number of fin-de-siècle Argentine texts, the term "fictions of exclusion" fails to sufficiently address the multiplicity of constructions of Jewishness in late-nineteenth- and twentieth-century Latin American fiction. I would argue that Jewishness does not always represent the margins of society, but rather appears in liminal spaces, and thus simultaneously becomes more threatening and more nuanced in its symbolic forms.

12 I will analyze the figure of Efraín in greater detail in chapter 3.

13 This act could be read as sending him to the cosmopolitan center from which his father came; in this sense, he is simultaneously assimilating *and* remaining other through this overdetermined voyage to London.

14 "The famous Lacanian motto not to give way on one's desire [ne pas céder sur son desir]—is aimed at the fact that we must not obliterate the distance separating the Real from its symbolization: it is this surplus of the Real over every symbolization that functions as the object-cause of desire. To come to terms with this surplus (or, more precisely, leftover) means to acknowledge a fundamental deadlock ('antagonism'), a kernel resisting symbolic integration-dissolution" (Žižek 1989, 3).

15 Molloy elaborates this act of translation from the perspective of the translator: "Here is the poet (or the event), and here am I, the witness, to interpret him (or it) for you" (1996b, 373). Her essay details the way in which Martí "repackages" Whitman for the Latin American reader.

16 While I am principally interested in exploring the Latin American reception of Nordau's work, Linda Maik (1989) analyzes the North American response to the theories proposed in *Degeneration*.

17 Julio Ramos has addressed this paradoxical dynamic in his book *Divergent Modernities* (2001), in which he discusses the autonomization of the field of literature, as well as the inherent impossibility of its institutionalization.

18 For more on Nordau's "romance" with Olga Alexeevna Novikova, see chapter 3 of Stanislawski's *Zionism and the Fin de Siècle* (2001).

19 I am thinking of postcolonial theory on the politicization of and the inherent inequality in the opposition North-South, elaborated by the Latin American cultural critic Neil Larsen (1995), among many others.

20 "The idea of freeing the world of moral disease was a radical version of the nineteenth-century concept of respectability, which linked the strength of civilization with the need for social coherence and sexual control. Supported by the entire weight of positive science, this illusion was in particular internalized by the assimilated Jewish *Bildungsbürgertum* [including Nordau]. If we accept that in the novel everything hinges on *Bildung* and *Sittlichkeit*, then nervousness, femininity, cowardliness and even genius referred to what were understood as the main attributes of the decadent, Jewish body" (van der Laarse 1999, 21).

21 For a discussion of the construction of aesthetic space in Spanish-American modernismo, consult Gerard Aching's *The Politics of Spanish American "Modernismo"* (1997), an analysis of the reino interior in modernista writers such as Rubén Darío. Aching details the way in which these writers utilize the aesthetic as an alternative entrance into modernity and modern subjectivity.

22 "Por una parte, Verlaine, el 'padre y maestro mágico' del 'Responso [a Verlaine]'; por la otra, Nordau, que llama a Verlaine 'el líder más famoso de los simbolistas' para concluir que es también un 'degenerado repulsivo.'"

23 Benigno Trigo acknowledges the contradictory nature of Darío's rhetorical performance in *Los raros*, referring to his "simultáneo uso y crítica del discurso alienista" (simultaneous use and criticism of the *alienista* discourse) (1994, 192).

24 Montero compares this maneuver to that of Enrique Gómez Carillo, who attempted to win over the cultural elite by showing his affinity toward the Parisian Decadents as well as the Latin American bourgeoisie by distancing himself from the very same degenerate poets (1996, 822–23).

25 José Ingenieros is not the only fin-de-siècle Latin American intellectual to pay Nordau a visit in Paris: the Guatemalan chronicler Enrique Gómez Carrillo also relates his "Visita a Max Nordau" in the 1898 *Almas y cerebros* (Souls and brains).

26 "El científico Ingenieros reconoce en el literato Darío . . . a un 'amigo de observar anomalías y rarezas'" (1996a, 196).

27 "La intersección de disciplinas y discursos en la que Ingenieros elabora sus diagnósticos, intersección en la que la literatura desempeña un papel preponderante" (1996a, 190).

28 Gabriel Giorgi evaluates the interaction of distinct discourses in *De sobremesa*: "El discurso médico debate con el discurso artístico las condiciones de apropiación del poder o la autoridad cultural alrededor de las relaciones entre diferencia y normalidad, enfermedad y salud, síntoma e invención estética" (medical discourse debates with artistic discourse over the conditions of appropriating cultural power or authority regarding relations between difference and normality, sickness and health, symptom and aesthetic invention) (1999, 1). Sylvia Molloy, for her part,

focuses on the "impersonation" of Marie Bashkirtseff in her 1997 essay "Voice Snatching: *De Sobremesa*, Hysteria, and the Impersonation of Marie Bashkirtseff."

29 "Esa concepción de la vida sirve de base a la estética de Max Nordau, que clasifica las verdaderas obras de arte como productos patológicos y a la asquerosa utopía socialista que en los falansterios con que sueña para el futuro repartirá por igual pitanza y vestidos a los genios y a los idiotas. . . . ¡La realidad! ¡La vida real! ¡Los hombre prácticos! . . . ¡Horror!" (That conception of life serves as the basis for the aesthetics of Max Nordau, who classifies true works of art as pathological products, and for the disgusting socialist utopia that in the phalansteries he dreams of for the future will dole out equal rations and clothing to geniuses and idiots. . . . Reality! Real life! Practical men! . . . Horrors [141]) (138–39).

30 I am thinking about Fernández's national political project, for example, in addition to the external pressure he receives from his friend Saenz to be productive.

31 In both works there is a tension between author, narrator, and protagonist, all of whom overlap and invent one another in a complex system of enunciation.

32 The idea of the nation as a disease and, more specifically, as a smoking addiction, encounters an uncanny echo in the following *Jerusalem Report* interview with an Argentine woman who emigrated to Israel during the economic crisis of 1999: "'I think of Argentina as being like a cigarette,' says Kuschevatzky, explaining her motive for leaving. 'I crave it, but it was killing me.' Systematically, every 5–10 years, she relates, something bad happened there: a war, or a dictatorship, or an economic crisis. 'But what's happening there now is different, debilitating, like suffering from a virus'" (Friedman 2002, 18).

33 Paris also represents the origin of life itself, according to many middle-class Argentine parents, who, according to the narrator, struggle to answer their children's inquiries about where babies come from: "Los nenes vienen de París y andá a jugar afuera porque ahora tengo que hacer" (Children come from Paris; now go and play outside because I'm busy) (14).

34 "Absolute hospitality requires that I open up my home and that I give not only to the foreigner . . . but to the absolute, unknown, anonymous other, and that I *give place* to them, that I let them come, that I let them arrive, and take place in the place I offer them, without asking of them, either reciprocity or even their name (Derrida 2000, 25).

35 For a discussion of the female body as liminal space, see Luce Irigaray's *An Ethics of Sexual Difference* (1993).

36 The Jew was excluded from becoming a foot soldier specifically in "the popular militia, which was the hallmark of all of the liberal movements of the midcentury" (Gilman 1991, 39–40).

37 In *Las genealogías* Glantz establishes a questionable relationship between Jewishness and disease, recalling that when her Uncle Albert "quien en Filadelfia murió de cancer dejando como único testamento un papel donde aseguraba que el cancer no es hereditario" (died of cancer in Philadelphia, the only will he left was a piece of paper assuring all heirs that cancer is not hereditary [40]) (20). By

negating the hereditary nature of the illness, of course, Uncle Albert (not to mention Glantz herself) is affirming the very link he ostensibly denies.

38 DiAntonio and Glickman 1993; Goldberg 2000; Igel 1997; Liwerant, Gojman de Backal, and Soriano 1999; Senkman 2000; Bernardo Sorj 1997; Bila Sorj 1997; Sosnowski 2000; and Stavans 2001.

TWO ⅋ THE SCENE OF THE TRANSACTION

1 First identified by the French poet Charles Baudelaire, a flâneur is a gentleman who wanders the streets of a city, observing urban public life from a distance without engaging.

2 Like prostitution, gambling resides on the margins of the law; further, gamblers resemble investors within the context of capitalism. Benjamin highlights the link between gambling and capitalism by quoting Paul Lafargue, who points out that investment in the stock exchange is often described as "playing the market" (quoted in Benjamin 1999, 497).

3 Though certainly immigration in general is mentioned as a threat: "150.000 inmigrantes al año significan algo. Pronto la cifra ascenderá a 300.000" (150,000 immigrants a year is significant. Soon the figure will ascend to 300,000) (18).

4 While the medieval Christian idea of the blood libel is one of the earlier forms of this conspiracy theory, it is consolidated in the Protocols of the Elders of Zion, a forged text that is still widely circulated today (see Cohn 1967).

5 The Brazilian Revolution of 1930 was not, like the Cuban Revolution, a revolution "from below" or from the Left, but rather initiated by oligarchies unsatisfied with the previous government, together with radical sectors of the Brazilian military. Vargas's administration became "fascist" with the implementation of the Estado Novo (New State) in 1937. For more on this period, see Jordan M. Young's The Brazilian Revolution of 1930 and the Aftermath and Boris Fausto's A revolução de 1930.

6 All translations from Portuguese to English, unless otherwise stated, are my own.

7 This line refers to an actual event in Brazilian soccer history.

8 The nickname "Russinho" (little Russian) is a term of affection for children of mixed-race descent who have light hair; it is interesting that the idea of the foreign is used to differentiate racially fair children from their more "Brazilian" relatives or friends, regardless of the fact that their nationality is identical.

9 See Freyre's Casa-grande e senzala (1943) and Santiago's The Space In-between (2001).

10 Founded in 1931 and directed by Victoria Ocampo, Sur published the writings of well-known intellectuals such as Adolfo Bioy Casares, José Ortega y Gasset, Octavio Paz, Juan Carlos Onetti, Alfonso Reyes, to name only a few contributors.

The election of Juan Domingo Perón in 1946 ushered in a period of populist nationalism, the corporatization of labor unions, and—relevant to my discussion here—the offering of asylum to Nazi criminals fleeing Europe after the war's end. Perón cultivated wide support among the working classes, and his political base spanned the ideological Right and Left for decades. For more on the cultural and political landscape of Peronist Argentina, see Mariano Ben Plotkin's *Mañana es San Perón* (2003).

11 For more on Borges's use of the Jewish kabbalistic tradition in his work, see Aizenberg 1984, Alazraki 1988, and Sosnowski 1976.

12 Sander Gilman dedicates a chapter of *The Jew's Body* to an analysis of "The Jewish Murderer" (1991, 104–27).

13 I would like to thank Daniel Balderston for his helpful comments on earlier drafts of my analysis of "Emma Zunz." Any errors or oversights are, of course, my own.

14 Ludmer points out that while Emma evades state justice, she abides by a divine justice instead: "The woman that kills represents all 'justices': that of God, that of the father, class justice, racial justice and sexual justice. And she finally mocks state justice. . . . Before justice, she stages a farce of the truth" (2004, 132).

15 In a highly original reading of "Emma Zunz" Juan Duchesne-Winter interprets Emma's actions as an *ethical* response to the call of the other: by recognizing herself as the addressee of the letter, Emma constitutes herself as an ethical subject, which is made possible only within the context of fiction (2000, 188–89, 198).

16 For a discussion of the phenomenon of "luxury prostitution" in late-nineteenth- and early-twentieth-century São Paulo, see chapter 1 of Margareth Rago's *Os prazeres da noite*. Rago maintains that while prostitution certainly represented a marginal (and more public) form of femininity, so-called luxury prostitutes (*prostitutas de luxo*) were seen as offering a more French (or more broadly European), "superior" cultural experience. In particular, foreign prostitutes were emblems not only of an exotic sexuality but also of modernity itself.

17 *Pré-modernismo* (the Brazilian counterpart of Spanish-American *modernismo*) is a literary generation that spanned the last two decades of the nineteenth century and the first two decades of the twentieth. Not to be confused with Spanish-American modernism, Brazilian modernismo (initiated in the 1920s) would be the rough equivalent of the Spanish-American *vanguardia*. While the former was heavily influenced by the Parnassian, Symbolist, and Decadent movements of the time, the latter sought to create more "local" cultural products (though they, too, were impacted by European avant-garde movements such as Expressionism, Futurism, and Cubism).

18 The choice of pseudonym by José Maria de Toledo Malta has been treated in Brait 1996 (136–37) and Aparecida Ferreira 1998 (27).

19 This edition was published as part of a larger project on the topic of Brazilian pre-modernism, which included a seminar, an exposition, the publication of a volume of scholarly essays on the literary period, as well as new editions of pre-modernist texts like *Madame Pommery*.

20 Rago points out that the Zwi Migdal exercised considerably more influence in Buenos Aires than in Brazil (1991, 286).

21 Oswald de Andrade's "Manifesto Antropofágico" (1970) and Mário de Andrade's *Macunaíma* (1984) are two examples of the parodic, cannibalizing trend in this avant-garde literary movement.

22 Like Jorge Isaacs's Efraín, Ida would not be considered Jewish by Orthodox and Conservative rabbinical authorities because of her Catholic mother. Yet I would like to insist that her "Jewishness" (inherited from her father) as well as her ethnic hybridity are traits central to her symbolic value in Tácito's text.

23 "Ida . . . peregrinou por cidades e nações de toda a Europa, a negociar os beijos e os sorrisos, como a mesma finura e com o mesmo talento que revelara de princípio" (Ida . . . wandered through cities and countries all through Europe, negotiating kisses and smiles, with the same delicacy and the same talent she revealed from the beginning) (54).

24 "Encasquetou-se-lhe a idéia de 'fazer América.' Só pensava na América" (55).

25 Madame Pommery has a rough beginning in Brazil: she participates in spectacles of Roman fights with other women, in which she turns into a celebrity by being named "heavy weight" champion. Later, she opens the Paradis Retrouvé, a house in decay with pretensions of a "school of refinement and society." Ironically, this refinement is realized through prostitution; in this way, society is paradoxically constituted through vulgarity (Aparecida Ferreira 1998, 43).

26 For an analysis of Tácito's allusions to *Madame Bovary*, see Brait 1996, 132–33.

27 *Paulistana* refers to an inhabitant of São Paulo. It is also used as an adjective to describe things related to that city.

28 "[A] humanidade vai melhorando graças a Noé, Dionísio e Baco, em vez de degenerar" (Humanity is improving thanks to Noah, Dionysus and Bacchus, instead of degenerating) (112).

29 For a more thorough discussion of the theories of eugenics and social engineering that became fashionable during this period, see Nancy Leys Stepan's "The Hour of Eugenics" (1991).

30 Here I am thinking of Baudelaire, Verlaine, Darío, and José Asunción Silva, among others.

31 Borges parodies the division between the two groups in his "La inútil discusión de Boedo y Florida," *La Prensa* (Bueno Aires), 30 September 1928, 5.

32 In her book *La broma literaria en nuestros días* (1979) the Latin American literary critic Estelle Irizarry suggests that Castelnuovo may have hidden his identity because he suspected that Clara Beter did not, in fact, exist.

33 Bernard McGuirk argues that the "blind spot" of Emma's "perfect crime" is that she leaves Loewenthal's blood-stained glasses in plain view. He suggests that this act reveals not only the imperfection of the crime but also the open quality of the text: "In offering to detective (or reader) the flaw in a 'perfect' crime, 'Emma Zunz' invites further speculation, refuses the closure of its own text, supplementing the already read with the trace of further writing" (1997, 202).

34 While I will not discuss it here, the figure of the "compadre" is also worth considering. See Jaime Alazraki's analysis (1975) of this figure in Borges and Cortázar.

35 In another crucial reading of the "feminine" in Borges, Edna Aizenberg details the exceptional agency of Emma Zunz in her essay "Emma Zunz: A Kabbalistic Heroine in Borges's Fiction" (1983).

36 Brant also traces this triangular structure in "El muerto," which I will not detail here.

37 In addition to Dove's brilliant analysis of "El Sur" (2004) are the well-known discussions of the problem of the gauchesque in Borges by Josefina Ludmer (1988), Beatriz Sarlo (2003), and Ricardo Piglia (1986).

38 "La idea de que 'nuestro patrimonio es el universo' sintentiza en cinco palabras el argumento de 'El escritor argentino y la tradición' y, junto con muchas otras alusiones universalistas, apuntala la postulación de un horizonte cosmopolita para la práctica discursiva borgeana" (The idea that "our patrimony is the universe" synthesizes in five words the argument of "The Argentine writer and tradition" and, together with many other universalist allusions, points in the direction of a cosmopolitan horizon for a Borgean discursive practice) (Mariano Siskind, "Margins of the Universal: Latin American Modernity and the Discourses of Globalization" [unpublished manuscript, n.d.], 5).

THREE ❧ TEXTUAL CONVERSIONS

An earlier, Spanish-language version of a section of this chapter was published as "Conversiones textuales, inquisiciones transatlánticas: La figura de la cristiana nueva en Dias Gomes y Antonio Gala," *Journal of Spanish Cultural Studies* 6.3 (2005): 259–69.

1 While not all New Christians were former Jews (i.e., some were pagans), I use the term here to refer specifically to Jewish converts to Christianity. In each of the texts I analyze in this chapter, the figure of the New Christian is a descendant of Jews or a Jewish convert herself or himself.

2 James Shapiro details the way in which Paul struggled to conceive of the notion of "spiritual circumcision" (as well as, paradoxically, spiritual and physical uncircumcision), which would maintain the human covenant with God while rewriting or erasing the specifically Jewish nature of this pact. (See Shapiro 1996, esp. "The Pound of Flesh.")

3 The converso (and Jewish) "problem" was unique to the Spanish and Portuguese Inquisitions, as the medieval historian Edward Peters discusses in *Inquisition*: "Unlike Spain, the Roman Inquisition did not primarily—or even significantly—deal with any phenomenon remotely comparable to that of the *conversos*. Although the Roman Inquisition, like earlier inquisitions, had certain authority over Jews and, of course, total authority over Judaizing Christians, the Roman Inquisition never faced the *converso* problem in any significant way. Indeed, many Spanish and Portuguese *conversos*, fleeing Spain and Portugal, often found themselves in Italy, where some were able to live as Jews again. The chief target of the newly founded Roman Inquisition was the 'heresy' of Protestantism" (1988, 110).

4 Solomón's daughter is named for the biblical Esther, whose name in Hebrew connotes hiddenness. Born Hadassah, the biblical figure is renamed Esther when she enters the royal harem, hence leaving her Jewishness behind. She becomes

queen, a move which leads to the liberation of the Jews, on marrying the non-Jew Ahashverus.

5 Sylvia Molloy refers to the significance of the father figure in her essay "Paraíso perdido y economía terrenal en María," suggesting that "si el destierro y la vuelta imposible constituyen el tema central de María, es necesario recordar que la figura paterna—idealizado judío errante—es su núcleo generador" (if exile and the impossibility of returning constitute the central theme of María, it is necessary to remember that the father figure—an idealization of the Wandering Jew—is its generating nucleus) (1984, 46).

6 I would like to thank Vivaldo Andrade dos Santos for his generous help with translating "A cristã nova" into English.

7 For more on the period surrounding abolition in Brazil, see Andrews et al. 1988.

8 Brazil is never named explicitly, perhaps because the action is situated in the early eighteenth century. However, the lyrical voice speaks from a later moment, ostensibly that of the publication of the poem at the end of the nineteenth century: "Guanabara ainda / Não era a flor aberta / Da nossa idade" (Guanabara was still / not the open flower / of our time) (Machado de Assis, 1962–71, 1.3.13–12). This temporal chasm between lyrical subject and object represents yet another displacement in the poem, this time on the level of form. Moreover, the "nossa" (our) seems to imply an inclusive identity between lyrical voice and reader, for whom Brazil's existence as a nation is already a reality.

9 Numbers indicate part, stanza, and lines.

10 While it is implied that the father has converted along with his daughter, he has not fully left his Jewishness behind, a dynamic that is echoed in O Santo Inquérito.

11 This ostensibly clear theological vision will be problematized in the next stanza.

12 A crypto-Jew is a New Christian who continues to secretly observe Jewish law.

13 While the repeated conversions—literal and figurative—of Branca make her a particularly convertible signifier, this term proves useful in thinking about the rhetorical treatment of all of the Jewish converts analyzed in this chapter.

14 Guerrilheiro refers to a member of a leftist armed militant group. There were many small groups of this sort in Brazil at the time (unlike, for example, in Nicaragua or Guatemala, where there were large, centralized guerrilla movements). For more on this, consult Jacob Gorender's Combate nas Trevas (1987) and Archbishop Paulo Evaristo Arns's preface to Brasil: Nunca mais (1985). The Machiguengas are an indigenous tribe from the Amazonian region of Peru.

15 Jews were disproportionately targeted in Argentina's Dirty War as well as by the Brazilian military governments of the same period, though it was not a central aspect of the Brazilian dictatorships. See Mário Sérgio de Morães's O ocaso da ditadura, caso Herzog (2006) on the Vladimir Herzog case in Brazil, as well as Jacobo Timerman's Preso sin nombre, celda sin número (2004) for a discussion of the role of anti-Semitism in the Dirty War.

16 For a more detailed analysis of the interpellation of the narrator, see Sommer 1996, 92.

17 In a lecture he delivered at New York University on 8 December 2003, Vargas Llosa made a distinction between "Third World" and "First World" artists, maintaining that in developed countries art was merely another form of entertainment.

FOUR ✺ THE LIMITS OF REPRESENTATION

An earlier version of this chapter was published as "Writing the Absent Face: 'Jewishness' and the Limits of Representation in Borges, Piglia and Chejfec," *Modern Language Notes* 122.2 (2007): 350–70.

1 Three years later, Louis published a second essay on the topic, in which she suggests that Borges "no intenta . . . demostrar la validez de su posición, simplemente expone la incoherencia argumentativa de la de los otros, las similitudes entre sistemas de pensamiento, la historia de ciertos conceptos" (does not try . . . to demonstrate the validity of his position, he merely displays the argumentative incoherence of others' positions, the similarities between systems of thought, the history of certain concepts) (2000, 62).

2 Aizenberg explains that "Deutsches Requiem" was "ignored for many years—it was either unmentioned or roundly dismissed" (2005, 34).

3 Louis points out that by sketching this philosophical genealogy, Borges highlights the attraction felt by many German intellectuals to the early forms of National Socialism (2000, 63n12).

4 "Se murmura que las consecuencias de esa herida fueron muy graves (*Nota del editor*)" (It is rumored that the wound had extremely serious consequences [ed.] [64n1]) (85n1).

5 "En el terreno de la ficción, en uno de los pocos cuentos de los años cuarenta que tratan explícitamente del nazismo, 'Deutsches Requiem,' se pone en escena un combate por imponer una verdad, mediante una estrategia *oblicua*: la de la exhibición de la versión (presentada como verdad) de un criminal nazi" (In the terrain of fiction, in one of the few stories written in the forties that explicitly deal with Nazism, "Deutsches Requiem," a fight to impose truth is staged through an *oblique* strategy: that of displaying the version [presented as truth] of a Nazi criminal) (Louis 2000, 63).

6 Patrick Dove points out that the opening question, "¿Hay una historia?" could be read as "Is there a story?" "Is there one story?" "Is there a history?" or "Is there one history?" (2004, 225).

7 Isabel Quintana also deals with this thematic in Piglia in her excellent study of the literary codification of "experience" in postdictatorship narrative, *Figuras de la experiencia en el fin de siglo* (2001).

8 Yet another example of Tardewski's marginality can be found in the fact that his only published article is in Spanish and, therefore, illegible to the author himself (Piglia 2000, 179).

9 The second alternate outcome of his life—finishing his doctorate and becoming a professor of philosophy at some British or North American university—imagines

a successful turn of events, whether viewed in comparison to Tardewski's failed intellectual endeavors in Argentina or to a far worse hypothetical outcome at the hands of the Nazis, and points to what "could have been" had the destruction of European culture not occurred.

10 Kafka, of course, is the more "empirically" Jewish and, at least posthumously, more successful version of Tardewski: like his less famous counterpart, Kafka possesses a strange last name ("cacophonous" [Piglia 1994, 177]) and speaks a minority language (German in predominantly Slavic Prague).

11 Of course, as are nearly all the assertions in *Respiración artificial*, the alleged connection between Hitler and Kafka is posited as a "working hypothesis" (Piglia 1994, 182), ultimately unprovable.

12 "Primera historia" has been translated as "First Hi/story" in order to take into account the double meaning of the Spanish word.

13 Emphasis has been added for all words in italics.

14 Gabriela Basterra's analysis of the relationship between ethics and politics is particularly fruitful: "Politics understood in the broadest sense is already ethical, already demanded in the demand. . . . If I am a political subject at all, it is because I am already obeying a demand to which I did not choose to respond, because I am acting on the decision that another has made in me. The problem is not how to bridge ethics and politics, for ethics is already political, and it exists for the sake of the political. My problem is, rather, how to make the ethical demand inflect every political act in each singular context, beyond socially sanctioned normativity. This would be a politics that exceeds the political space of reciprocity and representation. It would be a politics beyond theoretical consciousness and even beyond commitment" (2004, 168).

❧ BIBLIOGRAPHY

Aching, Gerard. 1997. *The Politics of Spanish American "Modernismo": By Exquisite Design.* Cambridge: Cambridge University Press.

Aizenberg, Edna. 1983. "Emma Zunz: A Kabbalistic Heroine in Borges's Fiction." *Studies in American Jewish Literature* 3: 223–35.

———. 1984. *The Aleph Weaver: Biblical, Kabbalistic and Judaic Elements in Borges.* Potomac: Scripta Humanistica.

———. 1997. "Postmodern or Post-Auschwitz: Borges and the Limits of Representation." *Variaciones Borges* 3: 141–52.

———. 2005. "Deutsches Requiem 2005." *Variaciones Borges* 20: 33–57.

Alazraki, Jaime. 1975. "Dos soluciones estilísticas al tema del compadre en Borges y Cortázar." In *Estudios sobre los cuentos de Julio Cortázar,* ed. David Lagmanovich, 23–39. Barcelona: Ediciones Hispam.

———. 1988. *Borges and the Kabbalah: And Other Essays on His Fiction and Poetry.* Cambridge: Cambridge University Press.

Alencar, José Martiniano de. 1967. *As minas de prata*. Rio de Janeiro: Edições de Ouro. (Orig. pub. 1865.)

Alves, Castro. 1997. "Hebraia" (1866). In *Espumas Flumantes*. São Paulo: Ateliê Editorial.

Anderson, Benedict R. 1991. *Imagined Communities: Reflections on the Origin and Spread of Nationalism*. London: Verso.

Andrade, Mário de. 1984. *Macunaíma*. Translated by E. A. Goodland. New York: Random House. (Orig. pub. 1928.)

Andrade, Oswald de. 1970. *Obras completas*. Rio de Janeiro: Civilização Brasileira.

Andrews, George Reid, Hebe Maria Mattos De Castro, Seymour Drescher, Robert M. Levine, and Rebecca J. Scott. 1988. *The Abolition of Slavery and the Aftermath of Emancipation in Brazil*. Durham, N.C.: Duke University Press.

Aparecida Ferreira, Sandra. 1998. "Entre a biblioteca e o bordel: A sátira narrativa em Madame Pommery, de Hilário Tácito." Master's thesis, Universidade de São Paulo.

Arendt, Hannah. 1962. *The Origins of Totalitarianism*. London: Allen.

Arlt, Roberto. 1992. *Los siete locos*. Madrid: Ediciones Cátedra. (Orig. pub. 1929.)

Arns, Paulo Evaristo. 1985. Preface to *Brasil: Nunca mais*. Petrópolis: Vozes.

Avelar, Idelber. 1995. "Cómo respiran los ausentes: La narrativa de Ricardo Piglia." *Modern Language Notes* 110.2: 416–32.

———. 1999. *The Untimely Present: Postdictatorial Latin American Fiction and the Task of Mourning*. Durham, N.C.: Duke University Press.

Badiou, Alain. 2002. *Ethics: An Essay on the Understanding of Evil*. Translated by Peter Hallward. London: Verso. (Orig. pub. 1993.)

Balderston, Daniel. 1995. "The 'Fecal Dialectic': Homosexual Panic and the Origin of Writing in Borges." In *¿Entiendes? Queer Readings, Hispanic Writings*, ed. Emilie Bergman and Paul Julian Smith, 29–45. Durham, N.C.: Duke University Press.

Basterra, Gabriela. 2004. *Seductions of Fate: Tragic Subjectivity, Ethics, Politics*. London: Palgrave Macmillan.

Bauman, Zygmunt. 1991. *Modernity and the Holocaust*. Ithaca, N.Y.: Cornell University Press.

———. 1998. "Allosemitism: Premodern, Modern, Postmodern." In *Modernity, Culture and "the Jew,"* ed. Bryan Cheyette and Laura Marcus, 188–96. Stanford, Calif.: Stanford University Press.

Benjamin, Walter. 1977. *The Origins of the German Tragic Drama*. Translated by John Osborne. London: Verso.

———. 1999. *The Arcades Project*. Translated by Howard Eiland and Kevin McLaughlin. Cambridge, Mass.: Belknap Press.

Bennington, Geoffrey. 1998. "Lyotard and 'the Jews.'" In *Modernity, Culture and "the Jew,"* ed. Bryan Cheyette and Laura Marcus. Stanford, Calif.: Stanford University Press.

Beter, Clara (Israel Zeitlin). 1998. *Versos de una. . . .* Rosario, Argentina: Ameghino. (Orig. pub. 1926.)

Beverley, John, and José Oviedo. 1995. Introduction to *The Postmodernism Debate in Latin America*, ed. John Beverley, José Oviedo, and Michael Aronna, 1–17. Durham, N.C.: Duke University Press.

Borges, Dain. 1993. "Puffy, Ugly, Slothful, and Inert: Degeneration in Brazilian Social Thought, 1880–1940." *Latin American Studies* 25: 235–56.

Borges, Jorge Luis. 1957. "El escritor argentino y la tradición." In *Discusión*, 128–37. Buenos Aires: Emecé Editores. (Orig. pub. 1952.)

———. 1986a. "El Aleph" (1945). In *Ficciones—El Aleph—El informe de Brodie*, 169–74. Caracas: Biblioteca Ayacucho.

———. 1986b. "El fin" (1944). In *Ficciones—El Aleph—El informe de Brodie*, 80–82. Caracas: Biblioteca Ayacucho.

———. 1986c. "El muerto" (1946). In *Ficciones—El Aleph—El informe de Brodie*, 103–106. Caracas: Biblioteca Ayacucho.

———. 1986d. "El Sur" (1944). In *Ficciones—El Aleph—El informe de Brodie*, 86–90. Caracas: Biblioteca Ayacucho.

———. 1986e. "La intrusa" (1970). In *Ficciones—El Aleph—El informe de Brodie*, 182–84. Caracas: Biblioteca Ayacucho.

———. 1998a. "The Dead Man." In *Collected Fictions*. Translated by Andrew Hurley, 196–200. New York: Viking.

———. 1998b. "The End." In *Collected Fictions*. Translated by Andrew Hurley, 168–70. New York: Viking.

———. 1998c. "The South." In *Collected Fictions*. Translated by Andrew Hurley, 174–79. New York: Viking.

———. 1999a. "Deutsches Requiem" (1946). In *El Aleph*, 83–91. Barcelona: Galaxia Gutenberg y Círculo de Lectores.

———. 1999b. "Emma Zunz" (1948). In *El Aleph*, 59–66. Barcelona: Galaxia Gutenberg y Círculo de Lectores.

———. 2004a. "Deutsches Requiem." In *The Aleph and Other Stories*. Translated by Andrew Hurley, 62–68. New York: Penguin.

———. 2004b. "Emma Zunz." In *The Aleph and Other Stories*. Translated by Andrew Hurley, 44–50. New York: Penguin.

Boyarin, Daniel. 1997. *Unheroic Conduct: The Rise of Heterosexuality and the Invention of the Jewish Man*. Berkeley: University of California Press.

———. 1998. "Goyim Naches: The Manliness of the Mentsh." In *Modernity, Culture and "the Jew,"* ed. Bryan Cheyette and Laura Marcus, 63–87. Stanford, Calif.: Stanford University Press.

Boyarin, Jonathan, and Daniel Boyarin, eds. 1997. *Jews and Other Differences: The New Jewish Cultural Studies*. Minneapolis: University of Minnesota Press.

Brait, Beth. 1996. *Ironia em perspectiva polifônica*. Campinas, São Paulo: Editora da Universidade Estudual de Campinas.

Brant, Herbert J. 1999. "The Queer Use of Communal Women in Borges' 'El muerto' and 'La intrusa.'" *Hispanófila* 125: 37–50.

Bravo, Pilar, and Mario Paoletti, eds. 1999. *Borges verbal*. Buenos Aires: Emece.

Brunner, José Joaquín. 1992. *América Latina: Cultura y modernidad*. Mexico City: Editorial Grijalbo.

Butler, Judith. 1998. *The Psychic Life of Power*. Stanford, Calif.: Stanford University Press.

Carneiro, Maria Luiza Tucci. 1988. *O anti-semitismo na era Vargas: Fantasmas de uma gera-ção (1930–1945)*. São Paulo: Editora Brasiliense.

Castillo, Debra A. 1995. "Postmodern Indigenism: 'Quetzalcoatl and All That.'" *Modern Fiction Studies* 41: 35–73.

Castro, Américo. 1984. *España en su historia: Cristianos, moros y judíos*. Barcelona: Editorial Crítica.

Castro Leal, Antonio. 1959. "Biografía." In *La hija del judío*, vol. 1, by Justo Sierra O'Reilly. Mexico City: Editorial Porrúa.

Chejfec, Sergio. 1999. *Los planetas*. Buenos Aires: Alfaguara.

Cheyette, Bryan. 1993. *Constructions of "the Jew" in English Literature and Society: Racial Representations, 1875–1945*. Cambridge: Cambridge University Press.

Cheyette, Bryan, and Laura Marcus, eds. 1998. *Modernity, Culture and "the Jew."* Stanford, Calif.: Stanford University Press.

Cohn, Norman. 1967. *Warrant for Genocide: The Myth of the Jewish World-Conspiracy and the Protocols of the Elders of Zion*. London: Eyre and Spottiswoode.

Cony, Heitor Carlos. 1967. *Pessach: A travessia*. Rio de Janeiro: Editôra Civilização.

Cornejo Polar, Antonio. 1978. "El indigenismo y las literaturas heterogéneas: Su doble estatuto socio-cultural." *Revista de Crítica Latinoamericana* 7–8: 7–21.

———. 1994. *Escribir en el aire: Ensayo sobre la heterogeneidad socio-cultural en las literaturas andinas*. Lima: Editorial Horizonte.

———. 2000. "A Non-Dialectic Heterogeneity: The Subject and Discourse of Urban Migration in Modern Peru." In *Unforeseeable Americas: Questioning Cultural Hybridity in the Americas*, ed. Rita De Grandis and Zilà Bernd, 112–23. Critical Studies 13. Amsterdam: Rodopi.

Costigan, Lúcia Helena. 1998. "Exclusões (e inclusões) na literatura latino-americana: Índios, negros, e judeus." *Revista Iberoamericana* 182–83: 55–80.

Critchley, Simon. 1992. *The Ethics of Deconstruction: Derrida and Levinas*. West Lafayette, Ind.: Purdue University Press.

Critchley, Simon, and Robert Bernasconi, eds. 2002. *The Cambridge Companion to Levinas*. Cambridge: Cambridge University Press.

Cytrynowicz, Roney. 2002. "Além do Estado e da ideologia: Imigração judaica, Estado-Novo e Segunda Guerra Mundial." *Revista Brasileira de História* 22.44: 393–423.

Darío, Rubén. 1972. *Los raros*. San José, Costa Rica: Ciudad Universitaria Rodrigo Facio / Editorial Universitaria Centroamericana. (Orig. pub. 1896.)

Derrida, Jacques. 1978. "Violence and Metaphysics: An Essay on the Thought of Emmanuel Levinas." In *Writing and Difference*. Translated by Alan Bass, 79–153. Chicago: University of Chicago Press.

———. 2000. *Of Hospitality: Anne Dufourmantelle Invites Jacques Derrida to Respond*. Translated by Rachel Bowlby. Stanford, Calif.: Stanford University Press.

DiAntonio, Robert, and Nora Glickman, eds. 1993. *Tradition and Innovation: Reflections on Latin American Jewish Writing*. Albany: State University of New York Press.

Dias Gomes, Alfredo. 1966. *O Santo Inquérito*. Rio de Janeiro: Editôra Civilização Brasileira.

Dopico Black, Georgina. 2001. *Perfect Wives, Other Women: Adultery and Inquisition in Early Modern Spain*. Durham, N.C.: Duke University Press.

Dove, Patrick. 2004. *The Catastrophe of Modernity: Tragedy and the Nation in Latin American Literature*. Lewisburg, Penn.: Bucknell University Press.

Duchesne-Winter, Juan. 2000. "Después de la pérdida de la justicia: Una lectura zizekiana de 'Emma Zunz.'" *Variaciones Borges* 10: 185–202.

Eiland, Howard, and Kevin McLaughlin. 1999. "Translators' Foreword." In *The Arcades Project*, by Walter Benjamin. Translated by Howard Eiland and Kevin McLaughlin, ix–xiv. Cambridge, Mass.: Belknap Press.

Eliot, George. 1961. *Daniel Deronda*. New York: Harper. (Orig. pub. 1876.)

Elkin, Judith Laikin. 1998. *The Jews of Latin America*. New York: Holmes and Meier.

Fausto, Boris. 1986. *A revolução de 1930: Historiografia e história*. São Paulo: Brasiliense.

Finkielkraut, Alain. 1994. *The Imaginary Jew*. Translated by Kevin O'Neill and David Suchoff. Lincoln: University of Nebraska Press.

Fishburn, Evelyn. 1981. *The Portrayal of Immigration in Nineteenth Century Argentine Fiction (1845–1902)*. Berlin: Colloquium Verlag.

———. 1998. "Reflections on the Jewish Imaginary in the Fictions of Borges." *Variaciones Borges* 5: 145–56.

Fogwill, Rodolfo Enrique. 1998. *Vivir afuera*. Buenos Aires: Editorial Sudamericana.

Fonseca, Guido. 1982. *História da Prostituição em São Paulo*. São Paulo: Resenha Universitária.

Foot Hardman, Francisco. 1997. "São Paulo de Pommery." In *Madame Pommery*, by Hilário Tácito, 9–11. Rio de Janeiro: Fundação Casa de Rui Barbosa.

Freud, Sigmund. 1959. "The 'Uncanny.'" In *Sigmund Freud: Collected Papers*. Translated by Joan Riviere, 4:368–407. New York: Basic Books.

Freyre, Gilberto. 1943. *Casa-grande e senzala: Formação da família brasileira sob o regime de economia patriarcal*. Rio de Janeiro: J. Olympio. (Orig. pub. 1933.)

———. 1964. *The Masters and the Slaves: A Study in the Development of Brazilian Civilization*. Translated by Samuel Putnam. New York: Random House.

Friedman, Ina. "So Happy To Be Here." *Jerusalem Report*, 11 March 2002: 18.

Futoransky, Luisa. 1986. *De pe a pa: De Pekín a París*. Barcelona: Editorial Anagrama.

———. 1999. *Son cuentos chinos*. Buenos Aires: Editorial Planeta. (Orig. pub. 1983.)

Gala, Antonio. 1983. *Las cítaras colgadas de los árboles*. Madrid: Preyson. (Orig. pub. 1974.)

Garb, Tamar. 1995. Introduction to *The Jew in the Text: Modernity and the Construction of Identity*, ed. Linda Nochlin and Tamar Garb. London: Thames and Hudson.

García Canclini, Néstor. 1989. *Culturas híbridas: Estrategias para entrar y salir de la modernidad*. Mexico: Grijalbo.

———. 1995. *Hybrid Cultures: Strategies for Entering and Leaving Modernity*. Translated by Christopher L. Chiappari and Silvia L. López. Minneapolis: University of Minnesota Press.

García Márquez, Gabriel. 1994. *Del amor y otros demonios*. Buenos Aires: Editorial Sudamericana.

Gerchunoff, Alberto. 1968. *Los gauchos judíos*. Buenos Aires: Centro Editor de América Latina. (Orig. pub. 1910.)

Gilman, Sander. 1985. *Difference and Pathology: Stereotypes of Sexuality, Race and Madness*. Ithaca, N.Y.: Cornell University Press.

———. 1991. *The Jew's Body*. New York: Routledge.

Giorgi, Gabriel. 1999. "Nombrar la enfermedad: Médicos y artistas alrededor del cuerpo masculino en *De sobremesa*, de José Asunción Silva." *Ciberletras* 1. http://www.lehman.cuny.edu/.

Glantz, Margo. 1991a. *The Family Tree*. Translated by Susan Bassnett. London: Serpent's Tail.

———. 1991b. "Zapatos: Andante con variaciones." *Debate Feminista* 2: 203–13.

———. 1997. *Las genealogías*. Mexico City: Alfaguara. (Orig. pub. 1981.)

———. 1999. "Shoes: Andante, with Variations." Translated by Elizabeth Rosa Horan. In *The House of Memory: Stories by Jewish Women Writers of Latin America*, ed. Marjorie Agosín. New York: Feminist Press, City University of New York.

———. 2001. "Zapatos: Andante con variaciones." In *Zona de derrumbe*, 197–207. Rosario, Argentina: Beatriz Viterbo Editora.

Glickman, Nora. 2000. *The Jewish White Slave Trade and the Untold Story of Raquel Liberman*, 73–92. New York: Garland Publishing.

Goldberg, Florinda F. 2000. "Literatura judía latinoamericana: Modelos para armar." *Revista Iberoamericana* 191: 309–24.

Gómez Carrillo, Enrique. 1898. "Max Nordau." In *Almas y cerebros*, 243–53. Paris: Garnier Hermanos Editores.

González Echevarría, Roberto. 1998. *Myth and Archive: A Theory of Latin American Narrative*. Durham, N.C.: Duke University Press.

Gorender, Jacob. 1987. *Combate nas Trevas: A esquerda brasileira: Das ilusiones perdidas a luta armada*. São Paulo: Editoria Atica.

Grandis, Rita de, and Zilá Bernd, eds. 2000. *Unforeseeable Americas: Questioning Cultural Hybridity in the Americas*. Critical Studies 13. Amsterdam: Rodopi.

Guy, Donna. 1991. *Sex and Danger in Buenos Aires: Prostitution, Family and Nation in Argentina*. Lincoln: University of Nebraska Press.

Helg, Aline. 1990. "Race in Argentina and Cuba, 1880–1930: Theory, Policies, and Popular Reaction." In *The Idea of Race in Latin America, 1870–1940*, ed. Richard Graham, 37–69. Austin: University of Texas Press.

Hippler, Fritz, dir. 1940. *Der ewige Jude*. Berlin: Deutsche Filmherstellungs und Vertriebs.

Igel, Regina. 1997. *Imigrantes judeus/Escritores brasileiros: O componente judaico na literatura brasileira*. São Paulo: Perspectiva, Associação Universitária de Cultura Judaica, Banco Safra.

Ingenieros, José. 1908. *Al margen de la ciencia*. Valencia: F. Sempere.

Irigaray, Luce. 1993. *An Ethics of Sexual Difference*. Translated by Carolyn Burke and Gillian C. Gill. Ithaca, N.Y.: Cornell University Press.

Irizarry, Estelle. 1979. *La broma literaria en nuestros días: Max Aub, Francisco de Ayala, Ricardo Gullón, Carlos Ripoll, César Tiempo*. New York: Eliseo and Sons.

Isaacs, Jorge. 1978. *María*. Caracas: Biblioteca Ayacucho. (Orig. pub. 1867.)

Joyce, James. 1981. *Ulysses*. New York: Random House. (Orig. pub. 1910.)

Kamen, Henry. 1998. *The Spanish Inquisition: A Historical Revision*. New Haven, Conn.: Yale University Press.

Kraniauskas, John. 2004. "Hybridity in a Transnational Frame: Latin Americanist and Postcolonial Perspectives on Cultural Studies." In *The Latin American Cultural Studies Reader*, eds. Ana del Sarto, Alicia Ríos, and Abril Trigo, 736–59. Durham, N.C.: Duke University Press.

Kristeva, Julia. 1991. *Strangers to Ourselves*. Translated by Leon S. Roudiez. New York: Columbia University Press.

Kumler Anderson, George. 1965. *The Legend of the Wandering Jew*. Providence, R.I.: Brown University Press.

Kushnir, Beatriz. 1996. *Baile de máscaras: Mulheres judias e prostituição: As Polacas e suas Associações de Ajuda Mútua*. Rio de Janciro: Imago Editora.

Kutzinski, Vera. 1993. *Sugar's Secrets: Race and the Erotics of Cuban Nationalism*. Charlottesville: University of Virginia Press.

Larsen, Neil. 1995. *Reading North by South: On Latin American Literature, Culture, and Politics*. Minneapolis: University of Minnesota Press.

Lesser, Jeffrey. 1995. *Welcoming the Undesirables: Brazil and the Jewish Question*. Berkeley: University of California Press.

———. 1999. *Negotiating National Identity: Immigrants, Minorities, and the Struggle for Ethnicity in Brazil*. Durham, N.C.: Duke University Press.

———. 2001. "Jewish Brazilians or Brazilian Jews? A Reflection on Brazilian Ethnicity." *Shofar* 19: 65–72.

Levinas, Emmanuel. 1969. *Totality and Infinity: An Essay on Exteriority*. Translated by Alphonso Lingis. Pittsburgh: Duquesne University Press. (Orig. pub. 1961.)

———. 1982. *Ethics and Infinity: Conversations with Philippe Nemo*. Translated by Richard A. Cohen. Pittsburgh: Duquesne University Press.

———. 1987. "Reality and Its Shadow." In *Collected Philosophical Papers*. Translated by Alphonso Lingis, 1–14. Dordrecht, Netherlands: Nijhoff.

———. 1993. "Philosophy and the Idea of the Infinite." Translated by Alphonso Lingis. In *To the Other*, edited by Adriaan Peperzak, 88–119. West Lafayette, Ind.: Purdue University Press.

———. 1996. *Basic Philosophical Writings*. Edited by Adriaan T. Peperzak, Simon Critchley, and Robert Bernasconi. Bloomington: Indiana University Press.

———. 1998. *Otherwise than Being, or Beyond Essence*. Trans. Alphonso Lingis. Pittsburgh: Duquesne University Press. (Orig. pub. 1974.)

Levine, Robert. 1968. "Brazil's Jews During the Vargas Era and After." *Luso-Brazilian Review* 5.1: 45–58.

Levinson, Brett. 2004. *Market and Thought: Meditations on the Political and Biopolitical*. New York: Fordham University Press.

Liwerant, Judit Bokser, Alicia Gojman de Backal, and Hellen B. Soriano, eds. 1999. *Encuentro y Alteridad: Vida y cultura judía en América Latina*. Mexico City: Universidad Nacional Autónoma de México / Universidad Hebrea de Jerusalem / Asociación

Mexicana de Amigos de la Universidad de Tel Aviv / Fondo de Cultura Económica (Mexico).

Llewelyn, John. 1995. *Emmanuel Levinas: The Genealogy of Ethics*. London: Routledge.

Lombroso, Cesare, and Guglielmo Ferrero. 2004. *Criminal Woman, the Prostitute, and the Normal Woman*. Translated and introduced by Nicole Hahn Rafter and Mary Gibson. Durham, N.C.: Duke University Press.

Louis, Annick. 1997. "Borges y el nazismo." *Variaciones Borges* 4: 117–36.

———. 2000. "Besando a Judas: Notas alrededor de 'Deutsches Requiem.'" In *Jorge Luis Borges: Intervenciones sobre pensamiento y literatura*, ed. William Rowe, Claudio Canaparo, and Annick Louis. Buenos Aires: Paidós.

Ludmer, Josefina. 1988. *El género gauchesco: Un tratado sobre la patria*. Buenos Aires: Sudamericana.

———. 2004. *The Corpus Delicti: A Manual of Argentine Fictions*. Translated by Glen S. Close. Pittsburgh: University of Pittsburgh Press.

Lund, Joshua. 2006. *The Impure Imagination: Toward a Critical Hybridity in Latin American Writing*. Minneapolis: University of Minnesota Press.

Lyotard, Jean François. 1990. *Heidegger and "the jews."* Minneapolis: University of Minnesota Press.

Machado de Assis, Joaquim Maria. 1962–71. "A cristã nova" (1875). In *Obra completa*. Vol. 3. Edited by Afrânio Coutinho, 110–125. Rio de Janeiro: J. Aguilar.

Maik, Linda. 1989. "Nordau's Degeneration: The American Controversy." *History of Ideas* 50.4: 607–23.

Martel, Julián (José María Miró). 1979. *La bolsa*. Buenos Aires: Imprima Editores. (Orig. pub. 1891.)

———. 1946. *La bolsa*. Buenos Aires: Clásicos Argentinos. (Orig. pub. 1891.)

McCann, Bryan. 2001. "Noel Rosa's Nationalist Logic." *Luso-Brazilian Review* 38: 1–26.

McGuirk, Bernard. 1997. "Z/Z: On Midrash and *Écriture féminine* in Jorge Luis Borges' 'Emma Zunz.'" In *Latin American Literature: Symptoms, Risks and Strategies of Poststructuralist Criticism*, 185–206. London: Routledge.

Mejía, Gustavo. 1978. "Cronología." In *María*, by Jorge Isaacs, 210–85. Caracas: Biblioteca Ayacucho.

Menocal, María Rosa. 2002. *The Ornament of the World: How Muslims, Jews and Christians Created a Culture of Tolerance in Medieval Spain*. Boston: Little, Brown.

Miller, Marilyn Grace. 2004. *Rise and Fall of the Cosmic Race: The Cult of Mestizaje in Latin America*. Austin: University of Texas Press.

Molloy, Sylvia. 1984. "Paraíso perdido y economía terrenal en *María*." *Sin Nombre* 14: 36–55.

———. 1996a. "Diagnósticos del fin del siglo." In *Cultura y tercer mundo 2: Nuevas identidades y ciudadanía*, ed. Beatriz González-Stephan, 171–200. Caracas: Nueva Sociedad.

———. 1996b. "His America, Our America: José Martí Reads Whitman." *Modern Language Quarterly* 5: 369–79.

———. 1997. "Voice Snatching: *De Sobremesa*, Hysteria, and the Impersonation of Marie Bashkirsteff." *Latin American Literary Review* 25: 11–29.

———. 1998. "The Politics of Posing." In *Hispanisms and Homosexualities*, ed. Sylvia Molloy and Robert McKee Irwin, 141–60. Durham, N.C.: Duke University Press.

Montero, Oscar. 1996. "Modernismo y 'Degeneración': Los raros de Darío." *Revista Iberoamericana* 176–77: 821–34.

Morães, Mário Sérgio de. 2006. *O ocaso da ditadura, caso Herzog*. São Paulo, Brazil: Barcarolla.

Moraña, Mabel. 1995. "*Escribir en el aire*: Heterogeneidad y estudios culturales." *Revista Iberoamericana* 170–71: 279–86.

Morris, David. 1985. "Gothic Sublimity." *New Literary History* 16: 299–319.

Musselwhite, David. 2006. "The Colombia of María: 'Un país de cafres.'" *Romance Studies* 24.1: 41–54.

Nancy, Jean-Luc. 1998. "The Surprise of the Event." Trans. Lynn Festa and Stuart Barnett. In *Hegel after Derrida*, ed. Stuart Barnett, 91–104. New York: Routledge.

Nochlin, Linda, and Tamar Garb, eds. 1995. *The Jew in the Text: Modernity and the Construction of Identity*. London: Thames and Huson.

Nordau, Max. 1895. *Degeneration*. New York: D. Appleton. (Orig. pub. 1892.)

Norris, Frank. 1903. *The Pit: A Story of Chicago*. New York: Doubleday, Page.

Nouzeilles, Gabriela. 2000. *Ficciones somáticas: Naturalismo, nacionalismo, y políticas médicas del cuerpo*. Rosario, Argentina: Beatriz Viterbo Editora.

Ortiz, Fernando. 1978. *Contrapunteo cubano del tabaco y el azúcar*. Caracas: Biblioteca Ayacucho. (Orig. pub. 1940.)

———. 1995. *Cuban Counterpoint: Tobacco and Sugar*. Durham, N.C.: Duke University Press.

Peperzak, Adriaan. 1989. "From Intentionality to Responsibility: On Lévinas's Philosophy of Language." In *The Question of the Other*, ed. Arleen B. Callery and Charles E. Scott, 3–22. Albany: State University of New York Press.

Pérez Galdós, Benito. 1963. *Gloria*. Madrid: Librería y Casa Editorial Hernando. (Orig. pub. 1877.)

Perpich, Diane. 2001. "Jill Robbins, *Altered Reading: Levinas and Literature*." *Bryn Mawr Review of Comparative Literature* 3.1 (fall). http://www.brynmawr.edu/.

Peters, Edward. 1988. *Inquisition*. New York: Free Press.

Piglia, Ricardo. 1986. *Crítica y ficción*. Santa Fe, Argentina: Cuadernos de Extensión Universitaria, Universidad Nacional del Litoral.

———. 1994. *Artificial Respiration*. Translated by Daniel Balderston. Durham, N.C.: Duke University Press.

———. 2000. *Respiración artificial*. Buenos Aires: Seix Barral, Biblioteca Breve. (Orig. pub. 1980.)

Plotkin, Mariano Ben. 2003. *Mañana es San Perón: A Cultural History of Perón's Argentina*. Translated by Keith Zahniser. Wilmington, Del.: SR Books.

Presner, Todd Samuel. 2003. "Clear Heads, Solid Stomachs, and Hard Muscles: Max Nordau and the Aesthetics of Jewish Regeneration." *Modernism/Modernity* 10: 269–96.

Quintana, Isabel. 2001. *Figuras de la experiencia en el fin de siglo: Cristina Peri Rossi, Ricardo Piglia, Juan José Saer y Silviano Santiago*. Rosario, Argentina: Beatriz Viterbo Editora.

————. 2004. "Ciudad y memoria en *Los planetas.*" *Latin American Literary Review* 32.63: 65–80.

Rago, Margareth. 1991. *Os prazeres da noite: Prostituição e códigos da sexualidade feminina em São Paulo (1890–1930).* Rio de Janeiro: Paz e Terra.

Ragussis, Michael. 1995. *Figures of Conversion: "The Jewish Question" and English National Identity.* Durham, N.C.: Duke University Press.

Rama, Angel. 1982. *Transculturación narrativa en América Latina.* Mexico City: Siglo XXI.

Ramos, Julio. 1989. *Desencuentros de la modernidad en América Latina: Literatura y política en el siglo XIX.* Mexico City: Fondo de Cultura Económica.

————. 2001. *Divergent Modernities: Culture and Politics in Nineteenth-Century Latin America.* Translated by John D. Blanco. Durham, N.C.: Duke University Press.

Riera, Carme. 1996. *En el último azul.* Madrid: Alfaguara.

Robbins, Jill. 1999. *Altered Reading: Lévinas and Literature.* Chicago: University of Chicago Press.

Rosa, Noel. 1930. *Quem dá mais: Samba-humorístico.* Sheet music. São Paulo, Brazil: Editora Mangione.

Santareno, Bernardo. 1966. *O Judeu: Narrativa dramática em três actos.* Lisboa: Edições Atica.

Santiago, Silviano. 1985. *Stella Manhattan.* Rio de Janeiro: Editora Nova Fronteira.

————. 2001. *The Space In-between: Essays on Latin American Culture.* Edited by Ana Lúcia Gazzola. Translated by Tom Burns, Ana Lúcia Gazzola, and Gareth Williams. Durham, N.C.: Duke University Press.

Sarlo, Beatriz. 1999. "El saber del cuerpo: A propósito de 'Emma Zunz.'" *Variaciones Borges* 7: 231–47.

————. 2003. *Borges, un escritor en las orillas.* Buenos Aires: Seix Barral. (Orig. pub. 1993.)

Sarmiento, Domingo Faustino. 1977. *Facundo, o, Civilización y barbarie.* Caracas: Biblioteca Ayacucho. (Orig. pub. 1845.)

Scarry, Elaine. 1985. *The Body in Pain: The Making and Unmaking of the World.* New York: Oxford University Press.

————. 1994. *Resisting Representation.* New York: Oxford University Press.

————. 1999. "The Difficulty of Imagining Other Persons." In *Human Rights in Political Transitions: Gettysburg to Bosnia,* ed. Carls Hesse and Robert Post, 277–309. New York: Zone Books.

Schmelz, U. O., and Sergio DellaPergola. 1991. *World Jewish Population, 1989.* Jerusalem: Institute of Contemporary Jewry, Hebrew University of Jerusalem.

Senkman, Leonardo. 2000. "La Nación imaginaria de los escritores judíos latinoamericanos." *Revista Iberoamericana* 191: 279–98.

Shakespeare, William. 2003. *The Merchant of Venice.* Cambridge: Cambridge University Press.

Shapiro, James. 1996. *Shakespeare and the Jews.* New York: Columbia University Press.

Showalter, Dennis E. 1982. *Little Man, What Now?* New York: Archon Books.

Siegel, Don, dir. 1956. *Invasion of the Body Snatchers.* Walter Wanger Productions.

Sierra O'Reilly, Justo. 1959. *La hija del judío*. Edited by Antonio Castro Leal. 2 vols. Mexico City: Editorial Porrúa, S.A. (Orig. pub. 1848.)

Silva, José Asunción. 1996. *De sobremesa*. Madrid: Hiperión. (Orig. pub. 1925.)

———. 2005. *After-Dinner Conversation: The Diary of a Decadent*. Translated by Kelly Washbourne. Austin: University of Texas Press.

Silverman, Max. 1998. "Re-figuring 'the Jew' in France." In *Modernity, Culture and "the Jew,"* ed. Bryan Cheyette and Laura Marcus, 197–207. Stanford, Calif.: Stanford University Press.

Simmel, Georg. 1990. *The Philosophy of Money*. London: Routledge.

Skidmore, Thomas E. 1990. "Racial Ideas and Social Policy in Brazil, 1870–1940." In *The Idea of Race in Latin America, 1870–1940*, ed. Richard Graham, 7–36. Austin: University of Texas Press.

———. 1993. *Black into White: Race and Nationality in Brazilian Thought*. Durham, N.C.: Duke University Press.

Sommer, Doris. 1991. *Foundational Fictions: The National Romances of Latin America*. Berkeley: University of California Press.

———. 1996. "About-Face: The Talker Turns." *boundary 2* 23: 91–133.

Sontag, Susan. 1990. *Illness as Metaphor and AIDS and Its Metaphors*. New York: Doubleday.

Sorj, Bernardo. 1997. "Sociabilidade Brasileira e Identidade Judaica." In *Identidades Judaicas no Brasil Contemporâneo*, ed. Bila Sorj, 9–31. Rio de Janeiro: Imago Editora.

Sorj, Bila, ed. 1997. *Identidades Judaicas no Brasil Contemporâneo*. Rio de Janeiro: Imago Editora.

Sosnowski, Saúl. 1976. *Borges y la Cábala: La búsqueda del verbo*. Buenos Aires: Ediciones Hispamérica.

———. 1987. "Latin American-Jewish Writers: Protecting the Hyphen." In *The Jewish Presence in Latin America: Thematic Studies in Latin America*, ed. Judith Laikin Elkin and Gilbert W. Merkx, 297–307. Winchester, Mass.: Allen and Unwin.

———. 2000. "Fronteras en las letras judías-latinoamericanas." *Revista Iberoamericana* 191: 263–78.

Spackman, Barbara. 1989. *Decadent Genealogies: The Rhetoric of Sickness from Baudelaire to D'Annunzio*. Ithaca, N.Y.: Cornell University Press.

Stanislawski, Michael. 2001. *Zionism and the Fin de Siècle: Cosmopolitanism and Nationalism from Nordau to Jabotinsky*. Berkeley: University of California Press.

Stavans, Ilan, ed. 2001. *The Inveterate Dreamer: Essays and Conversations on Jewish Culture*. Lincoln: University of Nebraska Press.

Stepan, Nancy Leys. 1991. *"The Hour of Eugenics": Race, Gender, and Nation in Latin America*. Ithaca, N.Y.: Cornell University Press.

Tácito, Hilário (José Maria de Toledo Malta). 1997. *Madame Pommery*. 5th ed. Rio de Janeiro: Fundação Casa de Rui Barbosa. (Orig. pub. 1920.)

Taunay, Alfredo d'Escragnolle Taunay, Visconde de. 1971. *O encilhamento: Cenas contemporâneas da bolsa do Rio de Janeiro em 1890, 1891 e 1892*. Rio de Janeiro: Itatiaia. (Orig. pub. 1894.)

Tiempo, César (Israel Zeitlin). 1974. *Clara Beter y otras fatamorganas.* Buenos Aires: A. Peña Lillo.

Timerman, Jacobo. 2002. *Prisoner without a Name, Cell without a Number.* Translated by Toby Talbot. Madison: University of Wisconsin Press.

———. 2004. *Preso sin nombre, celda sin número.* Madison: University of Wisconsin Press. (Orig. pub. 1981.)

Trigo, Benigno. 1994. "Los raros de Darío y el discurso alienista finisecular." *Revista Canadiense de Estudios Hispánicos* 18: 293–307.

van der Laarse, Robert. 1999. "Masking the Other: Max Nordau's Representation of Hidden Jewishness." *Historical Reflections/Reflexions Historiques* 25: 1–31.

Vargas Llosa, Mario. 1987. *El hablador.* Barcelona: Editorial Seix Barral.

———. 1989. *The Storyteller.* Translated by Helen Lane. New York: Farrar, Straus and Giroux.

Vasconcelos, José. 1925. *La raza cósmica: Misión de la raza iberoamericana.* Paris: Agencia Mundial de Librería.

———. 1997. *The Cosmic Race: A Bilingual Edition.* Translated and introduced by Didier T. Jaén. Baltimore: Johns Hopkins University Press.

Vianna, Hermano. 1999. *The Mystery of Samba: Popular Music and National Identity in Brazil.* Edited and translated by John Charles Chasteen. Chapel Hill: University of North Carolina Press.

Vieira, Nelson H. *Jewish Voices in Brazilian Literature.* Gainesville: University of Florida Press, 1995.

Wasserman, Renata R. Mautner. 2001. "Financial Fictions: Émile Zola's *L'argent,* Frank Norris' *The Pit,* and Alfredo de Taunay's *O encilhamento.*" *Comparative Literature Studies* 38.3: 193–214.

Webster's New World Dictionary of the American Language. 1980. 2d ed. Cleveland: Wiley Publishing.

Witalec, Janet, ed. 1999. "Isaacs, Jorge Ricardo: Introduction." eNotes.com. http://www.enotes.com/.

Young, Jordan M. 1966. *The Brazilian Revolution of 1930 and the Aftermath.* New Brunswick, N.J.: Rutgers University Press.

Žižek, Slavoj. 1989. *The Sublime Object of Ideology.* London: Verso.

Zola, Emile. 1928. *L'argent.* Paris: F. Bernouard. (Orig. pub. 1891.)

stock market, 39, 81; crash of (1890), 36–37; novels of, 79–80
storytellers, 153; ethnography and, 148–50; El hablador and, 145–48, 150; Machiguengas and, 151–52
subaltern, 92, 112
subjectivity, 3, 22–23, 27, 67, 72, 157; absence and, 176; Borges and, 108, 112, 159–60, 163; constitution of, 21; corporality and, 29; degeneracy and, 58, 61; doctors and, 42–43; ethnography and, 148; El hablador and, 147; malleability and, 106; discourse and, 30; masculinity and, 53; Nordau and, 46, 52, 60; Pessach and, 139–40; political transformation and, 122–23; "Quem dá mais?" and, 83, 87; transactions and, 74, 78, 116–17; transvestitism and, 107; violence and, 156
Sublime Object of Ideology, The (Žižek), 173
Sur (periodical), 88, 156
"Sur, El" (Borges), 111–12
surplus, 75, 80, 92, 116–17
surprise, 25, 108
Suwala, Halina, 79
Symbolists, 47, 100
symbolization, 3, 36, 40, 43, 64, 75; "Emma Zunz" and, 112; memory and, 43; Nordau as raro and, 49; promiscuity and, 94, 96–97; "Quem dá mais?" and, 85; value and, 78–80
syncretism, 18–19
syphilis, 43, 75

Tácito, Hilário: alcohol and, 98–99; Beter and, 105; "Emma Zunz" and, 108; Madame Pommery, 78, 93, 101, 105, 116; modernism and, 95; positivism and, 107; prostitution and, 94–98, 100, 103
Tacitus, 95
Talmud, 68
Tarde, Gabriel, 53
Teresa de Jesús, Santa, 70

texto sin afuera (text without an outside), 164. See also exteriority
textual conversion, 9, 24–27, 78, 123–27, 135; absence and, 176; Jewishness and, 153; New Christians and, 16, 129; political transformation and, 119–22; representation and, 154
thematization, 72, 111, 152–53, 169–70, 176; "Deutsches Requiem" and, 159; language and, 24; other and, 23; textual conversion and, 123–24
theology, 157–58
"Thou shalt not kill" injunction, 21–24; Borges and, 160–61
threshold, 77, 87
Tiempo, César, 94, 101–3, 106–7, 116
Toledo Malta, José Maria de, 95
Torah, 8
totalitarianism, 145, 153, 165, 170, 172; representation and, 155
totality, 92, 116–17, 154, 177; absorption into, 27; Borges and, 159–63
Totality and Infinity (Levinas), 23
totalization, 119–20, 124, 137, 155
tradition, 112
tragedy, 36, 39
transactions, 25–26, 74–78, 114, 116–18, 154; Beter and, 105; Borges and, 88–92, 109–10; malleability and, 106; political transformation and, 119; "Quem dá mais?" and, 83, 85–86; value and, 82
Transculturación narrativa en América Latina (Rama), 19
transculturation, 18–20
transference, 59, 114–15
transformation, 152–53; Pessach and, 139–40, 145
translation, 46, 97
transvestites, 107
tropics, 100
truth, 27, 78, 164, 177; Borges and, 88, 90, 110; fixedness of, 91

ERIN GRAFF ZIVIN is an assistant professor of Spanish and Portuguese at the
University of Southern California.

Library of Congress Cataloging-in-Publication Data

Graff Zivin, Erin.
The wandering signifier : rhetoric of Jewishness in the Latin American imaginary /
Erin Graff Zivin.
p. cm.
Includes bibliographical references and index.
ISBN 978-0-8223-4332-5 (cloth : alk. paper) —
ISBN 978-0-8223-4367-7 (pbk. : alk. paper)
1. Latin American literature—19th century—History and criticism.
2. Latin American literature—20th century—History and criticism.
3. Jews in literature.
I. Title.
PQ7081.G687 2008
860.9′3529924—dc22
2008013873